Waldron Smith

$450

K

9/23

THE IDEA OF A PARTY SYSTEM

*The Rise of Legitimate Opposition
in the United States, 1780–1840*

JEFFERSON MEMORIAL LECTURES

The Idea of
a Party System

*The Rise of Legitimate Opposition
in the United States, 1780-1840*

By RICHARD HOFSTADTER

University of California Press

BERKELEY AND LOS ANGELES 1969

UNIVERSITY OF CALIFORNIA PRESS
BERKELEY AND LOS ANGELES, CALIFORNIA

UNIVERSITY OF CALIFORNIA PRESS, LTD.
LONDON, ENGLAND

LIBRARY OF CONGRESS CATALOG CARD NUMBER: 76–82377
PRINTED IN THE UNITED STATES OF AMERICA

Preface

This book has grown out of the Jefferson Memorial Lectures, given at the University of California, Berkeley, October 1966. The lectures, which were intended for listeners who could not have been expected to be immersed in American history or political science, no doubt still show signs of a manner suitable to a leisurely oral exposition before a general audience. My first intention was to clarify the development of the early idea of party by tracing its treatment in Jeffersonian democracy. For the purpose of a few lectures it seemed wise to concentrate upon this idea as it found expression in the minds of the Virginia Dynasty. I could see an element of awkwardness in this, since it demanded, along with extended discussion of such a central thinker as Jefferson and such an important and interesting one as Madison, some attention to James Monroe which may seem warranted neither by the intrinsic interest of his mind nor by his place in the development of American political culture. But in practice it fell to Monroe to execute a certain conception of party, and in theory he represented with stark and ingratiating simplicity the sturdy perdurance of eighteenth-century political ideas.

As the book changed in revision, it expanded—not quite into a full account of the ideas of party held by the Jeffersonians (such a significant thinker for this purpose as John Taylor receives only peripheral notice), but at least into a fuller account of this phase of our history. In order to establish the partisan dialogue, something also had to be said about a few of the Federalist leaders. Finally, in order not to end at an anticlimactic point, I felt obliged to break the chronological bounds I had first set for myself and to carry the idea of the party beyond the first generation of political leaders. Hence this book closes not with Monroe but with Martin Van Buren, who reacted sharply against him, and with the political culture of the Albany Regency from which Van Buren came. Like Monroe, Van Buren is neither a glamorous figure in our political annals nor an important thinker; but he and his associates were of fundamental importance for what they did to develop the theory and practice of the political party. They not only formed the first fully articulate justification of the party as a competitive organization but also showed the first reasonably full comprehension of the idea of a party *system*. In this way, they carried the idea of party well beyond its first stage and into a new phase that is much closer to our own ideas than it is to those of the eighteenth century.

My starting point was the presence of certain observable paradoxes in the thought and practice of the Founding Fathers. The first was that they did not believe in political parties as such, scorned those that they were conscious of as historical models, had a keen terror of party spirit and its evil consequences, and yet, almost as soon as their national government was in operation, found it necessary to establish parties. They had framed a Constitution which, among its other ends, was meant to control and counteract parties, and yet they gradually began to realize that they could not govern under it without the help of such organizations. Indeed it may appear to us, with the benefit of long historical perspective, that the new Constitution which they had so ingeniously drawn up could never have been made to work if some of its vital deficiencies, not least the link between the executive and the legislature, had not been remedied by the political party. They did not believe, as modern democrats do, that partisan competition is an asset to the political order under what they called free government; nor had they yet even conceived of a party system. Yet despite themselves they gradually gave form to the first American party system, and under it gave the world its first example of the peaceful transit of a government from the control of one popular party to another.

Of course it is important to realize that the Founding Fathers were more accurately criticizing the rudimentary parties they had seen in action or had read of in their histories than the modern parties they were themselves beginning to build for the future. They stood at a moment of fecund inconsistency, suspended between their acceptance on one side of political differences and opposition criticism, and on the other their rejection of parties as agencies to organize social conflict and political debate. They well understood that conflicts of opinion are inevitable in a state of republican freedom, but they wanted to minimize such conflicts and hoped to achieve a comprehensive unity or harmony.[1] They did not usually see conflict as functional to society, and above all they could not see how organized and institutionalized party conflict could be made useful, or could be anything other than divisive, distracting, and dangerous.

For this reason the history of the United States during the first quarter century of government under the federal Constitution marked a focal episode in the development of the idea of legitimate opposition. In Anglo-American experience the idea of free political criticism had made vital gains in the eighteenth century. But in England what was then called a "formed opposition"—that is, an organized and continuous opposition group, as distinct from an individual speaking his mind in or out of a parliamentary body—still fell short of respectability, and in the minds of many men was tainted with disloyalty, subversion, or treason. Even in America, where the battle with royal governors had created a strong tradition of oppositional

---

[1] When I speak in the text of a quest for unanimity as characteristic of their generation, I trust it will be clear that I am not imputing to them a hope for total agreement of all men on all matters of policy, which they too would have thought naïve, but only a desire for such general oneness of spirit as would render lasting party divisions unnecessary.

politics, the idea of a mass party as an extension of parliamentary discussion and opposition was not widely accepted. It was held by most men to be particularly unsuited to government under a representative republic, where representative institutions themselves were believed sufficient to serve the public interest. In England, as late as 1826 when Sir John Cam Hobhouse first referred in a spirit of levity to "His Majesty's Opposition," the notion was greeted with the amusement he had anticipated, and was not yet taken as an important constitutional conception. In America, where party opposition had been much more fully developed, it had been carried on in the face of a firm conviction by each side in the party battle that the other was not legitimate, and in a healthy state of affairs would be put out of business. Neither party had thought of the other either as a legitimate opposition or as an alternative government; neither side thought of the two parties as engaged in a sustained competition that would result in rotations of power. Each party hoped to bring about the other's destruction by devouring and absorbing as many of its more amenable followers as could be won over, and by forcing the remaining top leadership into disorganization and impotence. Although the Federalists failed in this purpose, the Republicans at last succeeded when they were able to brand the Federalists as disloyal during and after the War of 1812. A period of one-party government followed in national politics. But the experience of the nation's political leaders with party politics was so imposing and the need for parties so strong that the second American party system began to form within no more than a decade, and in the course of its formation a much broader and more fully articulated rationale for a two-party system began to appear among the politicians themselves.

Another perspective on the politics of the early Federalist era kept insinuating itself into this work. If the events of that era are regarded from the standpoint of the gradual development of a party system and of a conception of legitimate opposition, and if we regard the idea of legitimate opposition as a pivotal element in the growth of democracy, then the crises of the young republic appear in a considerably different aspect from that in which they have been traditionally presented. In the prevailing view, the one profound crisis of the early union is held to have been the struggle over the acceptance of the Constitution in 1787–1788. To me it seems that the crisis that came upon the country in 1797–1801—or, if one wishes to read it more broadly, in 1794–1801—was at least as real and decisive for the early union as that which had been successfully passed in the 1780's. The French Revolution and the war that followed joined and intensified all the differences that separated Federalists from Jeffersonians: differences over what the character of the new society should be, over economic policies, over the interpretation of the Constitution, over foreign policy, clashing sectional interests, and republican ideology. It mobilized parochial and partisan prejudices to a point where the Union was threatened, and a civil war seemed possible. It also tested the ability of the founding generation to manage the non-violent transfer of power from one party to another during a period of intense party passions. The successful transition from the Federalists to the Jeffersonians in 1801—which needs more elaborate study than it has ever received and about which I have been able to offer only a few preliminary suggestions—did not by any means resolve the problems of political development, but it marked the nation's passage through an immensely significant trial of political capacity.

We are living through a period, certainly not the first, when discontent with the workings of the American party system is at a high pitch. It seems particularly important to be clear that this book was not written to justify, much less to extol, the American two-party system, which has some decisive merits but also many grave limitations that I have not tried to assess or balance here. My only interest has been in explaining some of the circumstances attending the origins of the party system, and no account of origins could in itself be sufficient to vindicate the workings of this system over its long span of life. I make, however, two assumptions of value which I have no desire to obscure: I do believe that the full development of the liberal democratic state in the West required that political criticism and opposition be incarnated in one or more opposition parties, free not only to express themselves within parliamentary bodies but also to agitate and organize outside them among the electorate, and to form permanent, free, recognized oppositional structures. And I believe that the gradual acceptance of parties and of the system of a recognized partisan opposition which I record here marked a net gain in the sophistication of political thought and practice over the anti-party thought and unlegitimated or quasi-legitimated opposition that had prevailed in the Anglo-American tradition in the eighteenth century and earlier. The emergence of legitimate party opposition and of a theory of politics that accepted it was something new in the history of the world; it required a bold new act of understanding on the part of its contemporaries and it still requires study on our part.

I hope others will be as aware as I am of the exploratory and unfinished character of these reflections. There are several aspects of this problem that require extended study, and I am sure that further exposure to the sources would cause me to change my interpretations on more than one count.

I wish to thank Mark Schorer and the committee on the Jefferson Memorial Lectures for the occasion to visit Berkeley, and my various hosts there for two pleasant weeks. To the research assistants who helped me over a period of four years, Edwin G. Burrows, Carol Gruber, and Michael Wallace, and to my secretary, Mrs. Jane Slater, I am especially obliged for their extraordinarily helpful interest, and to Beatrice K. Hofstadter for a close and acute reading of each draft. I am grateful also to the several scholars who have given me suggestions and corrected my errors. A very full and interesting historical literature, written mainly in the past fifteen years, was essential to the formulation of my ideas; most of it is referred to here and there in my footnotes, but these can hardly convey my admiration or my sense of indebtedness to contemporary students of early American parties.

For the sake of the modern reader's eye and his quick comprehension I have taken liberties with some eighteenth-century punctuation and capitalization, but not, I hope, with the meaning of quotations.

R.H.

Wellfleet, Mass.
New York, N.Y.
June 1965–January 1969

Contents

Then none was for a party;
  Then all were for the state;
Then the great man helped the poor,
  And the poor man loved the great.
              THOMAS BABINGTON MACAULAY,
                Lays of Ancient Rome, xxxii

Chapter One

Party and Opposition
in the Eighteenth Century

I

WHEN THOMAS JEFFERSON thought of setting down the lasting achievements he wanted inscribed on his tombstone, he mentioned the writing of the Declaration of Independence and of the Virginia Statute of Religious Liberty and the founding of the University of Virginia—thus omitting almost flamboyantly all the accomplishments of his long career in national politics. Yet surely this democrat and libertarian might have taken justifiable pride in his part in creating the first truly popular party in the history of the Western world, and in his leading role in the first popular election of modern times in which the reins of government were peacefully surrendered by a governing party to an opposition. Jefferson did more than assert the claims of democracy: he was also a central figure in developing responsible constitutional opposition, an accomplishment which alone would grace any man's tombstone.

But here we are brought face to face with the primary paradox of this inquiry: Jefferson, the founder, or more accurately, co-founder, of the first modern popular party, had no use for political parties. This seeming inconsistency is but one aspect of a larger problem: the creators of the first American party system on both sides, Federalists and Republicans, were men who looked upon parties as sores on the body politic.

Political discussion in eighteenth-century England and America was pervaded by a kind of anti-party cant. Jonathan Swift, in his *Thoughts on Various Subjects*, had said that "Party is the madness of many, for the gain of the few." This maxim, which was repeated on this side of the Atlantic by men like John Adams and William Paterson, plainly struck a deep resonance in the American mind. Madison and Hamilton, when they discussed parties or factions (for them the terms were usually interchangeable) in *The Federalist*, did so only to arraign their bad effects. In the great debate over the adoption of the Constitution both sides spoke ill of parties. The popular sage, Franklin (who was not always consistent on the subject), gave an eloquent warning against factions and "the infinite mutual abuse of parties, tearing to pieces the best of characters." George Washington devoted a large part of his political testament, the Farewell Address, to stern warnings against "the baneful effects of the Spirit of Party." His successor, John Adams, believed that "a division of the republic into two great parties . . . . is to be dreaded as the greatest political evil under our Constitution."[1] Similar admonitions can be found in the

---

[1] Swift's maxim first appeared in the 1727 edition of his *Thoughts*. For Paterson on Swift, see Richard McCormick, *Experiment in Independence: New Jersey in the Critical Period, 1781–1789* (1950), 72; for Adams see *Works*, ed. by C. F. Adams (1851), VI, 508. For Hamilton and Madison on parties see especially *The Federalist* Number 9 (Hamilton) and 10 (Madison), though the subject is reverted to elsewhere throughout; see also the commentary by Benjamin F. Wright in his edition of *The Federalist* (1961), 26–41. All subsequent references to

writings of the arch-Federalist Fisher Ames and the "philosopher of Jeffersonian democracy," John Taylor of Caroline. If there was one point of political philosophy upon which these men, who differed on so many things, agreed quite readily, it was their common conviction about the baneful effects of the spirit of party.

That the anti-party thought and partisan action of the Founding Fathers were at odds with each other is not altogether surprising. What they were trying to resolve—and they did so, after all, with a substantial measure of success—is a fundamental problem of modern democracy. We see this problem with a new interest today when so many new states, recently liberated from colonial status, are trying to develop viable governments and national economies. Although the political history and the particular circumstances of most of the new nations are marked less by similarities than by profound differences from, even antitheses to, the pattern of Anglo-American development, the presence in the world of so many countries undergoing rapid and formative change has awakened among scholars an interest in the general phenomena of political development almost as keen as their interest in economic development, and this has helped us to take a fresh look at our own early history. People in the new states may ask from time to time whether recognized opposition parties would be, under their circumstances, an asset to national development or, as

---

The Federalist are to this edition. For Franklin on parties, Max Farrand, ed., *The Records of the Federal Convention of 1787* (1911), I, 82. Elsewhere, it should be said, Franklin said of parties: "Such will exist wherever there is liberty; perhaps they help to preserve it. By the collision of different sentiments, sparks of truth are struck out, and political light is obtained." V. W. Crane, "Franklin's 'The Internal State of America, 1786,'" *William and Mary Quarterly*, 15 (1958), 226. For Adams on "the greatest political evil," see *Works*, IX, 511, and for his views on party, John R. Howe, Jr., *The Changing Political Thought of John Adams* (1966), chapter 7.

most of their leaders appear to have concluded from the very beginning, a dangerous and inadmissible luxury. The situation of the Americans in their formative years was unusually complex, and perhaps quite unique. The Founding Fathers had inherited a political philosophy which also denied the usefulness of parties and stressed their dangers. Yet they deeply believed in the necessity of checks on power, and hence in freedom for opposition, and were rapidly driven, in spite of their theories, to develop a party system.

The problem of the Jeffersonians as our first opposition party may then be seen as a part of a larger problem: How did this nation come to develop a responsible, effective, constitutional opposition? First, perhaps, a few clarifications are in order. When we speak of an opposition as being *constitutional*, we mean that both government and opposition are bound by the rules of some kind of constitutional consensus. It is understood, on one side, that opposition is directed against a certain policy or complex of policies, not against the legitimacy of the constitutional regime itself. Opposition rises above naked contestation; it forswears sedition, treason, conspiracy, *coup d'état*, riot, and assassination, and makes an open public appeal for the support of a more or less free electorate. Government, in return, is constrained by certain limitations as to the methods it can use to counter the opposition; the free expression of oppositional views is permitted both inside and outside the halls of the parliamentary body.

When we speak of an opposition as being *responsible*, we mean that it contains within itself the potential of an actual alternative government—that is, its critique of existing policies is not simply a wild attempt to outbid the existing regime in promises, but a sober attempt to formulate alternative policies which it believes to be capable of execution within the existing historical and economic framework, and to offer as its executors a competent alternative personnel that can actually govern.

4

Here I do not mean to prejudge the question whether a non-responsible critique of government may not also have some value. In fact, I believe that there is a useful agitational function to be performed under certain conditions by non-responsible groups: programs and critiques that are essentially utopian in content may have practical results if they bring neglected grievances to the surface or if they open lines of thought that have not been aired by less alienated and less imaginative centers of power. But this agitational function is not the same thing as the function of a responsible opposition.

When we speak of an opposition as being *effective*, we mean not merely that its programs are expected to be capable of execution, that its alternative policy is real, but that its capability of winning office is also real, that it has the institutional structure and the public force which makes it possible for us to expect that sooner or later it will in fact take office and bring to power an alternative personnel. If opposition, no matter how constitutional its methods and realistic its program, is too minuscule or too fragmented to offer this alternative, it hardly qualifies on the grounds of effectiveness.[2] It might then be an educational force, but it is not a political one. Now it is an essential question, to which Western theorists usually give a negative answer, whether the requirement of effectiveness can be adequately met without opposition party structures. Effectiveness and organization, they conclude, complement each other.

Free opposition, working through party organization, whether concentrated in a single party or shared by several, is regarded today in most of the Western world to be essential

---

[2] It may also be argued that if the opposition program offers nothing in fact but minuscule variations of that of the government, its status as an effective opposition is doubtful. This argument is related to the modern question whether an excess of consensus does not give rise to an opposition which, however free, is excessively compliant.

to a representative democracy. To the modern democratic mind, familiar as it is with the one-party states of authoritarian regimes, freedom of opposition seems almost meaningless not only in the absence of certain enforceable guarantees of political rights but also in the absence of effective oppositional *structures* in the form of one or more political parties. Such opposition as can manage to make itself felt within the framework of one-party regimes is not credited by such theorists with much effect or with a value in any way comparable to that expressed through an alternative party or parties.[3]

"The simplest and most realistic definition of democracy," writes Maurice Duverger in his standard work on *Political Parties*, "is the following: a regime in which those who govern are chosen by those who are governed, by means of free and open elections. . . . The existence of an organized opposition is an essential feature of 'Western' democracy, its absence a feature of 'Eastern' democracy." But like most other Western democratic theorists, Duverger expresses his skepticism of the possibilities of valuable opposition without an opposition party. For example, the internal opposition, in the form of "self-criticism," as practiced in the Russian Communist party, he finds to be more like public confession than genuine opposition. "Its aim is less to give form to any resistance to the regime than to overcome such resistance. . . . In the nature of things there-

---

[3] A new interest in the means of control over governmental decisions in one-party systems has led to a revived interest in mechanisms of control, operating both inside and outside the single party. See, for example, Jerzy J. Wjatr and Adam Przeworski, "Control without Opposition," *Government and Opposition*, 1 (1966), 227–239, and Ghita Ionescu, "Control and Contestation in Some One-Party States," *ibid.*, 240–250.

However, for a penetrating statement on the vital differences between oppositions under one-party and multi-party conditions, see Giovanni Sartori, *Democratic Theory* (ed. 1965), especially chap. V.

fore an analysis of the influence of parties upon the function of the opposition must primarily deal with systems of more than one party."[4]

Other democratic theorists concur. "Modern democracy," says Hans Kelsen, "depends directly on political parties, whose importance becomes the greater the more strongly the democratic principle is realized." "The political parties," writes E. E. Schattschneider, "created modern democracy . . . and modern democracy is unthinkable save in terms of the parties. The most important distinction in modern political philosophy, the distinction between democracy and dictatorship, can be made best in terms of party politics." "The principle of representation," says Robert MacIver, "had to be vitalized by the conflict of parties. When parties flourish we have in effect passed from a pre-democratic mode of representative government to a genuinely democratic one." "Representative government," says Herman Finer succinctly, "is party government."[5]

All of this is quite at odds with the view of party opposition that most governments have in fact adopted. The normal view of governments about organized opposition is that it is intrinsically subversive and illegitimate. Their normal procedure is to smother or suppress it, using force or more subtle techniques, depending upon what seems necessary or efficacious in the circumstances. I need hardly say that I am speaking of the present as well as the past. Robert A. Dahl has pointed out that of the 113 members of the United Nations in 1964, only 30 countries had political systems in which full legal opposition

---

[4] Maurice Duverger, *Political Parties* (1954), 353, 413–414.

[5] Kelsen, *Vom Wesen und Wert der Demokratie* (1929) 19; E. E. Schattschneider, *Party Government* (1942), 1; Robert MacIver, *The Web of Government* (1947), 210; Herman Finer, *Theory and Practice of Modern Government* (1949), 237; Finer uses this rubric as a chapter title.

by organized political parties had existed throughout the preceding decade.[6]

The idea of a legitimate opposition—recognized opposition, organized and free enough in its activities to be able to displace an existing government by peaceful means—is an immensely sophisticated idea, and it was not an idea that the Fathers found fully developed and ready to hand when they began their enterprise in republican constitutionalism in 1788. We will misunderstand their politics badly if we read them so anachronistically as to imagine that they had a matured conception of a legitimate organized opposition or of a party system. Such a conception would certainly have engendered different political ideas and would probably have brought about different political practices. The Federalists and Republicans did not think of each other as alternating parties in a two-party system. Each side hoped instead to eliminate party conflict by persuading and absorbing the more acceptable and "innocent" members of the other; each side hoped to attach the stigma of foreign allegiance and disloyalty to the intractable leaders of the other, and to put them out of business as a party. The high point in Federalist efforts in this direction came with the Alien and Sedition Acts of 1798. The high point in Republican efforts came after the Treaty of Ghent in 1814. Where the Federalists had failed, the Republicans succeeded: the one-party period that came with the withering away of Federalism was seen by the Republicans not as an anomalous or temporary, much less as an undesirable eventuality, but as evidence of the correctness of their views and of the success of the American system.

There are, of course, many ways of looking at what the first generation under the Constitution accomplished—setting administrative precedents, establishing the national credit, forging

---

[6] Robert A. Dahl, *Political Oppositions in Western Democracies* (1966), xi, 333.

8

a federal union in the teeth of provincial loyalties, winning a national domain, resisting European attempts to force the nation back into a quasi-colonial or inferior status—but one of the most important things they did was to come to terms with the idea of opposition and to experiment, despite their theories, with its incarnation in a party system. When they began their work, they spoke a great deal—indeed they spoke almost incessantly—about freedom; and they understood that freedom requires some latitude for opposition. But they were far from clear as to *how* opposition should make itself felt, for they also valued social unity or harmony, and they had not arrived at the view that opposition, manifested in organized popular parties, could sustain freedom without fatally shattering such harmony. Their skepticism about the value of parties made it inevitable that their discovery of a party system should be the product of drift and experimentation, that the rather nice system of implicit rules under which the modern two-party duel takes place could be arrived at only after many misunderstandings and some serious missteps. All their work in party development had to be undertaken without the advantage of adequate practical precedents, either in their own pre-revolutionary provincial experience, or in the political practices of Georgian England; and it had to be undertaken without much theoretical guidance. Under such circumstances, it is entirely understandable that they should have taken a certain amount of time in developing a party democracy. I think we are right to be more impressed by the measure of their success than by the elements of failure with which it was intermingled.

II

If we inquire into the place of parties in Anglo-American thought during the eighteenth century, the root idea we find is that parties are evil. It is true, as Caroline Robbins has taken

pains to show, that even before Edmund Burke's striking statement in behalf of the party principle in 1770, there was in
England a somewhat stronger strain of dissent from this root
idea than many historians have recognized. In the two centuries
before 1770, she remarks, "some commentators and a larger
number of participants in English political life had realized the
existence of parties, had accepted with varying degrees of enthusiasm or fatalism the role of parties in a free state, and had
developed theories about their function and to a lesser degree
their control." But she emphasizes that these men "were many
fewer than those who condemned party and faction, advo-
cated uniformity of opinion and praised nonpartisan public
service,"[7] and even when due credit is given to the strain of
dissent that she records, we are left with the acknowledged
fact that it was the dissent of a small minority. For the most
part, as we shall see, men did not ask whether parties were good
or bad. They asked only whether parties must be accepted as
necessary evils in a free polity or whether it is in fact possible
to prevent, abolish, or suppress them in the interests of a more
pervasive harmony and unity in the state.

The very terms, "party" and "faction," which were used
by some writers interchangeably, carried invidious overtones,
though this is more regularly true of "faction." That word, in
fact, seems to have had the meaning of a more sinister version
of "party"—party functioning at its worst. Thus the standard
anti-party writer, Bolingbroke, could say: "Faction is to party
what the superlative is to the positive: party is a political evil,
and faction is the worst of all parties."[8] It was only in a much

---

[7] Caroline Robbins, " 'Discordant Parties': A Study of the Acceptance
of Party by Englishmen," *Political Science Quarterly*, 73 (1958), 505.

[8] *The Idea of a Patriot King* (1749; ed. 1965), 46. It is clear in at least
one passage that Bolingbroke regarded parties, however mischievous,
as being at least directed toward some principles, while factions are
"always made subordinate to personal interests." *A Dissertation upon
Parties* in *Works* (ed. 1841), II, 11.

later period that faction came to mean simply and clearly what it now means to us—a subdivision of a larger party, or a party within a party. Nathan Bailey's *The New Etymological Dictionary*, published in its second edition in London in 1770, treated "party" and "faction" as synonyms. In Samuel Johnson's famous *Dictionary of the English Language* (London edition, 1822), faction is given two meanings: (1) a party in a state, and (2) tumult, discord, dissention. Most American writers seem to have assimilated these two senses of the word to each other. For Johnson, "party" was less clearly invidious, and he gave it quite neutrally as: "A number of persons confederated by a similarity of designs or opinion in opposition to others." Frederic Barlow's *The Complete English Dictionary* (1772) is clear on this, defining faction as Johnson does except for the addition of another synonym, "confusion," and saying quite explicitly of party that it is "used in a good or bad sense according to the object of the association"—which, to one accustomed to eighteenth-century political writing, might well be taken to mean: the term party is not *always* used pejoratively. Still, in the 1790's the leaders of the emerging Republican party in the United States were sometimes disposed at first to shy away from calling themselves a party, and often spoke instead in their private correspondence of "the republican interest." As for faction—that was out of the question: Jefferson indignantly denounced Hamilton in 1792 for "daring to call the Republican party *a faction.*"[9]

Before going on to the various refinements of the central proposition of the mischievous effects of party, it is important to be clear why the anti-party thinkers in the main stream of Anglo-American thought considered party an evil. It must be remembered here that American thought on this subject drew on English experience, and that most Englishmen looked back

---

[9] To Madison, June 29, 1792; *Writings* (Ford ed.), VI, 95.

with relief upon the passing of that long, convulsive epoch of English history that occupied the seventeenth century and the first two decades of the eighteenth, in which they saw clear party divisions at work, with consequences they disliked to contemplate. "By 1688," as J. H. Plumb has observed, "violence in politics was an Englishman's birthright." "Conspiracy and rebellion, treason and plot, were a part of the history and experience of at least three generations of Englishmen."[10] Impeachment or attainder, exile or death had at times been the penalties paid by the losers; and the opposition of the 1640's was, of course, associated with a most violent outcome. Party was associated with painfully deep and unbridgeable differences in national politics, with religious bigotry and clerical animus, with treason and the threat of foreign invasion, with instability and dangers to liberty. Even in 1715 the Tories, the opposition party, could still be seen as quasi-treasonable.

Party had thus come to be conventionally condemned by political writers on three separate but not inconsistent grounds. First, they often postulated that society should be pervaded by concord and governed by a consensus that approached, if it did not attain, unanimity. Party, and the malicious and mendacious spirit it encouraged, were believed only to create social conflicts that would not otherwise occur, or to aggravate dangerously those that normally would occur. It was a prolific cause of "turbulence," of the disorder that might lead to anarchy. Second, a party or faction was very likely to become the instrument with which some small and narrow special interest could impose its will upon the whole of society, and hence to become the agent of tyranny. Both anarchy and tyranny might arrive in succession, one breeding the other,

---

10 J. H. Plumb, *The Origins of Political Stability: England, 1675–1725* (1967), 19, 1. Bolingbroke's *A Dissertation upon Political Parties* (1734) is in essence a historical sketch in which the horrors of party warfare are fully spelled out.

both the common products of an unstable political order. The history of the past republics was full of instances of just such political cycles.

Finally, the party, with its capacity to arouse malice and hostility and to command loyalty to a political entity much narrower and less legitimate than the "public good" as a whole, was considered to be a force directly counterposed to civic virtue. Party loyalty was thought of as an insidious alternative to that disinterested good judgment on behalf of the public welfare that might be expected, in the absence of party forces, from the good citizen. This conception readily crossed the Atlantic. When the eighteenth-century American thought of a great and good man, he thought of a man free from such distortions of judgment. A contemporary, for example, praised the leading Virginia planter, Edmund Pendleton, in these terms: "None of his opinions were drawn from personal views or party prejudices. He never had a connexion with any political party, . . . so that his opinions were the result of his own judgment, and that judgment was rendered upon the best unbiased estimate he could make of the publick good." In 1807 Washington Irving could still say of a character in the *Salmagundi Papers*: "He pledged himself never to engage in party schemes, or party politics, but to stand up solely for the broad interests of his country."[11]

Parties were condemned in the Anglo-American tradition not only from the right but from the left. It is easy to understand how monarchical writers and, as some might now say, establishment thinkers, with minds bent toward the convenience of those in authority, could find dangers in factionalism.

---

[11] David J. Mays, *Edmund Pendleton* (1952), 330, quoting Timothy Alden, *A Collection of American Epitaphs and Inscriptions* (1814), V, 28; Washington Irving, *Works* (1910), XV, 406. Irving, it should be said, was quite aware that this posture of independence guaranteed political failure.

But writers in the radical Whig tradition had condemned parties with equal or greater fervor and looked to devices other than party contention to protect the liberties of the people. Perhaps the best example is *Cato's Letters* (1721) by John Trenchard and Thomas Gordon, a source so revered in eighteenth-century America that, as scholars have only recently come to realize, it outstripped Locke in frequency of reference and perhaps in influence as well. These two radical Whig journalists, with their anti-Catholicism and anticlericalism, their opposition to tyranny, corruption, and aggrandized power, their fear of standing armies, their egalitarianism and stout advocacy of freedom of speech and religion, gave the cues for many themes in American thought. Among these was the common anti-party bias. Writing in the 1720's, Trenchard and Gordon, along with many contemporaries, looked back with scorn upon an era when party conflicts were exacerbated by religious ones, and when parties could be regarded as the work not merely of ambitious politicians but of the scheming clergy, who, as Gordon put it, were "the constant incendiaries of every popular and wicked faction." The people, Gordon believed, having no unseemly ambitions to appease, had no need of such devices as parties: "they have no occasion for dissimulation or intrigue; they can serve no end by faction; they have no interest but the general interest."[12]

Trenchard was even more emphatic. He saw parties as a device by which "corrupt ministers" play the people against each other and prop up their authority. And what party ever lived up to its principles or reformed the abuses it condemned? Party leaders profess the public good and pursue their own. They are nothing but placemen and highwaymen, and it can

---

[12] *The English Libertarian Heritage* (1965), 5, 62; The Introduction by David L. Jacobson to this selection from the writings of Trenchard and Gordon has the best brief account of the influence of these men in America.

14

be of no use for "the gentry, the body of the people in a free nation" to "become the tools and instruments of knaves and pickpockets." It is always the practice of oppressors to "form parties, and blow up factions to mutual animosities, that they may find protection in those animosities. . . . Indeed, there had been no such thing as party now in England, if we had not been betrayed by those whom we trusted. . . . Most men are sick of party and party-leaders; and let us, by all proper methods, exemplarily punish the parricides, and avowed enemies of all mankind."[13]

Men who were so deeply convinced of the evil tendencies of parties were unlikely to start them, or even to start political associations that might too much resemble them. Caroline Robbins, who has written a sympathetic history of the long and honorable line of radical propagandists to which Trenchard and Gordon belonged, observes that men in this tradition were very late to organize, and that "without leaders and organization the reformers failed." "A part of their failure to organize," she remarks, "must be attributed to their detestation of party. None had the faintest conception of what was necessary and what was wrong, what was legitimate and what was unprincipled in the compromises and adjustments inevitably imposed upon groups anxious to implement reforming programs."[14] The

---

[13] *Ibid.*, 53–54, 124, 48–49.

[14] *The Eighteenth-Century Commonwealthman* (1961), 382.

Although scholars have not been able to find that Rousseau had any significant influence on American political thought in the Revolutionary era or for long afterwards, it is perhaps worth observing that any American radical who had gone to him for inspiration would have found a repudiation of party even more categorical than that which could be found in the English radical tradition. In Book II, chapter III of *The Social Contract*, Rousseau, writing in behalf of "the great association" which is society, opposes all "cabals and partial associations." When one of these associations becomes large enough to prevail over the others, he argued, "you no longer have the sum of many opinions dissenting in a small degree from each other, but one great dictating

effort to organize in behalf of reforming programs had to await the arrival of a breed of men who, parrot as they might the anti-party cant of their age and their inheritance, would have the happy inconsistency to act in disregard of it.

III

As one reads eighteenth-century American writers with an eye to their borrowings from English thought, one finds that there were three archetypal views of party. I say archetypal with special emphasis: my main concern here is to set forth certain basic views, as abstractions. It is easier to classify the possible views of party in the framework of eighteenth-century thought than it is to classify most individual writers with confidence. On this subject many men were equivocal or inconsistent, and some on occasion changed their minds. Therefore, my identification of individuals with this or that point of view should not be taken more rigidly than it is meant. Even the archetypes themselves may be set down here with too much clarity of outline to represent precisely the confused and fuzzy dialogue that was actually carried on; but it will be useful to set them forth as ideal types.

First, there was the orthodox view, which in England was identified especially with Bolingbroke and which in America, despite its general currency, may be called for convenience the Hamiltonian view—that parties are evils that can be avoided or abolished or suppressed, even if this must be done, para-

---

dissentient; from that moment there is no longer a general will, and the predominating opinion is only an individual one." He concludes: "It is therefore of the utmost importance for obtaining the expression of the general will, that no partial society should be formed in the State, and that every citizen should speak his opinion entirely from himself." He did see, however, that if partial societies do arise in the body politic, "it is politic to multiply their number, that they may be kept on an equality."

doxically, through the temporary agency of a party of national unification. Suppose one begins with the widely shared proposition that parties are simply organizations formed to advance various special interests against the common public interest. One need then be disposed only slightly toward a belief in utopian solutions to hope that by some combination of devices parties can be got rid of. A minority—though surely not a negligible minority—of Anglo-American thinkers believed that this might actually be done. Whether cruder or gentler techniques were thought to be necessary to the end of getting rid of parties might depend upon the situation and temperament of the thinker, and on the kind of state apparatus he had in mind. Alexander Hamilton was among those who agreed that the elimination of parties was a possible goal in a well-designed and well-run state. "We are attempting by this Constitution," he said to the New York ratifying convention in 1788, "to abolish factions, and to unite all parties for the general welfare." In *The Federalist* he spoke of the value of a confederation in "suppressing" faction, or again of "repressing" it, and still again, in quoting Montesquieu, of "quelling" it. His rhetoric here is colored by a touch of force, as it is when he speaks of a strong American union as "a barrier against domestic faction and insurrection"—a significant coupling—or when, talking about the dangers of sedition, he promises that the Union will be an overmatch for "a turbulent faction in any of the states."[15]

It may occasion some surprise to revert to these anti-party statements from Hamilton, whom we think of as having become a fierce partisan and a party organizer. In fact, however, the whole tradition of anti-party writing is full of the works of men who were strong partisans; this tradition is, in very large part, the work of partisan writers and political leaders who are

---

[15] Elliot, *Debates*, II, 320; *The Federalist*, 124–128. Montesquieu used the softer verb *apaiser*, for which the standard English translation "quell" seems a trifle harsh; but Hamilton was not alone here.

actually appealing to a general distrust of the idea of party in order to subvert some particular party or to advance the interest of another party whose greatest claim to glory is that it will surmount and eliminate the party battle itself. This generalization applies no less to Bolingbroke, that fountainhead of anti-party thought, than it does to several of the Americans. All these anti-party manifestos by party leaders can be set down, if we like, to hypocrisy; but I suppose it to be a natural recourse of a type of mind which could not accept strife as a permanent condition of civic existence, or was unable to conceive of a lasting regime of ordered conflict. Embroiled in conflict though such men were, they conceived of their own partisan affiliations as being justified by the prospect that these affiliations, and these alone, could bring about, at last, a condition of national unity and harmony. In their eyes the only true justification of any party would be its promise of ultimately eliminating all parties.

The primary ideal of apologists of the modern party system is regulated conflict that serves, on balance, the free expression of political differences and somehow arrives at a rough approximation of the public interest. The primary ideal of the anti-party writers of the eighteenth century was the elimination of organized conflict and the achievement of national unity through astute and magisterial non-partisan leadership. This was the ideal laid down by the classic anti-party writer, Bolingbroke, in his conception of the Patriot King. At first it may seem strange that this Tory peer, once a Jacobite and later imagined by Whig writers to have had a formative influence on the political notions of George III, should have been such an influence in Whig America, a writer congenial to Madison and read assiduously by John Adams and Jefferson. But even some English radicals of the 1770's did come to look upon him as a precursor, and the Americans, who were perhaps attracted by the subtlety and unction of his style, also saw in him much that they could use. Bolingbroke's ideas were not new—they had become rather commonplace in Parliament at the time he set them down—but he was their most articulate and eloquent spokesman. In the 1730's, when his notable works on party were written, Bolingbroke was an oppositionist, an alienated critic who disarmingly espoused the old Whig principles of 1688 to attack the new Whig regime of Robert Walpole and, as Bolingbroke would have put it, to liberate the Crown from the current oligarchy. His basic problem, as he saw and conveyed it, was one which the Americans a good generation later could well understand—to restore virtue to a state that had grown corrupt. The Americans of Jefferson's generation had themselves been raised on imported criticisms of the corruption of Walpole's era, and many of Bolingbroke's themes—the cry for a virtuous monarch, the plea that the Crown should not be the agent of a faction, above all, the attack on corruption and party—had powerful appeal to them.[16]

At the time Bolingbroke wrote his several works on the nature and influence of parties, he was a member of the "Patriot" group which still hoped to unseat Walpole; and, like so many of the denunciations of parties issued by political leaders, his writings were in fact highly partisan. But by the time Bolingbroke wrote the most notable of his pamphlets, *The Idea of a Patriot King* (written around 1738; published 1749), Frederick, the Prince of Wales, had fallen out with his parents, George II and Queen Caroline, and the "Patriots" had hoped upon his expected succession to return under his aegis. Although he was an unlikely figure for the exalted role of the Patriot King, Frederick had been the main hope of the discontented associates of Bolingbroke, and *The Idea of a Patriot King* was dedicated to him. However, by the time this work was written, the opposition to Walpole had so reconstituted

---

[16] On the response to these ideas in America, see Bernard Bailyn, *The Origins of American Politics* (1968), 31–52.

itself, that Bolingbroke no longer had hope of any important part in it, and his tract was written in impotent, if philosophical, retreat. The conception of the Patriot King was Bolingbroke's ideal counterfoil both to the factional strife that had ravaged England during the seventeenth century and to the hated machinery of patronage and "corruption" which Walpole had employed to restore stability. To Bolingbroke, seventeenth-century party spirit represented faction rampant and destructive; the Walpole regime represented faction enthroned and tyrannous. His proposed alternative to these evils was the utopian image of a monarch of surpassing virtue, competence, and political dexterity, a king so benign that opposition would no longer exist.

The political foolishness inherent in the notion of a totally and consistently benign monarch was probably as strikingly evident to eighteenth-century Americans as it is to the modern reader; but more sensible to them, one may guess, was the model Bolingbroke set forth of an ideal source of national unity, free from the need of resorting either to tyranny or corruption. Bolingbroke held out the promise that the divisions that plagued nations were not "incurable," that factions can be "subdued" by great and good statecraft. And, lest he be condemned out of hand as utopian, he invoked the historical example of Queen Elizabeth, who had found her kingdom full of factions that were considerably more dangerous than those of Bolingbroke's own day, and, finding it impossible to unite them, transcended them by uniting "the great body of the people in her and their common interest, . . . inflamed them with one national spirit: and, thus armed, she maintained tranquility at home, and carried succour to her friends and terror to her enemies abroad."[17]

---

[17] *The Idea of a Patriot King*, 60, 62. It does not appear to have troubled Bolingbroke that in the long history of the English monarchy

However lacking in persuasiveness Bolingbroke's image of the ideal monarch may have been to Americans, his conception of parties could only echo and strengthen the conception they received from many writers of other political persuasions. To Bolingbroke parties are, by definition, hostile to the common weal. "Parties, even before they degenerate into absolute factions, are still numbers of men associated together for certain purposes and certain interests, which are not, or are not allowed to be, those of the community by others." Their claim to forward the interest of the state is the baldest pretension. "A man who has not seen the inside of parties, nor had opportunities to examine nearly their secret motives, can hardly conceive how little a share principle of any sort, tho principle of some sort or other be always pretended, has in the determination of their conduct."[18]

All too casually, Bolingbroke had to concede that parties are as inevitable as they are undesirable, thus defaulting on his promise that there could be a partyless state. Factions, he said, are to a country as nations are to the world, invading and robbing each other and pursuing a single interest at the sacrifice of the common interest. But, he admitted: "This has been and must always be in some measure, the course of human affairs, especially in free countries where the passions of men are less restrained by authority: and I am not wild enough to suppose that a Patriot King can change human nature." What the King can do is to "defeat the designs, and break the spirit of faction, instead of partaking in one and assuming the other." He may not make the union of his subjects universal, but he can "render it so general as to answer all the ends of good government, pri-

---

he could find only one monarch to cite as an example of the Patriot King; nor did he see any lesson in the rapid disintegration of Elizabethan unity.

[18] *Ibid.*, 47, 59.

vate security, public tranquility, wealth, power, and fame."
Temporarily, when it becomes necessary, the King may favor
one party and discourage another, but he will espouse none,
join none, proscribe none, and work steadily to pursue "true
principles of government independent of all." What Bolingbroke anticipated, then, was not the party government under
constitutional monarchy that would one day emerge in England, but royal government, the "nearly divine" prospect of "a
king possessed of absolute power, neither usurped by fraud, nor
maintained by force but the genuine effect of esteem, of confidence, and affection."[19] The entire life of kingly statecraft
must, then, consist in a struggle for unity and against party.

Without trying to suggest too much about Bolingbroke's
direct influence in America—for his general approach to party
became such common currency that one could sanction it
by reference to many authorities—it is possible to find many
Americans whose view of party and of national unity were
similar to his. The Federalist conception of party opposition,
which I shall discuss in chapter 3, is frequently reminiscent of
him, and it is probably not too much a conceit to say that
George Washington thought of himself (and was thought of
by his idolators) as a sort of American republican equivalent
of the Patriot King, the Patriot President, a figure above party
whose task it was to unite the whole nation. The classic expression of this early view of party (drafted for him by Hamilton) was embodied in his Farewell Address. But this conception
of party was no monopoly of the Federalists; it was at times
Jefferson's also, and it rings through the pronouncements and
shapes the strategy of his party during its period of power.

In some ways the Jeffersonian who most resembles Bolingbroke is Monroe. Bolingbroke, hedging in a manner characteristic of partisan anti-party thinkers, believed that a role of

---

[19] *Ibid.*, 62, 52–53, 86.

temporary usefulness could be served by a "country party" formed not on particular prejudices but "on principles of common interest." Such a party, he hastened to add, would not really be a party: "A party thus constituted, is improperly called party. It is the nation speaking and acting in the discourse and conduct of particular men."[20] Monroe too was articulate about the role of the unifying party—and in the United States the Republicans were the "country party" as the Federalists were the "court party." It is party *conflict* that is evil, Monroe postulated, but a single party may be laudable and useful, even though not as a permanent instrument of the state, *if* it can make itself universal and strong enough to embody the common interest and to choke party strife. This view of the matter may have some resemblance to modern authoritarian conceptions of the one-party state; but Monroe did not think it legitimate to *prohibit* opposition by law. Rather he hoped that the single party would eliminate partyism through its ecumenical and absorptive quality. Monroe, moreover, united this view of the matter with what we might now call a theory of American exceptionalism.

Such an ideal nonpartisan unification through the agency of an ecumenical party was not, he thought, an achievement possible in all nations. But it was possible in the United States because of the basic homogeneity of its classes and interests and the absence of severely distinguished traditional orders in society. In due course I will discuss how Monroe deals with the implications, theoretical and practical, of this view. But it would be misleading here to leave him alone to carry the onus of it. It is, in effect, the latter-day Republican view, a view into which others readily fell when, as members of a group in power, they tried to combine active partisanship in practice with an expressed allegiance to the prevailing anti-party philosophy.

---

[20] *A Dissertation upon Parties, Works*, II, 48.

IV

Second among conceptions of party is the view—which in America could be called Madisonian, in England Humean—that though parties are indeed evil, their existence is an unavoidable by-product of a free state, and that they must therefore be endured with patience by all men who esteem liberty. The evils of party are thus held to be part of the price one pays for liberty. One can check and limit parties, but one cannot hope to do away with them.

This conception is usually accompanied by, indeed rooted in, a psychological assumption: the impulse to differ, and in differing to form parties, is founded in human nature. Or, as Madison put it in the Tenth *Federalist*, "the latent causes of faction are . . . sown in the nature of man." If so, nothing but the iron hand of tyranny can put faction down, and the evils of tyranny are far worse than those of faction.

David Hume was probably the only eighteenth-century English thinker of major consequence who hoped to control parties through a constitutional balance—the solution taken over and introduced into American thought most articulately by Madison. To the problems of politics Hume brought the attitude of the rationalist and the skeptic who was revolted by the bigoted party politics of the English past and by what he regarded as clerically inspired partisan fanaticism. In this respect, he was on common ground with Bolingbroke, but he also anticipated Edmund Burke's sense that if parties were now to be liberated from the fundamentally divisive, emotionally searing issues that had plagued the seventeenth century, they were far more susceptible to adequate control than in the past. By the middle of the eighteenth century, the great tradition of the Scottish philosophy—the tradition that produced, along with Hume, such men as Adam Smith, Lord Kames, Francis Hutcheson, and Thomas Reid—was establishing a primary influence in American colleges, including Princeton where Madison had been an undergraduate. Madison, the first of the Virginia dynasty upon whom we will concentrate our attention, owed, as Douglass Adair has shown, a very substantial direct debt to Hume's essays; and there can be little doubt that he pondered over them intensively when he formulated the view of faction that we find in *The Federalist*, or that he turned to Hume's essays while working on the Tenth *Federalist*.[21]

As to parties, Hume believed that "men are generally more honest in their private than in their public capacity," and would go to greater lengths to serve a party than to serve their private interests alone. Even the consideration of honor, which is "a great check on mankind," could be overridden by the solidarity of party. Hence: "If . . . separate interest be not checked, and be not directed to the public, we ought to look for nothing but faction, disorder, and tyranny from such a government. In this opinion I am justified by experience, as well as by the authority of all philosophers and politicians, both ancient and modern. When men act in a faction, they are apt, without shame or remorse, to neglect all ties of honour and morality, in order to serve their party. . . ." Hume conceded that when a faction was formed on a sound principle, the effect of party loyalty could also make men obstinate and determined in the interests of justice. However, on balance, as he wrote in his essay, "Of Parties in General," the "founders of sects and factions" ought to be "detested and hated" among men as much as great legislators and founders of states are revered, "because the influence of faction is directly contrary to that of laws. Factions subvert government, render laws impotent, and beget the fiercest animosities among men of the same nation who ought to give mutual assistance and protection to each other." Factions are

---

[21] For Madison's debt to Hume, see Douglass Adair, " 'That Politics May Be Reduced to a Science': David Hume, James Madison, and the Tenth *Federalist*," *Huntington Library Quarterly*, 20 (1957), 343–360.

like weeds: once rooted in the state, they naturally propagate themselves for centuries, and seldom end without causing "the total dissolution of that government in which they are sown." They grow best, moreover, in the richest soil—that is, in free governments, "where they always infect the legislature itself."[22]

In his essay, "Of the Coalition of Parties," which was added to the 1758 edition of his book, Hume made it wholly clear that "to abolish all distinctions of party may not be practicable, perhaps not desirable, in a free government," an injunction which was to be restated even more firmly by Madison. The only dangerous parties, Hume supposed, were those that "entertain opposite views with regard to the essentials of government" or on other vital questions "where there is no room for compromise or accommodation, and where the controversy may appear so momentous as to justify even an opposition by arms to the pretensions of antagonists." He endorsed a recent general tendency in England, as he saw it, to abolish party distinctions of the kind that had brought civil war and revolution.[23]

Hume was not optimistic about getting rid of parties altogether. He was disposed to believe that their evils could be controlled by a moderate spirit in the political public—a consideration on which he perhaps rested more faith than most of his contemporaries in America. The important thing, he thought, was to confine the issues between factions to those matters about which moderation was likely. Here he distinguished parties based on interests from those based on principles, or on affection (i.e., strong attachment to leading persons or great families). In a characteristically modern vein, he argued that parties based on interests, which were the kind that could not be prevented from arising, were the most excus-

[22] David Hume, *Essays, Moral, Political, and Literary* (ed. 1882), I, 110–111, 119, 127–128.
[23] *Ibid.*, I, 464.

able and the most reasonable; whereas those based on deep principle were capable of rising to the same madness and fury as in religious wars, and even those based on affection were "often very violent." Hume urged that the controversies of the past should be dealt with by historians in a controlled and urbane spirit in order to create a temperate climate of public opinion about civic affairs. "Moderation," he wrote, "is of advantage to every establishment: Nothing but zeal can overturn a settled power: And an overactive zeal in friends is apt to beget a like spirit in antagonists."[24]

Jefferson was among those who shared the Hume–Madison view, though not at all times with consistency. One of the more persistent notes in his writing is the common notion that parties are founded in human nature, a notion very often supplemented in his letters by the suggestion that it is a *twofold* party division that is really natural—that men are, by instinct or impulse, natural Whigs or Tories depending upon their disposition to trust and "cherish" the people or to distrust and fear them. Hence it would be of little point to talk of preventing parties altogether, though Jefferson too had some hope that a well-designed constitution and a healthy state of public opinion would check the worst evils of party. That he never succeeded in applying his abstract tolerance of a two-party division to the realities of the American party battle will, I trust, become evident in chapter 3. His basic conceptions of man and of political theory pointed toward the Madison–Hume view of parties; but his inability as a partisan to see any legitimacy in the Federalist party brought about a quiet drift toward the Monrovian view.

---

[24] For Hume on the imperative of moderation, see *Essays*, I, 107–109, 464, 469. A somewhat different view of Hume from that expressed here is taken by Geoffrey Marshall, "David Hume and Political Scepticism," *Philosophical Quarterly*, IV (1954), 247–257. Marshall stresses Hume's acceptance of party and regards him as a forerunner of Burke in this respect. See especially pp. 252–253.

Though our central concern here is with the mainstream of Republican views as represented by the Virginia dynasty, it seems necessary to point out that one of the primary political thinkers of the period—except perhaps for Madison, its most interesting political mind—also took the Hume–Madison view. At an early point in his life John Adams expressed his view that the spirit of party "wrought an entire metamorphosis of the human character. It destroyed all sense and understanding, all equity and humanity, all memory and regard to truth, all virtue, honor, decorum, and veracity." In one of those famous letters he exchanged with Jefferson in their old age, he still blamed the effects of parties for the failure of the "science" of government to advance. "What is the reason? I say, parties and factions will not suffer improvements to be made. As soon as one man hints at an improvement, his rival opposes it. No sooner has one party discovered or invented any amelioration of the condition of man, or the order of society than the opposite party belies it, misconstrues it, misrepresents it, ridicules it, insults it, and persecutes it." Adams never cherished any illusions about getting rid of parties. "All countries under the sun must have parties," he said. "The great secret is to control them." And with Madison he had confidence that the well-balanced state could do it by creating "a government so mixed that factions may always be ruled." He saw two ways of controlling rivalries—the unacceptable one of despotism, and the desirable one of devising a balance of power.[25]

The practical goal, then, of the well-run state as seen by this theory, is not to eliminate or suppress parties but only to check, control, and confine the evils that arise out of their existence; and this goal becomes a central one in the design of constitutions and in the conduct of politics by patriotic men. Men who reasoned thus are sometimes referred to as pro-party thinkers

---

[25] *Works*, II, 152; X, 50; VI, 181, 280–281.

because of their resigned acceptance of the fact of party. But this seems to me misleading. At the most the Madisonian view can be regarded as equivocal on the subject, and I think it more accurate to label it a qualified anti-party theory. In any case, this notion of parties as evils inevitable under liberty, though it was often deserted by partisans under pressure, seems to me to be the dominant philosophical conception of party in early American thought and the central problem of the Jeffersonians as anti-party party-builders. It is also intimately connected with the entire political theory of Madison and with his pluralistic approach to political problems. It demands lengthy attention in its own right, and I shall return to it.

V

Third among conceptions of party is the view—identified with Burke in England, and in America, so far as I am aware, with no one clearly and consistently among Jefferson's contemporaries—that parties are not only inevitable but necessary and, on balance, good. In his *Thoughts on the Cause of the Present Discontents* (1770), Burke for the first time cut through the prevailing anti-party cant to make the case for party principles and loyalties. Where Hume had been a skeptical conservative observer, Burke was an embattled participant, an oppositionist writing near the close of a period of intense ministerial instability. His *Thoughts* represented the consummatory statement of the political creed of the Rockingham Whigs, who had enjoyed a brief ministry in 1765–66, and who were trying to draw the salutary lessons that they thought could be learned from the difficulties of the Chatham ministry that had replaced them and from the intimately connected ministry of Chatham's successor, the Duke of Grafton. Chatham (William Pitt) had been a leading denouncer and renouncer of parties. Professing himself devoted to "measures not men," he had aimed to pulverize the parties and to form a ministry united not on partisan loyalties or principles but around his own talents and reputation, picking and choosing such associates as he might from the existing factions. By detaching from them the Duke of Grafton and General Conway, he had indeed stung the Rockinghamites, who prided themselves on their *esprit de corps*, and were disposed to think, as Rockingham wrote in 1769 that "we and *only we* of all the parts now in Opposition are so on principle."[26]

Burke's *Thoughts* was the last, and the most articulate and memorable, of three tracts written between 1766 and 1770 expounding the creed of his group and underlining the failure of Chatham's anti-party principles. In a sense, Burke may be seen as at last making the object of open justification on principle what all active participants in parliamentary politics had long been doing and then disavowing. It was the custom to act in parties, and then to denounce them. But we do so act, Burke was saying in effect, because it is necessary and even desirable. The *Thoughts* may be taken, then, as a kind of unsolicited apologia for the natural habits and group loyalties of the lordly oligarchs who had been running the politics of England with very little opposition for the past fifty years. But beyond the issues of the moment, on which it may be easy to find Burke vulnerable,[27] he had arrived at an idea centrally important both for the theory and practice of politics—the idea that parties can be respectable.

As Hume had seen, and as Madison would see, Burke recognized that "parties must ever exist in a free country," and had begun a tract of 1769 with the assertion: "Party divisions,

---

[26] Quoted by Archibald Foord, *His Majesty's Opposition, 1714–1830*, 315; see that work, 306–321, for a brief account of clashing party doctrines.

[27] Richard Pares accuses Burke of a "habit of constructing a theory of politics out of generalizations . . . on every incident in the career of the Marquis of Rockingham." *George III and the Politicians*, 80 n.

whether on the whole operating for good or evil, are things inseparable from free government."[28] But with his characteristically shrewd sense for the requirements of human institutions, he went beyond this, threw off the spell of the conventional wisdom about the evils of party, and emphasized the merits of party loyalty and the positive role that parties can perform. His purpose was to expound the superior merits of open opposition through parties based on common conviction and principle, as opposed to court cabal, favoritism, and intrigue.

In effect Burke was justifying what in the eighteenth century was known as "formed opposition," which was hitherto considered disloyal or at least highly discreditable and dangerous. It was deemed allowable to oppose ministerial measures in Parliament by speaking against them and trying to persuade others to vote against them; but to organize consolidated groups had the tincture of conspiracy against the crown. This ethos, Burke saw, made it possible for a court party to accuse every other interest of faction. But in fact, he contended, groups of men openly linked to each other by conviction and loyalty, and openly subject to judgment by the people, were those most likely to bring good government.

As Bolingbroke had looked back to the reign of Elizabeth as the precedent for his Patriot King, Burke found his precedent in the era of Queen Anne: "In one of the most fortunate periods of our history this country was governed by a *connection*; I mean the great connection of Whigs in the reign of Queen Anne." The Whigs of that era, he argued, had risen to power through "hard essays of practised friendship and experimented fidelity." "They believed that no men could act with effect, who did not act in concert; that no men could act in concert, who did not act in confidence; that no men could act with confidence, who were not bound together by com-

---

[28] *Works* (ed. 1865), I, 271.

mon opinions, common affections, and common interests." Parties, Burke perfectly understood, could act for evil as well as good; but it was certain that they were the only way of *preventing* great mischief. "Unconstitutional statesmen" liked to brand them all as illegitimate factions. But it was only through party connections that men could hope to gain enough strength to check evil designs and bad politics arising from the "united cabals of ambitious citizens." "When bad men combine, the good must associate; else they will fall, one by one, an unpitied sacrifice in a contemptible struggle." It was true that parties were capable of degenerating into "a narrow, bigoted, and proscriptive spirit." But every profession—the profession of the soldier too, and the priest—has its attendant vices, which do not argue against the necessity of the profession itself. "Of such nature are connections in politics; essentially necessary for the full performance of our public duty, accidentally liable to degenerate into faction."[29]

What raised parties above the level of scheming factions was their adherence to general principles, presumably related to the public good. Hence Burke's famous definition, the first in which party is put in a favorable light: "Party is a body of men united for promoting by their joint endeavors the national interest upon some particular principle in which they are all agreed." This is a normative definition, and a rather idealistic one, but it has the great merit of its awareness that party has a function. Burke also understood that party organization requires at times some sacrifice of individual judgment and discretion to the common cause. "Men thinking freely will, in particular instances, think differently. But still as the greater part of the measures which arise in the course of public business are related to, or dependent on, some great, *leading, general principles in government*, a man must be peculiarly unfortunate

---

[29] *Ibid.*, I, 529, 525–526, 527.

in the choice of his political company, if he does not agree with them at least nine times in ten. If he does not concur in these general principles upon which the party is founded, and which necessarily draw on a concurrence in their application, he ought from the beginning to have chosen some other, more conformable to his opinions." Once a man was committed to a group on principle, Burke thought him fractious and disloyal suddenly to exalt his personal judgment and to forsake his companions, and he urged men not to allow the seemingly high-minded rationale of principle, independence, and private judgment to serve as an excuse for deserting comrades of long standing. He cited what he called an old scholastic aphorism (in fact it originated in Aristotle's *Politics*) that "the man who lives wholly detached from others must be either an angel or a devil," and he was not credulous about the probability of human angels. He preferred men to act as men and to express the friendships and loyalties natural to their condition—and, indeed, necessary to effective political action. "All virtue which is impracticable is spurious. . . . Public life is a situation of power and energy." He recognized the possibilities of evil partisan action, but the ultimate in political evil he found in quite another circumstance: "men without popular confidence, public opinion, natural connection, or mutual trust, invested with all the powers of government."[30]

VI

On the subject of party, Burke was an advanced and prophetic thinker who took a long stride beyond what had been said before him by any of the leading writers. He went beyond Hume's acceptance of party as a necessary evil to defend it as a necessary good. He went far beyond Bolingbroke's acceptance of a single temporary court party as a transient means of

---

[30] *Ibid.*, 530, 533–535, 536.

getting rid of all parties. He saw parties as permanent, and he realized that their permanence implied a *party system*, a plurality of parties whose legitimacy must be accepted. The Whigs and Tories of the past, he once remarked, "by their collision and mutual resistance have preserved the variety of this constitution in its unity"—a characterization that seizes upon the essential value of party competition.[31] Some of his statements indicated that he looked upon other parties than his own "connection" as legitimate players in the political game. He did not expect others to surrender their principles and be absorbed into his own group, and he even opposed the idea of party coalition when a sufficient difference of principles existed to warrant separate identities. He understood that the common good, the "national interest," would not be achieved by a single interest or party alone, since none is entirely dependable without opposition or criticism by others.

In eighteenth-century America we cannot find a major thinker to set down as Burke's counterpart, as we can set down Madison for Hume or any one of several writers for Bolingbroke. Burke's great statement on parties came too late to be an influence in its own right, for by 1770 the Americans of Jef-

---

[31] Quoted by Harvey C. Mansfield, Jr., *Statesmanship and Party Government: A Study of Burke and Bolingbroke* (1965), 182, from Burke's *Letters on a Regicide Peace* (1796). For the argument that Burke's acceptance of party embraces a party system, see chapter VII, especially 181–186. I have been much enlightened by this study.

From the disappearance of the great divisions of the seventeenth century, Burke and Bolingbroke drew opposite conclusions. Like Bolingbroke, Burke welcomed the end of fanatical and profoundly divisive politics, and remarked with satisfaction that "the great parties which formerly divided and agitated the kingdom are known to be in a manner entirely dissolved." (*Works*, I, 438.) But where Bolingbroke concluded that the dissolution of the "great parties" meant that parties could now at last be done away with, Burke concluded that the passing of profound disruptive issues had now at last made it possible for parties to engage in tolerable competition rather than raw and disruptive conflict.

ferson's generation were busy not with questions raised by party conflict but with the forging of national unity and the pursuit of the rights of man. Twenty years later, when they were ready to consider the problem of party in a new light, Burke was on the verge of losing whatever authority he might have had with men in the Jeffersonian ranks because of his position on the French Revolution; and the Federalists, who might otherwise have found him more congenial, were, as the party in power, locked more firmly than ever into the notion that party was faction and that opposition was sedition.

Yet even though there was no American counterpart of Burke on party, the idea that parties might perhaps be vindicated by their services to the body politic was not unknown or unthinkable here. Americans had had much experience with intense factionalism in the colonial period, and though they had not learned to like it, they had become aware that it could be endured. They were becoming conscious of the healthy plurality of interests and sects that prevailed among them, and were growing increasingly aware of the necessity for mutual tolerance that this imposed—two elements of consciousness that provided the intellectual and moral prerequisites of an understanding of the party system. To be sure, most of their discussions of parties and factions, as Bernard Bailyn has observed, dwelt at length on "their destructiveness, the history of the evils they brought upon mankind, their significance as symptoms of disease in the body politic." Yet Bailyn notices an occasional flicker of dissent, the American counterpart of that dissent Caroline Robbins has remarked on in the English scene. A writer in the *New York Gazette* in the early 1730's suggests that opposition "is not only necessary in free governments but of great service to the public," argues that parties "are a check upon one another, and by keeping the ambition of one another within bounds, serve to maintain public liberty," and postulates that "opposition is the life and soul of public zeal." Fifteen years later another argues that "parties in a free state ought rather to be considered as an advantage to the public than an evil" because they are "so many spies upon one another, ready to proclaim abroad and warn the public of any attack or encroachment upon the public liberty."[32] A full study of the development of the idea of party might show that other obscure writers were stumbling upon or toying with the idea that parties, if they could be kept in healthy competition with each other, would act as mutual checks and thus contribute to the balance of society.

Near the end of the century one finds this occurring from time to time, even among some of those whom we must on balance classify as anti-party thinkers. For example, a delegate to the Massachusetts ratifying convention of 1788, arguing for the Constitution, thought that the "competition of interest . . . between those persons who are in and those who are out of office, will ever form one important check to the abuse of power in our representatives." Arguing on the other side of the issue, a Maryland Anti-Federalist writer put it this way: "And learn this most difficult and necessary lesson: That on the preservation of parties public liberty depends. Whenever men are unanimous on great public questions, whenever there is but one party, freedom ceases and despotism commences. The object of a free and wise people should be so to balance parties, that *from the weakness of all you may be governed by the moderation of the combined judgments of the whole, not tyrannized over by the blind passions of a few individuals.*"[33] This statement of the case is so shrewd that one is disappointed to find it imbedded in a rather soggy and almost incoherent essay.

Again, Representative Robert Goodloe Harper, one of the

---

[32] Bernard Bailyn, *The Origins of American Politics* (1968), 125, 126.

[33] For the Massachusetts spokesman, see Elliot's *Debates*, II, 167; for the Maryland writer, Morton Borden's collection of Anti-Federalist writings, *The Antifederalist Papers* (1965), 27.

most interesting minds among the Federalists, declared in the House in January, 1798, in the course of an argument over office-holding, that he considered parties not only inevitable but desirable. Opposition parties in government, he said, were like competitors in a public exhibition: "The public is the judge, the two parties are the combatants, and that party which possesses power must employ it properly, must conduct the Government wisely, in order to insure public approbation, and retain their power. In this contention, while the two parties draw different ways, a middle course is produced generally conformable to the public good." Party spirit, he conceded, might run to excess, as a wind gives rise to a storm or fire to a conflagration, "but its general effects, like those of the great elements of nature," he had no doubt, "were beneficial."[34] Again a highly suggestive statement; but one would be more inclined to attach profound significance to it if Harper had not been found six months later arguing zealously for the Sedition Act, which was intended to put the opposition out of business.

Even Hamilton himself, on at least one occasion, could see how partisan division within parliaments could have some merit now and then. In *The Federalist* Number 70, at a point where he is discussing the necessity of promptitude and firmness of decision in the Executive, he pauses to concede that the same is not true to the same degree of the legislature: "In the legislature, promptitude of decision is oftener an evil than a benefit. The differences of opinion, and the jarrings of parties in that department of the government, though they may sometimes obstruct salutary plans, yet often promote deliberation and circumspection, and serve to check excesses in the majority. When a resolution too is once taken, the opposition must be at an end. That resolution is a law and resistance to it is punish-

---

[34] *Annals of Congress*, 5th Congress, 2d sess., 873–874 (January 19, 1798); see below p. 116 n.

able."[35] There are, of course, some ambiguities in this: it is in no wise clear from this whether Hamilton saw that there might be merit in a mass party as well as a parliamentary party. Also one may ponder his assertion that opposition to a law, once passed, is "punishable." Does he mean only that the law must be obeyed, or is he trying to assert the far more objectionable proposition that criticism itself is no longer acceptable? His language indeed suggests the latter, for he speaks not of "disobedience" but of "opposition" as necessarily coming to an end. Be that as it may, we can at best make but little of this obiter dictum in behalf of opposition on the part of a man who sought to unite all parties in the general welfare.

John Adams was another anti-party theorist who had a glimmering of the possible value of an opposition. As early as 1779, speaking of the situation in Congress under the Articles, he wrote: "An opposition in parliament, in a house of assembly, in a council, in Congress, is highly useful and necessary to balance individuals, and bodies, and interests against one another, and bring the truth to light and justice to prevail." But an opposition in a foreign embassy, in the circumstances of this country and of Europe, is ruin, he went on, because it destroys the necessary secrecy and confidence. While he thus accepted the value of a parliamentary opposition, it is doubtful that he would also have accepted an opposition functioning among the people as an organized party. Certainly he did not seek such a thing for the United States. In the following year he wrote a letter in which he said: "There is nothing which I dread so much as a division of the republic into two great parties, each arranged under its leader, and concerting measures in opposition to each other. This, in my humble apprehension, is to be dreaded as the greatest political evil under our Constitution."[36]

---

[35] *The Federalist*, 454.
[36] *Works*, IX, 485, 511.

A few observers, then, saw that parties could be good because instead of making for aggrandizement of power they offered another possible source of checks and balances in addition to those already built into the constitutional structure. A few others saw the value of opposition, short of party organization. So far as I have been able to determine, none saw that parties might perform a wide variety of positive functions necessary to representative democracy and unlikely to be performed as well by any other institutions. This seems more understandable when we consider not only the state of party in eighteenth-century thought but also the state of party development in eighteenth-century practice. The Founding Fathers did not have, in their current experience or historical knowledge, models of working parties that would have encouraged them to think in such terms. First, parties had to be created; and then at last they would begin to find a theoretical acceptance.

Chapter Two

A Constitution
Against Parties

THAT POLITICAL PARTIES did not hold a respectable place in eighteenth-century American political theory was a reflection of the low estimate put upon their operation in practice. Wherever the Americans looked, whether to the politics of Georgian England, their own provincial capitals, or the republics of the historical past, they thought they saw in parties only a distracting and divisive force representing the claims of unbridled, selfish, special interests. I do not intend here to try to penetrate the thickets of eighteenth-century politics either in England or in the American provinces. We long ago learned not to identify the Whigs and Tories of the eighteenth century with the highly developed British political parties of modern times, and not to imagine that England had a well-developed two-party system at the close of the eighteenth century or even during the early decades of the nineteenth. Modern parties have grown up in response to (and in turn have helped to stimulate) the development of large electorates, and their institutional structures are in good measure an outgrowth of the efforts necessary to connect the parliamentary party and the mass party. The modern party is, in this respect, the disciplined product of regular party competition in the forum of public opinion. It also deals with legislative issues, over which the established parties differ. But this concern with issues and legislation—and hence with competing programs—which we now take for granted as a focus of party politics did not have at all the same degree of development in the politics of late eighteenth-century England or of the American colonies.[1] It is the need to legislate frequently that imposes a constant discipline within a parliamentary body, as it is the need to carry issues to an electorate of considerable size that requires permanent organizations within the constituencies.

Although a suddenly enlarged electorate, active political contests, and the presence before Parliament of important issues coincided with a strong tendency toward a two-party system in the early eighteenth century, this state of affairs, which began to wane after the death of Queen Anne, was a matter of the rather distant past by the time of George III's accession. British politics in the era of George III, with the cabinet system not yet developed, with its relatively small electorate, its pocket boroughs, its connections of leading

---

[1] Cf. Richard Pares: ". . . In the eighteenth century Cabinets existed to govern rather then to legislate, and parties to sustain government rather than legislation; . . . when a minister legislated, even on important matters, he often did so as an individual, not only technically but politically. It did not often happen that a party's programme consisted of legislation, or that the merits of a legislative proposal were, in any sense, put before the electorate." *King George III and the Politicians* (1953), 195. Cf. J. H. Plumb, *Sir Robert Walpole: The Making of a Statesman* (1956), 250–251.

families, its management by purchase and arrangement, its lack of highly focused issues, its multiple, shifting factions, its high proportion of unaligned members of Parliament, bore only a vague germinal relation to the highly developed modern British party system. Historians may argue about details, but even as late as the 1820's, Richard Pares once suggested, one should perhaps speak only of a tendency toward a two-party system. The modern procedure for a change of ministry was first fore-shadowed, though in a rudimentary way, only in 1830, when Wellington's cabinet was forced to resign and give way to the Whig ministry headed by Earl Grey.[2] An adverse vote in the House of Commons now became established as the occasion for the end of a ministry, but it was not until 1868 that a prime minister (in this case Disraeli) first took the popular verdict in an election as a clear mandate and resigned without testing his position in Parliament. It was only after the Reform Acts of 1832 and 1867 that Britain moved toward the extended elec-torate of the sort that had been established in the United States. Efforts to organize machinery to mobilize a large electorate, which had reached a high state of development in the United States by the 1820's were being made in England during the 1860's. In party development, therefore, the United States proved to be the avant-garde nation.

Though today we think of the party system, party organiza-tion, and party identifications among the electorate as being much more fully developed in Britain than in the United States, it is easy to see why eighteenth-century Americans found in the state of English politics little that was edifying and less to

---

[2] Pares, *King George III*, 191; cf. 182–207. The fluctuations and grad-ual growth of opposition and party politics are traced in Archibald S. Foord, *His Majesty's Opposition, 1714–1830* (1964). On tendencies toward party in early nineteenth-century England, see Austin Mitchell, *The Whigs in Opposition, 1815–1830* (1967), especially chapters 1–3, and Norman Gash, *Reaction and Reconstruction in English Politics, 1832–1852* (1965), chapters 5–6.

imitate. However we may now assess the English political system in the last half of the eighteenth century, it seems safe to say that most Americans saw in it even less merit than it had, that they regarded it with a certain self-righteous puritanism, emphasizing its evil and corrupt character, which they contrasted with the robust and virtuous character of their own politics. Although there were still Anglophiles of a sort, one finds few Americans near the close of the century who could, with Hamilton, look upon English political culture, with all its faults, as the most advanced in the West, or who could understand why he thought it was the only government in the world that united "public strength with individual security."[3] One can find perhaps none at all who could see in the historic division between Whigs and Tories any precursor of the highly functional party system of the future.

On the eve of the Revolution, most colonials thought of recent English history simply as a story of moral degeneracy, political corruption, and increasing despotism, marking a sharp and perhaps irreversible decline from the glories of that earlier England whose principles had been the inspiration of American liberties. Indeed one reason for the Revolution was the felt necessity of severing connections with a state that was losing the pristine purity of its constitution and was cutting itself adrift upon the seas of corrupt and tyrannical government. Americans saw this corruption when they visited the mother country; they read about it in the English political pamphleteers; they saw it at work on their own premises in the behavior of the Customs Commissioners during the 1760's. Benjamin Franklin had commented on the increasing "corruption and degeneracy of the people" in England during the 1750's, and

---

[3] Hamilton citing Necker to the Federal Convention, Max Farrand, ed., *Records of the Federal Convention of 1787* (1911), I, 288. On the elements of English freedom as of 1815, see Élie Halévy, *England in 1815* (ed. 1946), 588–591, and 108–200, passim.

shortly before Lexington and Concord was still complaining
about "an extream corruption prevalent among all orders of
men in this rotten state." All he could see was "Numberless
and needless places, enormous salaries, pensions, perquisites,
groundless quarrels, foolish expeditions, false accounts or no
accounts, contracts and jobbs" which "devour all revenue and
produce continual necessity in the midst of natural plenty."
James Otis thought that the House of Lords was filled with
peers who had not risen above what they learned at Oxford and
Cambridge—"nothing at all but whoring, smoking, and drink-
ing"—and that the Commons were "a parcel of button-makers,
pinmakers, horse jockeys, gamesters, pensioners, pimps, and
whore masters." John Adams believed that the virtue of England was done for: "Corruption, like a cancer . . . eats faster
and faster every hour. The revenue creates pensioners, and the
pensioners urge for more revenue. The people grow less steady,
spirited, and virtuous, the seekers more numerous and corrupt,
and every day increases the circles of their dependents and
expectants, until virtue, integrity, public spirit, simplicity, and
frugality, become the objects of ridicule and scorn, and vanity,
foppery, selfishness, meanness, and downright venality swal-
lowing up the whole society." Jefferson, writing under the
stress of wartime animosity in his *Notes on Virginia*, concluded
that Great Britain was nearly finished: "The sun of her glory is
fast descending on the horizon. Her philosophy has crossed the
channel, her freedom the Atlantic, and herself seems passing to
that awful dissolution whose issue is not given human foresight
to scan."[4]

---

[4] For Franklin, Otis, and Adams, see H. Trevor Colbourn, *The Lamp
of Experience* (1965), 72, 97, 130–131; for Jefferson, his *Notes on Virginia* (1785), ed. by T. P. Abernethy (1964), 66. Colbourn is especially
illuminating on American versions of English and European history.
See also Cushing Strout, *The American Image of the Old World* (1963),
12–17, 25–29, 33–38; William L. Sachse, *The Colonial American in*

II

Although the Americans thought of their own political condition as being much healthier than England's—it was in the New World that they expected old English liberties to be preserved—they thought they had no reason to attribute the comparative soundness of their own politics, as they saw it, to any evidences of party government. Though many historians would probably want to make an exception for Pennsylvania, and some perhaps for New York, most would agree with the general judgment that "no colony had what could be appropriately designated as a party structure."[5] Certainly if a rigorous definition of party structure is laid down, demanding not merely parliamentary factions in the assemblies but clearly developed and permanent mass parties, this judgment would hold.

A great deal of political energy went into the repeated battles with the royal governors, and this put a premium on methods of organization that united rather than divided the assemblies. In the conduct of their struggles, and in securing legislation, the colonists had recourse to more or less disciplined caucusing groups, sometimes called "Juntos" which made life difficult for the governors but greatly increased the effectiveness of those who wanted to assert colonial prerogatives. After 1776, with royal governors out of the way, the state legislatures, released from the unifying discipline imposed by the struggle for their prerogatives, were more free to break up into factional groupings. Political contests could now take on more clearly the form of struggles between rival groups of citizens within the state. But of course many respectable men saw this period as one of alarming disorder, and they could see little promise

---

Britain (1956), 204–207; Edmund S. Morgan, "The Puritan Ethic and the American Revolution," *William and Mary Quarterly*, 24 (1967), 14–19.

[5] Clarence Ver Steeg, *The Formative Years, 1607–1763* (1964), 273.

of good in the local factionalism that developed. "To many, the very word 'party' carried anti-republican connotations."[6]

Pennsylvania, which had the closest thing to a two-party system, was sometimes pointed to as an example of the evil effects of party strife under constitutional government. Madison, for example, in the Fiftieth *Federalist*, cited the "two fixed and violent parties" of Pennsylvania as a primary reason for the failure of that state's Council of Revision. The state had been "for a long time before, violently heated and distracted by the rage of party," Madison pointed out, and this was a difficulty that the other states must also expect to experience.[7] Yet one may wonder about the justice of this judgment on Pennsylvania. The factions in Pennsylvania may have been as bad as they were thought to be—the politics of that province had always been contentious—but the existence of parties did not prevent the Pennsylvanians from going through the fires of the Revolution, the British ensconced on their very doorstep, without slipping into tyranny or giving way to indiscriminate reprisals, or from emerging with a free and quite democratic constitution.

No doubt the factors that combined to produce free government were numerous, and party conflict was only one of them. Provincial factionalism had its seamy side and its social costs; and the pre-party factions may be criticized by contrast with the highly developed parties of a later day. But factional

---

6 Richard P. McCormick, *Experiment in Independence*, 79; see chapter IV of his work for an excellent account of political machinery in the 1780's. Carl L. Becker, in his *History of Political Parties in the Province of New York, 1760–1776* (1909), considered that parties, not very clearly defined, came into being in the 1760's, but concedes that before that date New York was still in the thrall of "aristocratic methods of political management." See 11–18.

7 *The Federalist*, ed. by B. F. Wright (1961), 353–354. On the party struggle before 1766, see Theodore Thayer, *Pennsylvania Politics and the Growth of Democracy, 1740–1776* (1953).

differences taught the Americans to argue, polemicize, legislate, and on occasion to make compromises; the modern political party is an evolutionary product resting on a large fund of political experience, of which this early factional politics was a part.

The truth seems to be, however, that free government could struggle along with or without these rudimentary forms of party. Virginia must here concern us especially; and Virginia—which, along with Connecticut, was the least faction-ridden of the colonies—represents the strongest challenge to the notion that the political party had to be a decisive force in the development of a free state. If we compare the political culture of the Old Dominion, which was, after all, the political culture that the Virginia dynasts knew best, with most other colonies, we are impressed by its partyless condition and the relative uneventfulness of its domestic politics in the eighteenth century up to about 1763. One may argue whether the government of colonial Virginia was brilliant, but it was certainly competent as governments went then and as most of them go now; and Virginia bequeathed to the new nation an impressive, if preponderantly parochial, gallery of talents, unmatched by any of the other states.

It is Virginia that may serve to remind us that, for all the claims that have been made for the "democratic" character of colonial politics, colonial society was a deferential society and its politics were ordered accordingly. In his elegant little study of the methods of political control in Washington's Virginia, there was one conception for which Charles S. Sydnor had no use, beyond a need to explain its absence, and that is the conception of party. In eighteenth-century Virginia men were elected not because of the group they were associated with or what they proposed to do about this or that issue but because of what they were. An election promise might be made here or there—though political promises were rather frowned on and

47

might even be made the object of investigation or cause an elected candidate to be refused his seat—but in the main men put themselves forward on their social position and character and manners, and on their willingness to treat their constituencies in the right and liberal fashion, not least on their willingness to ply them with rum punch. It was rare for a man to run on issues or policies; and no one could run on factional identifications, since these were thin, ephemeral, and spare of meaning.[8]

"Perhaps the most striking characteristic of Virginia politics between 1689 and 1763," writes Jack P. Greene in his study of the Southern colonial assemblies, "was its tranquillity." Even the governors, he concludes, were in the main able, prudent, and moderate. The aristocracy was tightly knit and mutually accommodating. There was no serious rivalry between the Council and the Burgesses. Sectional divisions there were, but before the Revolution they were not of grave consequence. Class differences there were also, and occasional personal rivalries, but they produced no parties, not even permanent factions, and St. George Tucker was able to recall with satisfaction long after the Revolution that he had never seen anything in the Burgesses "that bore the appearance of *party spirit*."[9]

---

[8] See C. S. Sydnor, *Gentlemen Freeholders* (1952), especially 106–108, 115, 120–121. On the nature and significance of deferential society, see the brilliant essay by J. R. Pole, "Historians and the Problem of Early American Democracy," *American Historical Review*, 67 (1962), 626–646. On the transition from the politics of deference to those of public opinion and party debate in England and America, see Lloyd Irving Rudolph, "The Meaning of Party," doctoral dissertation, Harvard University, 1956.

[9] Jack P. Greene, *The Quest for Power* (1963), 29–30; see also David Alan Williams, "Political Alignments in Colonial Virginia, 1698–1750," doctoral dissertation, Northwestern University, 1959, and Thad W. Tate, "The Coming of the Revolution in Virginia: Britain's Challenge to Virginia's Ruling Class," *William and Mary Quarterly*, 19 (1962), 339–340, 343.

A generation nurtured in this environment had no successful example of party government anywhere in its experience, but it had an example of a partyless government of a free and relatively benign character, and the statements of the Virginia dynasts about party, though conventional among their entire generation in America as well as in their own particular cherished locale, have a uniquely firm root in Virginia soil.

III

Let us turn from the state of practice to the state of theory. The Founding Fathers, thinking along lines drawn by the old struggle against British authority, by the works of dissenters, radical Whigs, and libertarian publicists, and by the violent pre-Revolutionary controversy itself, were concerned with one central issue: liberty versus power. Because men are fallible, wicked, and self-aggrandizing, they thought, power tends always to extend itself and to encroach upon liberty. "From the nature of man," said George Mason at the Federal Convention, "we can be sure that those who have power in their hands . . . will always, when they can, . . . increase it." "Power," said Madison, "is of an encroaching nature."[10] The basic problem of republicanism, as most of them saw it, was to protect liberty by devising foolproof checks upon power. The basic problem of good American republicans like Madison, who nevertheless wanted a stronger Union, was to protect liberty by checking power, without at the same time weakening government to a point at which its stability would be in danger.

Liberty, then, was the basic value. As to what it consisted of, Americans sometimes assumed so much that their passionate

---

[10] Farrand, *Records*, I, 578; *The Federalist*, Number 48, 343. On the theme of power and liberty, see Bernard Bailyn, *The Ideological Origins of the American Revolution* (1967), and on the late acceptance of parties in formal political theory, Austin Ranney, "The Reception of Political Parties into American Political Science," *South-Western Social Science Quarterly*, 32 (1951), 183–191.

claims for liberty seemed to mask a demand for license or anarchy. But they would have answered that liberty prevailed when men were free to exercise their natural rights. As an answer to the abstract question, What is liberty? this was enough for them, and they had no difficulty at all in spelling out what natural rights were or what institutions threatened liberty or sustained it. It was endangered by many things they saw in contemporary England: monarchy and aristocracy, a standing army, corruption, bribery, and patronage, a decadent state of morals. It could best be protected under a government which had within it a strong popular house in the legislature, a broad freehold suffrage, a system of mutual checks and balances among the arms of government, an independent judiciary, explicit guarantees of rights (among these, civil and religious liberties and trial by jury), and frequent (some said annual) elections.

The necessity of checks on power is a theme struck over and over. But it is important that for the Fathers these checks had to be built *into the constitutional structure itself*. They were not content—and still less were the people they had to persuade—to rest their hopes on those checks that might arise in the political process alone, and this is one reason why they put no faith in party competition. Their hopes were pinned on a formal, written system of internal checks and balances, the precise enumeration of limited powers, and the explicit statement of constitutional guarantees, such as the opponents of the Constitution insisted on adding to it. Such informal forces in politics as the temper of the public, the process of opposition, the institutionalization of party structures, which to us seem so vital in democracy, seemed to them too slender a reliance, too inadequate a substitute for explicit constitutional specifications.

Here, it is important to realize, the ideas about constitutional structure that prevailed in America were derived both from Anglo-American experience and from the traditions of classical political thought. What had come down as the authoritative prescription for just and stable government from the times of Polybius and Aristotle was the idea of mixed government—that is, a government that would incorporate representation of the three basic orders in society. The three indispensable arms of government would act for the sovereign, the nobility, and the people. The prevalent eighteenth-century passion for balanced government, which was founded on the conviction that liberty and justice would be most secure if the elements of the state and of society were counterposed in such a way as to check and control each other, was sought for in constitutional systems that separated the powers of government and put the several arms of government in a state of watchful mutual tension. The necessary mutual checks would thus be provided by the elements of the constitution, and not by parties, which were indeed usually thought of, when they were thought of at all, as forces likely to upset the desired constitutional balance by mobilizing too much force and passion in behalf of one limited interest.

When they were thought of at all: in classical political theory, in the great books from Aristotle and Machiavelli to Locke and Montesquieu, which were read by the Founding Fathers when they consulted literature for political wisdom, parties played only an incidental, illustrative historical role, usually as examples of some difficult problem or some historical mischief. Most of the classical political writers had mentioned party here and there, but none of them discussed parties at substantial length or offered a theory of the role of the party in the state. Even such empirically minded thinkers as Aristotle and Machiavelli had little to say on the subject;[11] and so strong was this

---

[11] It is a point that deserves further exploration, but what seems to dominate in the classical tradition is the sense that parties will normally be more or less identical with one of the orders in the state. Machiavelli generally speaks of a party as being identical with an order. Cf. *The*

tradition that even as late as 1861, long after his own country was well launched upon the development of its two-party system, John Stuart Mill could write an entire treatise, *Considerations on Representative Government*, in which he never elaborated upon the role of party. Indeed, it was the great cumulative and collective merit of writers like Bolingbroke, Hume, Burke, and Madison that they showed a new understanding of the importance of party and a strong disposition to move it somewhat closer to the center of concern in political thought.

However, the point remains that in the thinking of the Founding Fathers, the truly useful and reliable antitheses of politics, the counterpoises upon which they were disposed to rely for liberty and stability, were still embodied not in the mutual checks of political parties but in the classic doctrine of the separation of powers, in the mutual checks of the houses of legislature, or in the checks exerted upon each other by the executive and the legislature, and in that exerted by the judiciary over the other two. Checks were to be built into planned constitutional forms instead of being left to the hurly-burly of politics. James Madison, for example, assuring the Federal Convention that the new constitution would have safeguards against the betrayal of trust by officials, explained: "An obvious precaution against this danger would be to divide the trust between different bodies of men, who might watch and check

---

Prince in *The Prince and the Discourses* (Mod. Lib. ed., 1940), 35, 119; he refers to two hostile groups within the nobles as "factions." *Ibid.*, 42. In *The Discourses* he writes: "In every republic there are two parties, that of the nobles and that of the people; and all the laws that are favorable to liberty result from the opposition of these parties to each other, as may easily be seen from the events that occurred in Rome." *Ibid.*, 119. "Democracies," Aristotle had written, "are only exposed to sedition between the democratic party and the oligarchical, and there are no internal dissentions—at any rate none worth mentioning—which divide democratic parties against themselves." *Politics*, V, chap. 2, 16.

each other." John Jay, speaking for the Constitution in the New York ratifying convention, said: "The two houses will naturally be in a state of rivalship. This will make them always vigilant, quick to discern a bad measure, and ready to oppose it."[12] It was two *houses*, not two parties.

While most of the Fathers did assume that partisan oppositions would form from time to time, they did not expect that valuable permanent structures would arise from them which would have a part to play in the protection and exercise of liberties or in reconciling the stability and effectiveness of government with the exercise of popular freedoms. The solution, then, lay in a nicely balanced constitutional system, a well-designed state which would hold in check a variety of evils, among which the divisive effects of parties ranked high. The Fathers hoped to create not a system of party government under a constitution but rather a constitutional government that would check and control parties.

This conviction, as Cecelia Kenyon has pointed out, was shared by both sides in the debate over the adoption of the Constitution. Although Federalists and Anti-Federalists differed over many things, they do not seem to have differed over the proposition that an effective constitution is one that successfully counteracts the work of parties. The Anti-Federalists often expressed a sweeping opposition to the idea

---

[12] Farrand, *Records*, I, 421, 260; Jonathan Elliott, *Debates in the Several State Conventions* (1888), II, 285. Cf. Madison in Number 51, where he argues that one should so contrive "the interior structure of the government as that its several constituent parts may, by their mutual relations, be the means of keeping each other in their proper places." Again, the way to avoid excessive legislative predominance is "to divide the legislature into different branches; and to render them, by different modes of election and different principles of action, as little connected with each other as the nature of their common functions and their common dependence on the society will admit." *The Federalist*, 355, 357.

of political organization as such, and, as Miss Kenyon has observed, "the contemporary opponents of the Constitution feared parties or factions in the Madisonian sense just as much as did Madison, and . . . they feared parties in the modern sense even more than Madison did. They feared and distrusted concerted group action for the purpose of 'centering votes' in order to obtain a plurality, because they believe this would distort the automatic or natural expression of the people's will."[13]

IV

We have come now to the point at which we can examine the problem of party as it was expressed in the minds of the Virginia dynasts. It seems fitting to begin with Madison: he was a more systematic, and I believe a more deliberate and profound thinker than Thomas Jefferson; as the philosopher of the Constitution, he gives the clearest and most authoritative statement of the conflict between the rationale of the Constitution and the spirit of party; and, as the man who began, before Jefferson, to play the central role in organizing what came to be considered Jefferson's party, he illustrates even more sharply than Jefferson our central paradox of party government instituted by anti-party thinkers.

The great achievement of Madison was to provide for his contemporaries a statement of the checks-and-balances view

---

[13] See her "Introduction" to her documentary anthology, *The Antifederalists* (1966), cx; cf. lv, lxxxv, xciii–xciv; see also her essay, "Men of Little Faith: the Antifederalists on the Nature of Representative Government," *William and Mary Quarterly*, 12 (1955) 40; cf. 13, 36.

During the debates over the ratification of the Constitution, factions and parties were occasionally mentioned, and almost always invidiously, by spokesmen on both sides, though more often by Federalists than by Anti-Federalists. Elliot, *Debates*, II, 14, 71–72, 168, 248, 253–254, 266, 292, 310, 317, 320, 322, 532; III, 37, 46, 87, 90, 107–108, 125, 233, 282, 290, 310, 316, 492, 583; IV, 38, 40, 59, 60, 66, 74–75, 127, 329.

of government in which a pluralistic view of society itself was linked to the plural constitutional structure. Like John Adams, he saw with great clarity the importance of supplementing the internal balance of the constitution with the external balance of the various interests and forces that made up society.

Here Madisonian pluralism owes a great deal to the example of religious toleration and religious liberty that had already been established in eighteenth-century America. The traditions of dissenting Protestantism had made an essential contribution to political pluralism. That fear of arbitary power which is so marked in American political expression had been shaped to a large degree by the experience men of dissenting sects had had with persecution. Freedom of religion became for them a central example of freedoms in general, and it was hardly accidental that the libertarian writers who meant so much to the colonials so often stemmed from the tradition of religious dissent. In the colonies, Americans fought unrelentingly against the proposal to introduce an Anglican episcopate among them, an idea that excited in their minds a remarkable terror that religious liberty, and then all liberty, would be invaded. In their campaign against an American episcopate, the colonials cooperated with dissenters in the mother country with such admirable system and regularity that they established a veritable trans-Atlantic Protestant anti-episcopal union, whose members gave a great deal of thought to the problems of liberty, toleration, and pluralism.[14]

In 1768 an Anglican chaplain was quoted by one of his anti-establishment opponents in New York as having said that American experience showed that "republican principles in religion naturally engender the same in civil government." It was an appropriate remark. The whole Protestant enterprise had made for the decentralization of structure within the

---

[14] For a full account of this movement, see Carl Bridenbaugh, *Mitre and Sceptre* (1962).

churches themselves, and at the same time within the structure of society. There were no longer a State and a Church standing together as unified, firm ordered hierarchies, but two spheres of values that could sometimes compete. The presence of dissenters, and the necessity of appeasing them in the interests of secular stability, meant that the imperatives of the state and those of the church might not coincide, and that the latter might in some respects be sacrificed for the former. The presence of a variety of theologies, a plurality of views within Protestantism itself, also made toleration a necessary precondition for the secular values of peace and social stability. The coexistence of the sects and the growth of toleration led to a premium on argument and persuasion, as against main force. The dissenters, with the law against them and no other instrument of suasion available to them, had had to defend their interests in this way. It became clear in England that there could no longer be such a thing as a single enforceable orthodoxy. Even error had to be tolerated, and if error could be endured where profound matters of faith were concerned, a model had been created for the political game, in which also one might learn to endure error in the interests of social peace.[15]

Of course the advancing secularism of educated men brought strong reinforcement to this tendency. One notices the common sense of relief shared by such different theorists of party as Bolingbroke, Hume, and Burke at the passing of the old religiously inspired, bigotry-animated political divisions of the seventeenth century, and Hume indeed had made a central principle of it in his political writings. The advanced, enlightened, more or less secular man could take a genial view of the competitions of sects, so long as they were all free and not at each others' throats. So Franklin, a Deist, patronized the churches, and Jefferson in time forged a curious political alli-

---

[15] *Ibid.*, 306 n, 52.

ance between Enlightenment liberalism and the passion of the minority sects for religious freedom.[16]

The intellectual transition from the pluralism engendered by religious denominations to that of parties was clearly illustrated by William Livingston in New York during the 1750's. A young man still in his late twenties when he started writing in 1752, Livingston was soon to cut quite a figure in the politics of the province as a partisan in the De Lancey–Livingston party battle. The De Lanceys were Anglicans, the Livingstons and their allies Presbyterians and keen enemies of episcopacy. In 1752 Livingston launched his *Independent Reflector*, a journal which aped the style of the *Tatler* and the *Spectator* but which took much of its argument from *Cato's Letters*. Though a strong partisan, Livingston had been put off by dogmatic doctrinal religion at Yale. His Presbyterianism was qualified by a certain broad tolerance of other dissenting groups and yet fortified by an intense, almost anti-clerical animus against the Anglican Church. His own doctrines on faction were hewn out of the current orthodoxy. ("Unspeakably calamitous have been the consequences of party-division. It has occasioned deluges of blood, and subverted kingdoms.") But still, as an ardent partisan, Livingston, like Bolingbroke with his country party to end all parties, had to have an exception: "To infer . . . that the liberties of the people are safe and unendanger'd, because there are no political contests, is illogical and fallacious." We all have a right to look into the conduct of our superiors, and if we find in them "a combination of roguery" it is our common right to "form a party against their united strength: and such a party, I hope we may never want the spirit to form."[17]

---

[16] For this alliance see Sidney E. Mead, "American Protestantism during the Revolutionary Epoch," *Church History*, 12 (1953), 279–297.

[17] *The Independent Reflector*, ed. by Milton Klein (1963), 146, 148. On the significance of this controversy, see Klein's Introduction and

Livingston, who never lacked such spirit, was roused to one of his keenest efforts in 1753 during the controversy over the founding of King's College (later Columbia). He was afraid that the college, should it receive a charter from the Crown, would become an exclusively Anglican institution, "an academy founded in bigotry and reared by party-spirit." He proposed instead that the college should be created by the legislature, and established on such a non-sectarian basis that all the groups in the province could use it together, and that all the youths sent there could be educated free of indoctrination in any particular set of religious or partisan tenets. *"For as we are split into so great a variety of opinions and professions; had each individual his share in the government of the academy, the jealousy of all parties combating each other, would inevitably produce a perfect freedom for each particular party."* Next to a patriot king and wise laws, Livingston argued, "an equal toleration of conscience is justly deem'd the basis of the public liberty of this country. And will not this foundation be undermined? Will it not be threatened with a total subversion, should one party obtain the sole management of the education of our youth?"[18]

Note that the term "party" is applied by Livingston more or less indifferently to a religious or a political group, a circumstance that arises not only out of their interconnection in the

---

Richard Hofstadter and Walter P. Metzger, *The Development of Academic Freedom in the United States* (1955), 187–191.

[18] *Independent Reflector*, 184, 195, 213: italics added. An Anglican spokesman, William Smith, saw the issue as follows: "As to the political uses of national establishments, he must indeed be a very shallow politician who does not see them. The statesman has always found it necessary for the purposes of government, to raise some one denomination of religion above the rest to a certain degree. This favor'd denomination, by these means, becomes as it were the creature of the government, which is thus enabled to turn the balance and keep all in subjection." Bridenbaugh, *Mitre and Sceptre*, 152. And this is precisely what the dissenting factions intended to prevent.

provincial politics of New York but also, and more important-
ly, out of his understanding of the principles of mutuality involved both in religious liberty and civic peace. For him libertarian principles in religion did indeed have a bearing on the
problems of civil government.

A similar awareness of the relation between multiple sects
and liberty is evident in a remarkable address before a convention of the Congregational clergy of Rhode Island delivered by the Reverend Ezra Stiles in 1760 and published the
following year. Stiles was really addressing the Congregational
world of New England, which, though badly divided for
twenty years by the effects of the Great Awakening, was still
united in its anxiety about episcopal incursions. In *A Discourse
on the Christian Union* Stiles pleaded for an ecumenical tolerance. "Every sect," he said, "have a right to vindicate their
particular forms." Theological differences, which he hoped to
minimize among good Christians, might survive, but: "Their
conviction . . . is not to be laboured by the coercion of civil or
ecclesiastical punishment, but by the gentle force of persuasion
and truth—not by appeals to the tenets of parties and great
men; not by an appeal to the position of Arminius or Calvin;
but by an appeal to the inspired writings." In arguing that even
church councils or consociations had no authority over individual churches, Stiles added strikingly: "Coercive uniformity is neither necessary in politics nor religion." This conclusion
was premised upon a remarkable statement of harmony in
plurality: "Providence has planted the British America with
a variety of sects, which will unavoidably become a mutual
balance upon one another. Their temporary collisions, like the
action of acids and alcalies, after a short ebullition will subside
in harmony and union, not by the destruction of either, but in
the friendly cohabitation of all. . . . Resplendent and all-
pervading TRUTH will terminate the whole in universal harmony. All surreptitious efforts and attempts on public liberty

will unavoidably excite the public vigilance of the sects, till the terms of general union be defined and honorably adjusted. The notion of erecting the polity of either sect into universal dominion to the destruction of the rest, is but an airy vision . . . all the present sects will subsist and increase into distinct respectable bodies, continuing their distinctions for a long time yet to come in full life and vigor. Indeed mutual oppression will more and more subside from their mutual balance of one another. Union may subsist on these distinctions, coalescence only on the sameness of public sentiment, which can again be effected in the Christian world only by the gentle but almighty power of truth. . . . The sects cannot destroy one another: all attempts this way will be fruitless—they may effect a temporary disturbance, but cannot produce a dissolution— each one subserves the mutual security of all. . . . Nothing however will content us but actual experiment—this experiment will be made in one century, and then perhaps we shall be satisfied."[19]

It remained for James Madison to make still more explicit than Livingston or Stiles the analogy between the religious and the civic spheres. From his earliest days Madison had had a deep and passionate commitment to religious liberty. The Madison family was never warmly disposed toward the Anglican establishment in Virginia, and Madison's father appears to have been unsympathetic to the persecution of Baptists that raged during James's youth in neighboring Culpeper County. Madison him-

---

[19] *A Discourse on the Christian Union* (1761), 53, 95, 96–97; cf. Bridenbaugh, *Mitre and Sceptre*, chap. 1. "Our grand security," Stiles wrote to a Saybrook minister in 1767, "is in the multitude of sects and the public Liberty necessary for them to cohabit together. In consequence of which the aggrieved of any communion will either pass over to another, or rise into new sects and spontaneous societies. This and this only will learn us wisdom *not* to persecute one another." Edmund S. Morgan, *The Gentle Puritan: A Life of Ezra Stiles, 1727–1795* (1962), 252.

self, who was tutored by a Princeton-educated Presbyterian, made the significant choice to go to Princeton rather than to Anglican William and Mary. His undergraduate years at Princeton coincided with the regime of President John Witherspoon, who was later to be a signer of the Declaration of Independence. Although his religion was more severe than Madison's, Witherspoon may have heightened his antipathy to establishments. At Princeton Madison also appears to have read Voltaire surreptitiously, and of all the Voltairean aphorisms that he might have chosen to fasten upon, he became particularly fond of Voltaire's saying that in England one sect would have produced slavery and two a civil war, but that a multiplicity of sects caused the people to live at peace.[20] He was also apparently familiar with William Livingston's *Independent Reflector*, which was often read at Princeton. When he went back to Virginia, it was as a firm advocate of religious liberty and an alert foe of an Anglican episcopate. The editors of his papers have concluded that religious issues were more important than economic ones in stimulating his earliest interest in politics. When he began to correspond with a college friend from Pennsylvania, William Bradford, it was religious issues that chiefly aroused him, and he began to make unfavorable comparisons between Virginia's persecutions and the broad tolerance displayed in Pennsylvania.

At twenty-three, he denounced "that diabolical Hell conceived principle of persecution" and the Anglican clergy for abetting it, and professed that this troubled him more than any other public issue. Concerning a new outbreak of persecution in Culpeper County he wrote to Bradford in January 1774: "There are at this [time] in the adjacent county not less

---

[20] In the *Lettres Philosophiques* Voltaire had written: "If there were only one religion in England, one would have to fear despotism; if there were two, they would cut each other's throats; but they have thirty, and they live happy and in peace."

than five or six well-meaning men in close [jail] for publishing their religious sentiments which in the main are very orthodox. I have neither patience to hear, talk, or think of anything relative to this matter, for I have squabbled and scolded, abused and ridiculed about it to so little purpose, that I am without common patience." By contrast he admired "that liberal catholic and equitable way of thinking as to the rights of Conscience, which is one of the characteristics of a free people" that he believed to be prevalent in Pennsylvania. Later it was Madison who would take the leadership in the struggle to go beyond the limited principle of toleration to espouse complete religious liberty and achieve disestablishment in the first constitution of Virginia.[21]

As Madison was well aware in the less discouraged moments of his maturity, an answer to the "hell-conceived principle" was already apparent in America. The growth of a multiplicity of denominations and sects had made religious freedom a practical necessity, and had provided the political forces to make it possible. Madison's insight into the strength and viability of a pluralistic society seems at least to have been heightened by, if it did not derive from, the model already before him of various religious groups coexisting in comparative peace and harmony. He told the Virginia ratifying convention of 1788 that the remarkable freedom of religion now achieved "arises from that multiplicity of sects, which pervades America, and which is the best and only security for religious liberty in any society. . . . The United States abound in such a variety of sects, that it is a strong security against religious persecution, and it is

---

[21] *Papers*, ed. by W. T. Hutchinson and W. M. E. Rachal, I (1962), 101–106, 107, 111–113, 159, 170 ff.; Irving Brant, *James Madison: The Virginia Revolutionist* (1941), 65–77, 85, 128–130, 243 ff. On religious persecution in Virginia, see William Taylor Thom, *The Struggle for Religious Freedom in Virginia: the Baptists* (1900) and Garnett Ryland, *The Baptists of Virginia, 1699–1926* (1955), chap. III.

sufficient to authorize a conclusion that no one sect will ever be able to outnumber or depress the rest."[22]

A monopolistic religious establishment, Madison saw, is in a position to persecute, just as a single interest in society or a single arm of government, when unchecked, is in a position to be tyrannical. A plurality of sects militates against religious oppression just as a plurality of varying social interests militates against political oppression. Madison put this analogy very explicitly in Number 51 of *The Federalist*, where he spoke of the desirability of guarding against the oppression of minorities by a single consolidated majority. This, he thought, could be done in the proposed federal republic of the United States "by comprehending in the society so many separate descriptions of citizens as will render an unjust combination of a majority of the whole very improbable, if not impracticable." While all authority in the proposed republic, he went on, "will be derived from and dependent on the society, the society itself will be broken into so many parts, interests, and classes of citizens, that the rights of individuals, or of the minority, will be in little danger from interested combinations of the majority. *In a free government the security for civil rights must be the same as that for religious rights. It consists in the one case in the multiplicity of interests, and in the other in the multiplicity of sects.* The degree of security in both cases will depend on the number of interests and sects; and this may be presumed to depend on the extent of country and number of people comprehended under the same government."[23]

---

[22] Elliot, *Debates*, III, 330: see also *Writings*, Hunt, ed., II, 185; V, 176. For a much later statement on pluralism and tolerance in connection with the founding of the University of Virginia, see *Writings*, IX, 125–127.

[23] *The Federalist*, 358; italics added; cf. Farrand, *Records*, I, 134–136 for his speech in the Convention of 1787; and *Writings*, V, 123–129 for his speech in the Virginia Convention.

V

The best statement of Madison's pluralism, of course, is in the familiar Number 10 of *The Federalist*, a work which shows a powerful obligation to the theory of party laid down in David Hume's essays.[24] Madison's basic concern in that essay was to show that a large federal union would be better than a small republic at sustaining free representative government; but his point of departure was the problem of controlling parties and the "violence" and threat to liberty that are connected with them. Always, in *The Federalist* the fundamental thing government has to control is the "assertive selfishness of human nature." But the basic manifestation of this selfishness in political life is the party, or faction. Possibly the greatest of the many advantages that would come with a well-constructed Union, Madison argued, was "its tendency to break and control the violence of faction." (Madison, it should be noted, used the terms party and faction as synonyms.)[25] The classical problem of the republics known to previous history, their instability, injustice, and confusion, had already been much remedied by the constitutions of the American states, he admitted. But now complaints were being heard everywhere by public-spirited men that "the public good is disregarded in the conflicts

---

[24] For the text, see *The Federalist*, 129–136. The composition of this remarkable essay had gone on for some period of time. The basic analysis had been stated and restated in letters and in his "Observations" of April 1787. See *Writings*, II, 273, 346–347, 366–369; V, 28–32. It is important also, on this theme, to read *The Federalist*, Numbers 14, 37, 47, 48, 50, and 51.

[25] For example: ". . . and the most numerous party, or, in other words, the most powerful faction must be expected to prevail." *The Federalist*, Number 10, 132. See, on this, the useful textual comparisons made by Gottfried Dietze in *The Federalist: A Classic on Federalism and Free Government* (1960), 119 n; Dietze also points out (106) that Hamilton and Jay used the terms in the same way; cf. B. F. Wright in his edition of *The Federalist*, 33.

of rival parties"—and particularly that measures were being decided "by the superior force of an increased and overbearing
majority." Such injustices were largely if not wholly the consequence of "a factious spirit" in government. "By a faction,"
Madison goes on, "I understand a number of citizens, whether
amounting to a majority or a minority of the whole, who are
united and actuated by some common impulse of passion, or of
interest, adverse to the rights of other citizens, or to the permanent and aggregate interests of the community."[26]

How best to remedy this state of affairs? You can destroy
liberty, which makes faction possible, but that remedy is clearly
far worse than the disease. You can try to give all citizens the
same opinions, passions, and interests, but that is impracticable.
Men have different faculties and different abilities in acquiring
property; and protecting these faculties is the first object of
government. But out of these differences arise different kinds
and degrees of property, hence differing political interests and
parties. "The latent causes of faction are thus sown in the
nature of man." Passions will make men form factions and
"vex and oppress each other." But different propertied interests
—landed, moneyed, mercantile, manufacturing, debtors, and
creditors—are the most common and durable sources of factions. "The regulation of these various and interfering interests
forms the principal task of modern legislation, and involves
the spirit of party and faction in the necessary and ordinary
operations of government."

This last sentence, because of the ambiguity of the word
"involves," has led some readers to think that Madison had
found, after all, a strong positive function for parties. But it is
one thing to say that legislation or government cannot be carried on without having parties make their appearance—i.e., that

---

[26] Note that where Burke had defined party as based on principles
aiming to advance the common interest, Madison defines it as based
on passions or interests that threaten the general welfare.

they are *involved*—and another that they are *valuable* in the process; and I think the whole context of Madison's work, with its pejorative definition of party and its many invidious references to party, make it clear that it was the former meaning he was trying to convey.

Since the causes of faction cannot be safely or wisely removed, Madison was saying, we have to look for relief in the means of controlling its effects. The most dangerous faction is the most powerful, the majority faction, and it is above all the tyranny of the majority that we must be concerned with. A minority faction, he admitted, could be temporarily obstructive, and could even convulse society. But in the normal course of events in a republic, it will be outvoted, and it will be "unable to execute and mask its violence under the forms of the Constitution." However, a majority faction can sacrifice the public good and the rights of other citizens to its ruling passion, and it is this above all that must be prevented. "To secure the public good and private rights against the danger of such [majority] faction, and at the same time to preserve the spirit and form of popular government, is then the great object to which our inquiries are directed."

How can this be done? It is useless to rely on enlightened statesmen: they may not always be there; and it is the very essence of good constitution-making to provide safeguards against ordinary human frailties.[27] The answer lies in a representative republic, which will avoid the turbulence of direct democracy, and in an extensive republic rather than a small one.

In making this last point, Madison was trying to establish a view which thus far had had the status of a heresy. It was standard eighteenth-century doctrine—made canonical by

---

[27] Cf. Hume, *Essays*, I, 99: "But a republican and free government would be an obvious absurdity, if the particular checks and controls, provided by the constitution, had really no influence, and made it not the interest, even of bad men, to act for the public good."

Montesquieu though questioned by Hume—that republican governments, whatever their merits, are not strong enough for the government of an extended territory. Madison was concerned to assert the opposite: that an extended territory such as that of the United States bodes well for the survival and stability of representative republican government precisely because, being large, it embraces a healthy and mutually balancing variety of economic and social interests. It is just this plurality and variety that he believes will prevent the emergence of a cohesive and oppressive majority. "Extend the sphere, and you take in a greater variety of parties and interests; you will make it less probable that a majority of the whole will have a common motive to invade the rights of other citizens; or if such a common motive exists, it will be more difficult for all who feel it to discover their own strength, and to act in unison with each other."[28]

In a large federal republic, Madison argued, a majority faction was less likely to be achieved than in a small one. The greater variety of parties is the greatest security "against the event of any one party being able to outnumber and oppress the rest." Thus the parties themselves are mobilized against the great danger of party. A multilateral equipoise, a suspended harmony of conflicting elements, very Newtonian in conception, is established. In Pope's words:

> *Not chaos-like, together crushed and bruised*
> *But, as the world harmoniously confused*
> *Where order in variety we see,*
> *And where, though all things differ, all agree.*

With the Madisonian formulation, thinking on the role of party had thus reached a stage of profound but fertile am-

---

[28] In The *Federalist*, Number 9, Hamilton had tackled the same problem by trying to show that even Montesquieu had seen the confederation of republics as an answer to the problem of size.

biguity. To unravel the ambiguity would require an entire additional generation of political experience.

VI

Certain aspects of the Madisonian model require comment here, since they point to difficulties unresolved either in the theory or the construction of the Constitution. Madison is not, for example, wholly clear by just what mechanism the formation of an oppressive majority is to be prevented. It is not certain whether he is saying that in a properly balanced society under a properly balanced constitution it will be impossible for a majority to form at all, or whether he simply believes that the majority, if formed, will be too weak or too impermanent, or both, to execute its "schemes of oppression." But more important than this is the question whether Madison has left room enough in his ingenious model for the formation of a majority sufficiently effective to govern at all. If the "energetic" government he and Hamilton sought was to become a reality, it would surely carry out a number of policies of sweeping consequence for the people, policies which in most cases would be the object of doubt and dispute. How could any such policies be formed and executed, if not through the periodic formation of majority coalitions? Again, how could they be better legitimated under a republican system than by reference to the majority will? Madison himself would soon enough begin to see the cogency of these questions.

Another problem that has stimulated much comment is that Madison seems to show so little fear of minority tyranny or even of minority obstruction, both of which he dismisses in a phrase. He does not address himself to the possibility that, since majorities are to be weak and precarious, a large, aggressive minority, though incapable of taking the reins of government, might veto whatever policy it likes, and thus in effect tyrannize over the majority.[29] There is, in short, no protection of the majority against grave deprivations imposed by the minority. (And as we shall see in due course, Madison was forced to confront this possibility near the end of his life, when he was compelled by his opposition to nullification to rephrase his view of the majority.) Neither, it must be added, does Madison address himself to the possibility that a minority interest in the population, by virtue of superior wealth, organization, and influence, can actually come into the firm possession of power against a pluralistic and divided majority. Yet within a few years after the Constitution was in operation this was precisely what the leaders of the emergent Republican party were saying about the Federalists.

Then, again, Madison's argument hardly anticipates the next step in the political game. What was he to say about the dangers of a majority coalition when his own party, the Republicans, had finally organized one? Were the Republicans a faction or party in the sense in which Madison had used that word? Were they too, then, a danger to liberty? Were they a danger to liberty when, having two of the arms of government and finding the opposition entrenched in the third, the judiciary, they tried to subordinate the third arm also? Was this a fatal invasion of the sacred principle of the separation of powers?

There is another set of problems arising from the tension between Madison's two great objectives, to create a more "energetic" national government and to protect liberty. Professor Alpheus T. Mason has remarked that *The Federalist* was a "split personality." Certainly there was a breach between Hamilton's clear and uncluttered concern for greater governmental energy and his tendency to consider that in a country like America liberty would be sure to take care of itself, and

---

[29] See Robert A. Dahl, *A Preface to Democratic Theory* (1956), 27–29, and more generally, chap. I, "Madisonian Democracy."

Madison's passionate desire, without sacrificing energy, to check the majority, to be sure that liberty was secured in a more certain way than had ever been done in the history of republics.[30]

The balance of social interests, the separation and balance of powers, were meant to secure liberty, but it was still uncertain, after the instrument had been framed and ratified, whether the balance would not be too precarious to come to rest anywhere; and whether the arms of government, separated in the parchment, could come together in reality to cooperate in the formation and execution of policy. As we shall see, a mechanism had to be found, for example, by which men could put together what God, in the shape of the Constitution, had sundered—to make it possible for the President and Congress to work in harness. Both the Federalists and the Republicans had to find a solution to this—the Federalists by making Hamilton a kind of prime minister to bridge the gap, and the Republicans by having President Jefferson exert through his agents and his direct influence a great power in Congress. The framers, discussing the method of election of the President, had expressed a good deal of concern that this should not happen—that the Executive should not be in league with, or the leader of, a party. But both sides, in order to make policy, found the agency of party a practical necessity. And in the end it seems doubtful whether this Constitution, devised against party, could have been made to work if such a functional agency as the party had not sprung into the gap to remedy its chief remaining deficiencies.

At an early point, then, parties were to become a part of the machinery of government in a manner that went well beyond Madison's resigned acceptance of them as evils that would always be there. In a country which was always to be in need

---

[30] Alpheus T. Mason, "The Federalist—A Split Personality," *American Historical Review*, 57 (1952), 625–643, especially 636 ff.

of the cohesive force of institutions, the national parties, for all their faults, were to become at an early hour primary and necessary parts of the machinery of government, essential vehicles to convey men's loyalties to the State under a central government that often seemed rather distant and abstract. So much so that we may say that it was the parties that rescued this Constitution-against-parties and made of it a working instrument of government. When Lord Bryce came to evaluate American government in *The American Commonwealth*, he noted: "The whole machinery, both of national and State governments, is worked by the political parties. . . . The spirit and force of party has in America been as essential to the action of the machinery of government as steam is to a locomotive engine; or, to vary the simile, party association and organization are to the organs of government almost what the motor nerves are to the muscles, sinews, and bones of the human body. They transmit the motive power, they determine the direction by which the organs act. . . . The actual working of party government is not only full of interest and instruction, but is so unlike what a student of the Federal Constitution could have expected or foreseen, that it is the thing of all others which anyone writing about America ought to try to portray."[31]

A final word must be said about the character of Madison's pluralism. His was a pluralism *among* the parties, whereas the course of our national history has produced a pluralism *within* the parties. It was natural for Madison in 1787–88 to think of the country as having not merely a wide variety of interests but also a rather wide variety of party groupings and subgroupings within the states. Historians will almost certainly disagree about the details, but Forrest McDonald's delineation of the various political factions existing during the Confederation may be suggestive. He found, leaving out a miscellany of

[31] *The American Commonwealth*, 3d ed. (1897), I, 6; II, 3, 4.

very small factions, one state (Pennsylvania) with two parties, five states with two major factions, five with three or four major factions, and one (Delaware) with multiple cliques.[32] We need not be surprised that Madison's thought had to be adapted to this existing political disorganization—thirteen states, each in its way a kind of separate political interest, and all together containing within them something like thirty discernible political groupings. What Madison did not see in advance was that the Constitution, by focusing more attention on nationwide issues, and indeed by itself first becoming a nationwide issue, would become a major force, perhaps *the* major force, in creating two great parties, and thus ironically making more probable the very majority coalition he so much feared; and, still more ironically, putting first Jefferson and then himself at the head of such a majority. What happened in due course, as it is so easy for us to see, was that our social pluralism made itself effective within each of the two major parties, a process that was strikingly evident in the Jeffersonian ranks by 1804, if not earlier. In our politics each major party has become a compound, a hodgepodge, of various and conflicting interests; and the imperatives of party struggle, the quest for victory and for offices, have forced the parties themselves to undertake the business of conciliation and compromise among such interests. This business goes on not merely in the legislative process, where Madison expected it would, but also in the internal processes of the great political parties themselves.

Madison's pluralism, then, had substantial merits as a generalized model, but as to the parties it was mislocated. Envisaging political parties as limited, homogeneous, fiercely aggressive, special interests, he failed to see that the parties themselves might become great, bland, enveloping coalitions,

---

[32] Forrest McDonald, *We the People* (1958), chap. II. On Delaware, however, see John A. Munroe, *Federalist Delaware* (1954), 97–109, who finds two basic factions here also.

eschewing the assertion of firm principles and ideologies, embracing and muffling the struggles of special interests; or that they might forge the coalitions of majorities that are in fact necessary to effective government into forces sufficiently benign to avoid tyranny and sufficiently vulnerable to be displaced in time by the opposing coalition. Liberty, he had always understood, would sustain a political atmosphere in which a conflict of parties would take place. The reverse of that proposition, the insight that underlies our acceptance of the two-party system, that the conflict of parties can be made to reinforce rather than undermine liberty, was to be well understood only in the future.

Chapter Three

The Jeffersonians
in Opposition

I

I HAVE SAID so much about the absence of exemplary models of political parties and of a theory of politics that accepted parties, that it seems necessary now to emphasize another side of the matter and to acknowledge how many other ingredients of a mature political culture were present in the experience of the Founding Fathers. For while the absence of a party theory or a party system helps to explain the form some of their problems took, it is only the presence of certain auspicious traits and habits that accounts for their considerable measure of success in meeting these problems. It is of the utmost consequence that our first political parties developed in a benign environment.

The structural features of American society were exceptionally favorable to a moderate course of political development. Property was widely diffused. The political public was a large one, resting in part upon this propertied base and in part upon a generous suffrage. Relatively speaking, it was a literate public, and a large portion of it was accustomed to taking part in political life. It was proud of its rights, alert to violations of them, and suspicious of authority. Leadership and officeholding, of course, were largely in the hands of a patrician class—it seems hardly accurate to call it an aristocracy—and yet between the patrician leaders and the voting citizens there usually existed a fair degree of confidence, mutual respect, and accommodation. Colonial history had its record of class resentments, class conflicts, and even rebellions, but it had left no legacy of class hatred nor any fixed patterns of class hostilities. The political and social elite itself, though torn by certain conflicts of interests, personal suspicions and resentments, and factional clashes, was capable of sitting down in conclave without unmanageable distrust or frequent upheaval.

Moreover, both the elite and the democratic mass had been trained and tried by the political experiences of the recent past. Upon their long-developed tradition of English liberties and their historic habit of local self-government, the years since 1763 had superimposed a testing period of constant, hectic, and stimulating political protest, and the governing generation had been reared upon this immensely educative political experience. Each of the thirteen provinces, while undergoing the first trials of the Revolutionary War, had managed the political feat of peacefully forging a new constitution for itself, and the new constitutions usually reaffirmed basic religious and political liberties. Perhaps most important, the Revolution itself was brought about with a remarkable economy of violence. Although many Loyalists were driven into exile, and many lost their lands by confiscation, no systematic executions took place. There was no guillotine, no wholesale purge of counter-revolutionary conspirators. There was not, of course could not be, the occasion or the need for regicide, with the shock such an act inflicts upon the minds of legitimists or the stimulus it gives to increasing violence among their foes. The revolutionists did not turn against each other with the instruments of terror and violence. Unlike many other colonial revolutions, the American Revolution did not end in military dictatorship; unlike many more profound social revolutions, it did not end by devouring its own children. The leaders of 1776 were still alive, free, and active in 1790. "Was there ever a revolution brought about," Sam Adams asked, "especially so important as this, without great internal tumults and violent convulsions!"[1]

In addition to the constitution-making of the states, the Revolutionary generation had the experience of forging not one but two federal constitutions between the first draft of the Articles of Confederation in the summer of 1776 and the final ratification of the Constitution in 1788. In the case of the Constitution, following the example of Massachusetts, the Fathers set a historical democratic precedent by referring a basic instrument of national government to conventions chosen by a broad popular electorate and constituted solely for the act of ratification itself—a unique institutional expression of their commitment to the idea that lawful government rests upon the consent of the governed.

In waging revolution and making constitutions, the leading men of the revolutionary generation had learned to do business with each other through discussion and concession, and had grown somewhat self-conscious and justifiably proud of their flair for compromise. In the Pennsylvania ratifying convention James Wilson remarked that the science of government still seemed in its infancy and that "governments, in general, have been the result of force, of fraud, and accident." He went on: "After a period of six thousand years has elapsed since the

---

[1] *Writings*, ed. by H. A. Cushing (1904–08), III, 304. For a statement from another point of view of the auspicious elements in American political experience, see John C. Ranney, "The Bases of American Federalism," *William and Mary Quarterly*, 3 (1946), 1–35.

creation, the United States exhibit to the world the first instance of a nation, unattacked by external force, unconvulsed
by domestic insurrections, assembling voluntarily, deliberating
fully, and deciding calmly, concerning that system of government under which they would wish that they and their poster-
ity should live." It was to the operation of popular government
and the principle of consent that he attributed "the scene,
hitherto unparalleled, which America now exhibits to the world
—a gentle, a peaceful, a voluntary, and a deliberate transition
from one constitution of government to another."[2]

The Constitutional Convention, in transmitting its work to
the Confederation Congress, reported that "the Constitution
which we now present is the result of a spirit of amity, and of
that mutual deference and concession which the peculiarity of
our political situation rendered indispensable." It observed that
not every state would be expected wholly to approve of the
document, but pointed out: "Each will doubtless consider that
had her interest alone been consulted, the consequences might
have been particularly disagreeable and injurious to others."[3]
Though much has been written about the ratification of the
Constitution on the assumption that its friends and foes were
implacable enemies, and though much of the rhetoric, indeed,
in which the argument was put was couched in high and in-
flammatory tones, it is significant that the issue was resolved by
discussion and concession and not by force; that many original
skeptics were actually converted in the course of argument;
that many who doubted the merits of the Constitution doubted
them not dogmatically but tentatively, and were prepared to
pocket their reservations in the interest of a fair experiment;
and finally that many of those whose reservations remained
strong were calmed and reconciled by the process of discussion

[2] Jonathan Elliot, *The Debates in the Several State Conventions*
(1888), II, 422, 433.
[3] Farrand, *Records*, II, 667.

and decision they had experienced. Benjamin Franklin, before signing the Constitution in Philadelphia, stated candidly: "I confess there are several parts of this Constitution which I do not approve, but I am not sure that I shall never approve them. For having lived long, I have experienced many instances of being obliged by better information, or fuller consideration, to change opinions even on important subjects, which I once thought right, but found to be otherwise."

This was an auspicious note. Edmund Randolph, alluding to Franklin's remarks, "apologized"—so the record tells us—for refusing to sign the Constitution, "notwithstanding the vast majority and venerable names that would give sanction to its worth. He said, however, that he did not mean by this refusal to decide that he should oppose the Constitution without doors. He meant only to keep himself free to be governed by his duty, as it should be prescribed by his future judgment." He was later among those converted to the support of it. Gouverneur Morris added that he too had objections, "but considering the present plan as the best that was to be attained, he should take it with all its faults. The majority had determined in its favor, and by that majority he should abide." Even Hamilton, who admitted that the document itself was more remote from his own ideas than from those of anyone present, said he saw no possibility of deliberating between anarchy on one side and the chance of some good on the other. Elbridge Gerry said he could not sign because he feared the debate over adoption would excite a warfare of parties in his own state, Massachusetts, and that his fear of "the heat and opposition of parties" forced him to withhold his signature; but he promised that, if the fact were not otherwise revealed, he would not noise abroad his refusal to sign.[4]

Gerry, it must be added, did not live up to his promise, but

---

[4] *Ibid.*, II, 641–646.

then neither did his home state live up to his fears. A spirit of comity and compromise was manifest in the Massachusetts ratifying convention, in which a substantial opposition to the Constitution had been mounted, and a spirited debate had taken place. At the end, a member from new Gloucester who had been articulate in opposition rose to say that he would go back and tell his constituents that he had opposed the adoption of the Constitution, "but that he had been overruled, and that it had been carried by a majority of wise and understanding men; that he should endeavor to sow the seeds of union and peace among the people he represented; and that he hoped, and believed that no person would wish for, or suggest, the measure of a PROTEST; for . . . we must consider that this body is as full a representation of the people as can be convened." His sentiments were reiterated by other members who had voted with the opposition.[5]

The argument between Federalists and anti-Federalists was not only conducted in a creditable way procedurally but it had a substantive outcome which demonstrated the constructive potentialities of an opposition. In omitting a bill of rights from the original draft of the Constitution, the constitution-makers had been guilty at least of a tactical error, if not a substantive one. They were not, of course, opposed to the principles asserted in bills of rights, which were incarnated in most of the state constitutions; but they apparently thought the new government would affect the lives of individuals so little that such an additional guarantee was wholly unnecessary, and many of them mistook the widespread fear of a threat to sanctified rights as a mere pretext for rejecting the document entirely. However, they recouped this error quickly and flexibly when the debate over ratification made it clear how important a sticking point the issue had become to their opponents. In effect they

---

[5] Elliot, *Debates*, II, 182; cf. 181–183.

traded modification of the Constitution in a manner which most of them saw as harmless if inessential, and some even came to see as beneficial, for mollification of the opposition. And while some Anti-Federalists were not satisfied with the bill of rights as it was enacted, the compromise was for the most part effective. George Mason, a firm and thoughtful Virginia opponent of the Constitution, found enough satisfaction in the amendments as passed by the House so that he acknowledged: "With two or three further Amendments . . . I could cheerfully put my Hand and Heart to the New Government." Jefferson, who had basically approved the Constitution but who also felt the necessity of a bill of rights, concluded that the Anti-Federalists had made a vital contribution. "There has been just opposition enough," he said, "to produce probably further guards to liberty without touching the energy of the government, and this will bring over the bulk of the opposition to the side of the new government."[6]

II

When the Jeffersonians found it necessary to organize an opposition party in the 1790's, they were less troubled by the anti-party bias of their own thought than they were heartened by this precedent of adversary politics on a continental scale. Once again, the most articulate statement on the subject was made by Madison. In 1792 he wrote a series of brief papers on the developing political controversy for the Republican party paper, *The National Gazette*, among which two are of particular interest for us.[7]

In the first of these, Madison restated two assumptions which link his thought of this period with that of *The Federalist*: parties are unavoidable; they are also evil, and the problem of

---

[6] Helen Hill, *George Mason, Constitutionalist* (1938), 242; for Jefferson, see *Documentary History of the Constitution*, V, 189.

[7] For these papers, see *Writings*, VI, 86, 87, 104–105, 106–123.

politics is to combat them and to suppress the conflicts they embody. But more interesting is the new emphasis on equality that emerges when Madison enumerates ways of combating them. One might say that while in *The Federalist* Madison's basic note is anti-majoritarian, in his papers of 1792 it is egalitarian. To combat the evil of parties, he suggests five devices: first, that "political equality among all" should be established; second, that the new laws should withhold *"unnecessary"* opportunities from the few to increase the inequality of property by an immoderate, and especially unmerited, accumulation of riches"; third, the laws should silently "reduce extreme wealth towards a state of mediocrity, and raise extreme indigence towards a state of comfort"; and fourth (though this proposition hardly seems consistent with the two preceding ones) that government should abstain from measures that favor one interest at the expense of another. But it is the fifth and final device for checking the evils of party that holds special interest for us here: "By making one party a check on the other, so far as the existence of parties cannot be prevented, nor their views accommodated."

The expressed hope, then, is still to prevent parties from arising or to absorb one into another by the accommodation of views; but in the high probability that this cannot be done, it is suggested that they be played off against each other, in the hope that this competitive process can be made to work in the public interest. We have here another glimmering, if not more than that, of a realization of the positive function of two-party politics, and it is Madison's experience in opposition that seems to have brought him around to this view. He strikes another note of novelty: since different interests and parties will arise, the art of the politician, he explains once more, is to make them "checks and balances to each other." But to this familiar argument he has something to add: If to the natural distinctions that always exist we make the mistake of adding artificial ones

—kings, nobles, plebeians, the orders of the Old World—then still more checks are needed, and the weight of the governmental apparatus becomes greater, its machinery more complex and difficult. To follow this course "is as little the voice of reason, as it is of republicanism."

Another essay, "A Candid State of Parties," was somewhat more historical in content. Here Madison in effect tries to legitimate his oppositional activities by showing that party opposition is a familiar fact of American political experience. Disregarding the various state parties, which he said had existed in abundance from 1783 to 1787, he found that nationwide parties had gone through three periods: first, the division between those who wanted independence and those who "adhered to the British claims"; second, the division over the adoption of the Constitution; and now at last under the Constitution "a third division, which being natural to most political societies, is likely to be of some duration in ours." As he described it, one side consisted of those who, out of temperament, habit, or interest, were "more partial to the opulent than to the other classes of society; and having debauched themselves into a persuasion that mankind are incapable of governing themselves, it follows with them . . . that government can be carried on only by the pageantry of rank, the influence of money and emoluments, and the terror of military force"— rather a partisan and extravagant characterization of the Federalists at that time. Against these proponents of government by the few stood the other party, consisting of those who, "believing in the doctrine that mankind are capable of governing themselves, and hating hereditary power as an insult to the reason and an outrage to the rights of man, are naturally offended at every public measure that does not appeal to the understanding and to the general interest of the community, or that is not strictly conformable to the principles, and conducive to the preservation of republican government."

Since the character and commitments of the parties were of this nature, Madison suggested, it would not be hard to predict their future conduct. The anti-republican party, "being the weaker in point of numbers," would try to strengthen itself with the influential, particularly with the moneyed men, "the most active and insinuating influence." Also it could be expected to try to weaken its opponents "by reviving exploded parties" and making use of whatever local or occupational prejudices it could exploit that would "prevent or disturb a general coalition of sentiments." The republican party, on the other hand, conscious that "the mass of the people in every part of the union . . . must at bottom be with them, both in interest and sentiment," would find their interest in surmounting old political questions and in "banishing every other distinction than that between enemies and friends to republican government," and in promoting good harmony among its friends.

Which party would ultimately establish its ascendance, only time could tell, and Madison did not dismiss the possibility that on the anti-republican side, wealth and stratagem might make up for the lack of numbers. But on the republican side, "the superiority of numbers is so great, their sentiments are so decided, and the practice of making a common cause . . . is so well understood, that no temperate observer of human affairs will be surprised if the issue in present instance should be reversed, and the government be administered in the spirit and form approved by the great body of the people." In short, one might expect that the Republicans would in time oust their foes and take over.

Like Madison's contributions to *The Federalist*, this little essay was, of course, a piece of partisan propaganda, but the occasion may explain certain differences. In *The Federalist* Madison had been trying to rally all possible supporters to the idea of a stronger central government. That government having now been formed, and he having rather promptly gone into opposition to some of its central policies he was trying to rally the former Anti-Federalists, as well as those who had followed his own nationalistic course of thought, into a single party. Hence his references to the *outmoded* character of the old issues, and to the desire of his opponents to revive exploded parties. But new purposes brought new emphases. Gone, now that Madison is a party leader, are the old references to the turbulence and violence of faction. Gone too, now that Madison is the leader of a party which he is convinced can soon well command the loyalty of an overwhelming majority, are his speculations about the best way to check the most dangerous of all factions, the majority faction. Emphasized instead is the assertion that the existing ins are a minority faction, and the simple confidence that the outs, having the sentiments of the masses behind them, will probably triumph. The suggestion that this party will *"ultimately* establish its ascendance" suggests that the triumph is expected to be final and permanent. This much is consistent with Madison's argument in *The Federalist* that a minority faction is unlikely to rule long. But he has lost interest, at least for the moment, in thinking about necessary checks on the incoming majority. What troubles him now is the control of an ascendant minority—a problem he had dismissed in *The Federalist*. The pragmatic pressure of political conflict has already begun to modify his theoretical system.

A final aspect of these essays is worthy of remark, since it represents a strain in Republican thought which we encounter again and again: it is the effort to reduce the issue between the two sides to a dispute over the merits of republican government as such. Today this seems a false question; the issues of funding, assumption, the bank, taxation, and foreign policy seem real and substantial enough without superimposing on them an artificial quarrel over a question of monarchy and hereditary power on which all but the tiniest handful of Americans agreed. But the exaggerated passions of both sides can be understood if we remember that most politically conscious Americans were acutely aware of being involved in a political experiment in republicanism that was attended by difficulties of the most acute kind and that might face many hidden and unpredictable pitfalls. Both sides were nervous about the stability of republicanism in an extensive federal union pervaded by many differences of sensibility and interest. They were anxious about its ability to preserve itself in a world of predatory monarchical powers, to avoid fatal foreign entanglements (each side having a different idea of which foreign entanglement would be most fatal), and to avoid either drifting backward toward monarchy and the hereditary principle, as the Republicans feared, or, as their opponents feared, onward into an unrestrained popular regime that would in the end be fatal to property and order. There can be little reason to doubt that notable Republican partisans like Madison, Jefferson, and Monroe were quite sincere in charging that many of their leading opponents favored monarchy and would scheme for its restoration, perhaps in some thinly disguised form under a "consolidated" state.

The charge was, though sincere, also opportune: since the Revolution the tide of American opinion had set in firmly and irresistibly against monarchy and all its attendant institutions and practices, and any party that could be successfully saddled with secret monarchical preferences would carry a fatal burden. If the Federalists were indeed opponents of republicanism, then they were, by American canons, in a sense and to a degree an illegitimate party. If they believed in monarchy and in restricting popular government, then, no matter how properly they may have at first come into their power, the use they intended to make of it violated the general republican consensus upon which the Constitution had been based, and thus represented a betrayal of the common understanding at the outset. Madison's use of such phrases as "the influence of money and

emoluments," "the terror of military force," "hereditary power," and the like, and charges in a companion essay about the
desire of his opponents "to pervert the limited government of
the Union into a government of unlimited discretion" on the
part of those "who avow or betray principles of monarchy and
aristocracy"[8] substantiate this view of his intent. But this disposition to doubt the legitimacy of the other side was hardly
a monopoly of the Republicans. Quite the contrary, this way
of thinking is even more congenial to incumbent governments than it is to parties of the opposition, and in this country it became quickly enough a feature of Federalist rhetoric.
The habit of casting mutual doubts upon the basic legitimacy both of government and opposition parties was a primary symptom of the newness and instability of the party
system, as well as a logical corollary of eighteenth-century
thought on parties. Charges and countercharges of this kind,
heated by the European conflict and by mutual suspicions of
treasonable foreign loyalties, were to grow and feed upon each
other until they culminated in the Alien and Sedition Acts.
But this part of the story requires that we turn from the Republicans for a moment to look at the state of mind of the
Federalists.

III

One of the great dangers in newly organized states is that
the party in power, which is usually the party that claims credit
for the revolutionary liberation of the country and for the successful organization of the new nation, claims for itself the exclusive custodianship of the essence of nationality and the
exclusive right to interpret the meaning of national welfare.[9]
This disposition, natural enough in new nations, is heightened

---

[8] *Ibid.*, VI, 112, 115–116.

[9] See Edward Shils, "Opposition in the New States of Asia and
Africa," *Government and Opposition*, I (1966), 175–204.

by the great uncertainties that enshroud so many problems of policy. The margin for allowable differences seems slight, and every outburst of serious criticism can be taken as a dangerous broadside levelled not against this or that policy but against the ship of state itself. Those who are in power are disposed to think of themselves not as a party that has taken the reins of government but as the government itself. Hence, the opposition is identified as a wholly unconstructive faction, an anti-government. Its criticism of policies is taken to be criticism of the government. Its criticism of a particular government is taken to be criticism of all government. It is therefore identified with anarchy, subversion, and disloyalty. When the Federalist William Vans Murray imagined that to organize opposition to the Jay Treaty in Congress was "subversive of the Constitution and . . . poisonous to our national faith," he voiced precisely this state of mind.[10]

Under these circumstances, it was a stroke of good fortune for the Americans that the first domestic issues, though immensely controversial among some leaders, and in themselves sufficient to bring about a measure of party polarization by 1792, were limited in their divisiveness. In the debate over Hamilton's system, a substantial portion of the House of Representatives, for example, was not lined up on one side or another with a clear partisan voting record. Moreover, the purposes behind the legislation had greater sympathy from the opposition than some of the highly colored accounts of the period have made clear. Madison, the floor leader of the opposition to Hamilton's system, was his former co-worker in the battle for the Constitution, and shared most of his aspirations for a stronger national union. Although he fought over details of funding and assumption, and against Hamilton's bank, he had, significantly, a uniform positive voting record on mea-

---

[10] Quoted in Alexander DeConde, *Entangling Alliance* (1958), 133.

sures calculated to raise the necessary revenues for the new government. Even Jefferson understood much better than he is credited with understanding—indeed, much better than he later admitted having understood—the rationale behind Hamilton's measures.[11]

It was the French Revolution, and particularly the ensuing war, with the demands it made upon American leaders to make decisions about foreign policy that were bound to have either a British or a French bias, that made the party breach unnegotiable and almost irreconcilable. The Hamiltonian system, particularly the United States Bank, had created first an opposition in Congress, and then by 1792 the beginnings of opposition organization in the constituencies themselves; still, in 1792, as Noble E. Cunningham, Jr. has remarked, "parties did not yet reach very deeply into the political life of the country."[12] But the French Revolutionary War quickly moved the American party contest (as it did the English) into a new phase. From

---

[11] Concerning assumption, for example, Jefferson wrote as early as June 13, 1790, to George Mason: "In general, I think it necessary to give as well as take in a government like ours." Concerning the bargain over assumption and the location of the capital, he wrote Monroe a month later that unless a compromise was arrived at, "there will be no funding bill agreed to, our credit . . . will burst and vanish, and the States separate." Not much later he said that funding the public debt "will secure to us the credit we now hold at Amsterdam. . . . Our business is to have great credit and to use it little." Again: "In the present instance, I see the necessity of yielding to the cries of creditors in certain parts of the Union; for the sake of union, and to save us from the greatest of all calamities, the total extinction of our credit in Europe." On Jefferson's earlier and later versions of this episode, see Broadus Mitchell, *Alexander Hamilton*, II, 80–84.

[12] *The Jeffersonian Republicans*, 49. On the gradual advance of early party organization, see this work, 7–9, 22, 51–54, 82–84, and passim. See also Joseph Charles, *Origins of the American Party System* (1956), William N. Chambers, *Political Parties in a New Nation* (1963), and for an important work on an avant-garde party state Alfred F. Young's magisterial *The Democratic-Republicans of New York: The Origins, 1763–1797* (1967).

the spring of 1793, when the provocative French Minister Citizen Gênet arrived at Charleston, there came a series of events which rapidly polarized the leaders and their followers and finally inflamed them to the point at which the entire political system was threatened: the Whiskey Insurrection of 1794, the scourging of the Democratic Societies by Washington, the heated debate over the Jay Treaty in 1795, the frenzy over the conduct of the French in the XYZ affair in 1798, the undeclared naval war with France, the Alien and Sedition Acts and other measures of war preparation. The war had brought into one common focus three sets of issues: the domestic issues, which mobilized interest against interest; the foreign policy issues, which, because of the intimate dependence of Hamilton's system on British trade, linked the conflict of interests with basic foreign policy decisions; and finally a set of ideological passions of a surprisingly intense kind. As Jefferson himself put it in a letter of June 1793 to Monroe, the war "kindled and brought forward the two parties with an ardour which our own interests merely, could never excite."[13] The country was

---

[13] *Writings*, Ford ed., VII, 361–362. To Madison he declared that the war "has brought forward the Republicans and Monocrats in every state so openly that their relative numbers are perfectly visible." *Ibid.*, VII, 420.

Domestic issues had never quite succeeded in bringing about this kind of polarization. Even after the bank issue had intensified the rudimentary parties in Congress, Cunningham finds (p. 22) that in the session of October 1791 to May 1792 about one half of the Congressmen were not voting consistently for or against Madison, though two small, relatively tightly knit groups were obviously contending for power. Even in 1793, when William Branch Giles introduced a series of resolutions that sweepingly condemned Hamilton's conduct and policies as Secretary of the Treasury, Giles was unable to muster on these purely domestic issues more than fifteen votes (as against thirty-three nays) on any of his proposals. These resolutions came to a vote at the beginning of March. The following month news arrived of the execution of Louis XVI and the French declaration of war against Britain and Holland, and from this point, party division flared into intense heat.

moving rapidly into the era in which the willingness of the reigning party to tolerate serious opposition was put to the test, an era in which the disposition of each side to doubt the legitimacy and Americanism of the other, manifest from the first in milder forms, came to an angry climax. Each party saw the other as having a foreign allegiance, British or French, that approached the edge of treason. Each also saw the other as having a political aspiration or commitment that lay outside the republican covenant of the Constitution: the Federalists were charged with being "Monocrats," with aspiring to restore monarchy and the hereditary principle; the Republicans with advocating a radical, French-inspired democracy hostile to property and order.

This succession of provocative events largely broke down the spirit of comity that had been built up among American political leaders through the years of revolutionary comradeship and constitution-making. By the summer of 1797 Jefferson reported from Philadelphia that "men who have been intimate all their lives cross the streets to avoid meeting, and turn their heads another way, lest they should be obliged to touch their hats." The following year Deborah Logan, the wife of a leading Republican, found the social life of Philadelphia "a state of society destructive of the ties which in ordinary times bind one class of citizens to another," and observed that "friendships were dissolved, tradesmen dismissed, and custom withdrawn from the Republican party."[14]

By April, 1796, when the Republicans in the House tried to block appropriations necessary to carry out the Jay Treaty, they failed, with some defections in their ranks, by a very narrow margin, even though their partisans in this Congress now for the first time outnumbered the Federalists. Cunningham, *op. cit.*, 76–85. The best account of the Giles resolutions is that of Dumas Malone, *Jefferson and the Ordeal of Liberty* (1962), chap. 2.

[14] *Ibid.*, VII, 154–155; Alexander DeConde, *The Quasi-War* (1966), 82.

IV

This sequence of events also destroyed the bipartisan prestige of George Washington—a prestige a monarch might have envied—gradually stripped him of his aspirations and pretensions to nonpartisanship, and blasted his hopes for a partyless state. His election in 1788 had no doubt misled him, since it voiced the one national sentiment upon which there was true unanimity. In the first years of the party division, he considered that it was his role to hold together both sides of his divided administration and to prevail upon them to meet each other in the spirit of compromise. In August, 1792, he wrote moving letters to both Jefferson and Hamilton urging mutual forbearance, lamenting that "internal dissensions should be harrowing and tearing at our vitals," and voicing his fear that the Union would be torn asunder.[15]

Washington apparently hoped at first that the unanimity shown in his election would be echoed in at least a near-unanimity on basic issues. He was bitterly disappointed at the early show of sharp opposition, and in good time, without ever giving up his conception of himself as a man above party, he became a strong partisan of the views of the Hamiltonian Federalists. So far as he was concerned, the onus for strife, which at first he distributed almost with impartiality, was in the end placed entirely upon the opposition. When the Jay Treaty was at stake, he angrily charged that the opposition to it was the work of a party, without seeming to realize that its supporters also constituted a party. By July 1795, when Jefferson's retirement to private life and the forced resignation of Edmund Randolph had created a Cabinet of entirely Hamiltonian persuasion, and when he had ceased altogether to consult men of a

---

[15] *Writings*, ed. J. C. Fitzpatrick, XXXII, 130–131, 132–133; cf. the letter written to Edmund Randolph at the same time, 136–137.

different cast of mind, he still thought of himself as entirely above party, as "one who is of no party, and whose sole wish is to pursue, with undeviating steps a path which would lead this Country to respectability, wealth and happiness."[16]

In his denunciation of the Democratic Societies in 1794 Washington first gave full public expression to the difficulties he was experiencing with the idea of opposition and criticism. The Democratic Societies which sprang up in 1793 in response to the heightened polarization of sentiment that followed the war in Europe, numbered at their peak at least thirty-five throughout the several states. These political clubs were outspokenly pro-French and pro-republican, and in some cases acted as pressure groups on particular issues. Although their sympathies with the Republican party were manifest, they did not normally appropriate its activities or presume to manage its affairs, but rather asserted themselves as lively pressure groups functioning on its left wing. When the Whiskey Rebellion occurred in the summer of 1794, Washington concluded that one of these societies was responsible for instigating it, and issued a stinging rebuke which no doubt contributed to the rather rapid disappearance of the clubs in 1795 and 1796.

Washington's annual message to Congress (November 1794), in which he assailed the Democratic Societies, gave rise to a full-dress discussion of the principles of opposition and the limits of legitimate criticism of government. In the main, Washington's message was an account of the insurrection and the means taken to put it down. And in fact, when one considers that an armed insurrection, however brief and feeble, had been mounted against the authority of this new and (in this

---

16 *Ibid.*, XXXIV, 251. Some Republicans found that they too could play the nonpartisan game. One Republican address presented Jefferson as a man "of no party but the great party of human benefactors," and another asserted that "he alone can reconcile contending parties, and steer the bark into safety." Cunningham, *op. cit.*, 100–101.

respect) still untried federal government, it is the mildness of Washington's message (which presaged the pardon he soon extended to the two leaders who were convicted of treason) that is most impressive. In his words, the whole affair becomes, somehow, not a threatening *coup d'état*, a major trial of state, but a scuffle among farmers, in which one of the main issues was how the thing could be put down at least expense. He had not, he pointed out, been precipitate: commissioners had dealt with the rebels, offering them pardons from the state and federal governments, and a force had been at last ordered to march against them only after another warning. Then there was a nice, farmer-like deference to economy of means. Washington was very apologetic for having called forth almost 13,000 militiamen from four states to control this minor uprising. It was very hard, he explained, to decide "with precision the lowest degree of force competent to the quelling of the insurrection. From a respect, indeed, to economy and the ease of my fellow-citizens belonging to the militia, it would have gratified me to accomplish such an estimate. My very reluctance to ascribe too much importance to the opposition, had its extent been accurately seen, would have been a decided inducement to the smallest possible numbers." He chose to stress, as the chief lesson of the incident not the dangers it had presented to the government nor the government's instability, but rather the overwhelming loyalty and unity, the understanding of the "true principles of government and liberty" shown by the great majority of his fellow-citizens.

However, it was here that he went on to worry the opposition. "A spirit inimical to all order" had moved many of the offenders, he concluded, and he asked the people to determine whether the rebellion had not been "fomented by combinations of men who, careless of consequences and disregarding the unerring truth that those who rouse cannot always appease a civil convulsion, have disseminated, from an ignorance or perversion of facts, suspicions, jealousies, and accusations of the whole Government."

Particularly troublesome to the Republicans was his damnation of the Democratic Societies as "self-created societies" which in formal concert were trying to destroy the government.[17] This could be read as an attempt to brand all spontaneous opposition as sedition. Washington seemed to be trying to establish an alarming pattern of tandem guilt by association that threatened to tar all opposition sentiment with the brush of rebellion: insurrection and sedition were fostered by the Democratic Societies, and these societies in turn by the Republicans. "The game," Madison thought, "was to connect the democratic societies with the odium of the insurrection, to connect the Republicans in Congress with these societies, [and] to put the President ostensibly at the head of the other party in opposition to both. . . ." Jefferson thought it "an attack on the freedom of discussion." Washington's statement about "self-created" societies seemed to imply that voluntary political organizations critical of government policies had no right to exist. Even John Adams, who had no more use than Washington for the Democratic Societies, expressed a clear sense of the nature of the problem when he wrote to Abigail that "political clubs must and ought to be lawful in every free country."[18]

---

[17] Richardson, *Messages and Papers of the Presidents*, I, 155–158; for Washington's views of the Democratic Societies, see also his letter to Henry Lee, *Writings*, XXXIII, 474–476.

[18] Madison, *Writings*, VI, 221–222; Jefferson, *Writings*, VI, 517; C. F. Adams, ed., *Letters of John Adams Addressed to his Wife* (1841), II, 171. That Washington's response to opposition was not pure partisanship, however, may be suggested by the response of Edmund Randolph, still his Attorney General, who thought that the insurrection should be seized upon as an opportunity to crush the Democratic Societies. Moncure D. Conway, *Omitted Chapters of History Disclosed in the Life and Papers of Edmund Randolph* (1888), 194–195.

Although Adams's sense of the matter is closer to our own, Washington, in voicing alarm at the idea of "self-created" societies was expressing a view of political organizations that was widely accepted as an integral part of the anti-party creed, and even of republicanism itself. As exponents of this view had it, the representative institutions of republicanism were in themselves sufficient as instruments of government, and any attempt to set up political clubs or societies outside them would be an attempt not to extend but to destroy republican institutions. As George Cabot objected in 1795, when he saw the Republican party rising in strength, "After all, where is the boasted advantage of a representation system . . . if the resort to popular meetings is necessary?" Even after Jefferson's election, many Federalists continued to take this view of separate political organizations. A New Jersey mass meeting of 1803 denounced Republican clubs in these terms: "A representative government is properly composed of electors and elected under Constitutions. These self-created societies are neither one nor the other, but political machines which fatal experience (notwithstanding their fair professions) has proved to be the destroyers and the tyrants of the people."[19] It was only somewhat later, as the exigencies of political opposition impressed themselves upon the Federalists in greater force, that they began to found considerable numbers of their own political clubs, the Washington Benevolent Societies.

The Jeffersonians, however, might have felt their fears justified in 1794 when Washington, aroused by the opposition to the Jay Treaty, reached the point of declaring to Adams that "meetings in opposition to the constituted authorities" were "at all times, improper and dangerous,"[20] and they might have been forgiven for wondering by what devices he imagined the

---

[19] David H. Fischer, *The Revolution of American Conservatism*, 5, 112 n; on the Washington Benevolent Societies, see *ibid.*, chap. 6.

[20] *Writings*, XXXIV, 280.

freedom of political criticism under republican governments was to be maintained.

All Washington's misgivings about the legitimacy of opposition continued to be founded on his idea that he stood above party—which seems to suggest that the public measures he endorsed should also be regarded as nonpartisan. In a reproachful letter to Jefferson, written from Mount Vernon in July 1796, he still protested his impartiality, declaring that "I was no party man myself, and the first wish of my heart was, if parties did exist, to reconcile them." Until the last year or two, he added, "I had no conceptions that Parties would, or even could go, the length I have been witness to," and that he never anticipated that his efforts would lead to his being branded partial to one foreign country and the enemy of another.[21]

His anxiety about party division became the main theme of his Farewell Address and a nagging concern of his remaining years. That this address, somewhat misconstrued, has been a major text for American isolationism has obscured its central purpose. Its words dealt much more with domestic than foreign policy, and especially with the danger of parties. It was also in itself a partisan act, much resented by the opposition. Washington had been under pressure to remain President for a third term, and by delaying this announcement of his unavailability until September 19, 1796, only weeks before a national election was scheduled, he had materially hampered the Republican forces, rapidly marshaling themselves behind Jefferson, in their effort to mount a campaign. The partisanship of the Farewell Address is the more evident when we recall that the central passage warning against parties was drafted by Hamilton.[22]

Washington begins the Farewell Address with a firm state-

---

[21] *Ibid.*, XXXV, 119–120.

[22] For the evolution of the text, see Victor H. Paltsits, *Washington's Farewell Address* (New York, 1935).

ment of his determination to retire, with some well-chosen words reminding the people how free and well off they are under the Union, and with an exhortation to guard it and give it their patriotic devotion. He then passes on to some words of fatherly warning: he cautions against the effects of sectionalism, the divisions of Atlantic versus Western or Northern versus Southern states; against undue attachments to foreign countries; against overgrown military establishments. Then, as he warms to his subject, he launches upon an extended and concentrated counterblast against parties. It would be the tendency of parties, in order to acquire influence in a particular district, to excite its animosity against others, and thus "to render alien to each other those who ought to be bound together by fraternal affection." As against such divisiveness the people should attach themselves firmly to their own freely chosen Union and to the Constitution. There follows what can only be taken as a most categorical warning against opposition: "All obstructions to the execution of the Laws, all combinations and associations, under whatever plausible character, with the real design to direct, controul, counteract, or awe the regular deliberation and action of the constituted authorities, are destructive of this fundamental principle [i.e., the duty of every individual to obey the established government], and of fatal tendency. They serve to organize faction and give it an artificial and extraordinary force—to put, in the place of the delegated will of the Nation, the will of a party;—often a small but artful and enterprizing minority of the community;— and, according to the alternate triumphs of different parties, to make the public administration the mirror of the ill-concerted and incongruous projects of faction, rather than the organ of consistent and wholesome plans digested by common councils, and modified by mutual interests."

Such combinations, he goes on, may here and there seem to be serving popular ends, but in the end they will become engines by which the power of the people will be subverted and the reins of government usurped. This being the case, he advised, it was of the utmost importance that the people not only "steadily discountenance irregular oppositions to the acknowledged authority of government but resist innovations in its principles, however specious the pretexts." Here Washington had the gravest difficulty in distinguishing between the undeniable duty of the citizens to obey the laws and their presumed duty to refrain from supporting opposition. He cautions against "irregular" or illegitimate opposition, but provides no definition of "regular" or legitimate opposition against which it may be distinguished.

Having thus far declaimed against parties with particular reference to their effect on geographical differences, Washington now goes on to warn "in the most solemn manner against the baneful effects of the Spirit of Party generally." As he saw, this spirit is unfortunately a part of human nature. It therefore exists under all governments, somewhat stifled and controlled, but it is at its very worst in popular governments. To its workings he charged an impressive list of mischiefs: it distracts public councils and enfeebles administration, agitates the community with jealousies and false alarms, sets one part of it against another, occasionally foments riot and insurrection, opens the door to foreign influence which may subject one country to the will of another. In the end it is very likely to lead to permanent despotism, when the chief of some faction finally succeeds in elevating himself to power on the ruins of liberty.

There was an opinion, Washington noted, "that parties in free countries are useful checks upon the Administration of Government, and serve to keep alive the Spirit of Liberty." This justification for opposition, he conceded, was probably true within limits under governments "of a Monarchical cast," where, he assumed, the spirit of opposition might need encour-

agement. But under popular governments with elected representatives "it is a spirit not to be encouraged," and there is
more likely to be a constant danger of an excess of it. He closed
this passage by branding the spirit of party in a metaphor: "A
fire not to be quenched; it demands a uniform vigilance to prevent its bursting into a flame, lest instead of warming, it should
consume."

No one can doubt that by the end of his administration
Washington's role had become that of a committed partisan,
indispensable to his party, eminently usable, as Hamilton saw,
and, as Hamilton said of him after his death, *"an Aegis very
essential to me."* Historians have differed as to how conscious
his partisanship was. Joseph Charles, in his penetrating little
book, *The Origins of the American Party System*, observing
that the more partisan Washington became the more bitterly
he denounced parties, concludes that "he is to be blamed, not
for allying himself with a party but for not knowing that he
had done so, and for denouncing those opposed to his party
as opposed to the government."[23] Others have argued that he
was too intelligent a man and had in recent years shown too
much aptitude for politics to permit us to believe that he was
unaware of the significance of an appeal against parties just
on the eve of a national election, or that he was a mere front
and dupe for Hamilton's schemes.

In either case, I think his intellectual confusion about the
problem of government and opposition was altogether genuine and that it partook of an intellectual difficulty quite
common among his contemporaries.[24] He had on the one hand

---

[23] Hamilton, *Works*, X, 537; Joseph Charles, *Origins of the American
Party System* (1956), 44; for a different view see Stephen G. Kurtz,
The Presidency of John Adams (1957), 88–90.

[24] And at both extremes in the party contest. John Taylor, the most
ardent of the Republican pamphleteers, was as keen for unanimity and
as ingenuously uncomprehending of the difference between a system
that tries to establish an orthodoxy in thought and one that aims to

given a great part of his life to assuring the American people a popular republican form of government and a broad base of liberty. But he could not, at the same time, reconcile himself to the oppositional politics that liberty brought with it. His real goal was first the maintenance, and then the restoration, of that spirit of happy unanimity which had been manifested in his own election in 1788 and 1792. It was with keen gratification that he had written in 1790 that the government of the United States was already "one of the best in the world," and he was grateful for the near "miracle that there should have been so much unanimity, in such points of importance, among such a number of Citizens, so widely scattered, and so different in their habits" in many respects as the Americans were. He was, of course, aware, as he wrote to Jonathan Trumbull early in 1797, that "in all free governments, contention in elections will take place; and whilst it is confined to our own citizens it is not to be regretted; but severely indeed it ought to be reprobated when occasioned by foreign machinations"—which implies that he did not think serious differences would arise if there were no alien interference in our affairs. Otherwise the normal and proper thing would be unanimity—a word that recurs in his later letters. To avoid ruin from the war in Europe, he wrote to Benjamin Goodhue in 1798, America required "nothing . . . but unanimity," and less than four months before his death he was calling again for "more unanimity in our public councils." If there was only a way of erecting "a standard of infallibility in political opinions," he wrote to General Knox

---

arrive at an adjustment of interests. In a pamphlet of 1794, Taylor wrote: "The situation of the public good, in the hands of two parties nearly poised as to numbers, must be extremely perilous. Truth is a thing, not of divisibility into conflicting parts, but of unity. Hence both sides cannot be right. Every patriot deprecates a disunion, which is only to be obviated by a national preference of one of these parties." *A Definition of Parties* (1794), 2.

in 1795, "there is no being that inhabits this terrestrial globe that would resort to it with more eagerness than myself."[25]

Washington was increasingly tormented by the disparity between what he could infer about the persistence of strife from his conception of politics and human nature as well as from his practical experience, and what he yearned for as a man unused to impassioned criticism and partisan venom. He could never quite put out of his mind the wistful notion that, if there were no opposition to carry on "intrigues," the public would be unanimous. "For the *Mass* of our citizens," he wrote to John Marshall in 1797, "require no more than to understand a question to decide it properly." But this assumed precisely what was at issue—that the right public policies were really quite obvious to men of good will. In his most realistic moments, Washington knew that it would be asking for "a change in the order of nature" to expect all men to think alike on political or religious subjects. Nonetheless, he could not restrain his irritation with those whom he saw as standing in the way of an agreeable unanimity. Explaining the American situation to Lafayette a year before his death, he charged that the entire behavior of the Republicans made it clear that they were determined, by clogging the wheels of government, "to change the nature of it, and to Subvert the Constitution"—to do which they would resort to any means. This suggested that all neces-

---

[25] *Writings*, XXX, 496–497; XXXV, 412; XXXVI, 48; XXXIV, 310. Cf. a letter to Pickering 24 July, 1795: "But (much indeed to be regretted!) party disputes are now carried to that length, and truth is so enveloped in mist and false representation that it is extremely difficult to know in what channel to seek it. This difficulty to one, who is of no party, and whose sole wish is to pursue with undeviating steps a path which would lead this Country to respectability, wealth and happiness, is exceedingly to be lamented. But such (for wise purpose it is presumed) is the turbulence of human passions in party disputes; when victory, more than truth, is the palm contended for, 'that the Post of honor is a private Station.' " *Ibid.*, XXXIV, 251.

sary means must be used to stop them. This was the frame of mind of the Sedition Act—in which, as his biographers have said, he "saw simply an effort toward stronger national unity."[26]

Washington had lent his great prestige to making the new government a possibility, and without him we can well believe that it might have foundered. But his relation to the formation of parties is truly ironic. As Joseph Charles said of him: "More than any other man of his time, he tried to prevent the growth of parties, holding that there was no necessity or place for them in our form of government. Had he been successful in this, the main effort of his declining years, it is most doubtful that representative government in this country would have outlived him for long."[27]

V

The crisis of 1797–1801, precipitated by our troubled relations with France, marked by the XYZ affair, the Alien and Sedition Acts, the quasi-war of 1798–1800, and John Adams's peace missions, and climaxed by the election of 1800–1801, proved to be the most decisive crisis of the early Union. In this series of events the fundamental problem of the legitimacy of organized opposition and the possibility of a peaceful turnover of power to an opposition party was posed with unmistakable

---

[26] *Writings*, XXXVI, 93, 254; XXXVII, 66; cf. the letter to Patrick Henry, January 15, 1799, in which he charges the opposition with being "a dead weight" on government, pursuing measures "which must eventually dissolve the Union or produce coercion." *Ibid.*, XXXVII, 88–89. For his views on the Alien and Seditions Acts, see J. A. Carroll and M. W. Ashworth, *George Washington: First in Peace*, VII of D. S. Freeman's *George Washington* (1957), 540–541. On his inability to accept the processes of opposition, see Harold W. Bradley, "The Political Thinking of George Washington," *Journal of Southern History*, 11 (1945), 478–480.

[27] Charles, *op. cit.*, 42–43.

force. Under a federal system such as the American states had contrived, and with partisan loyalties unevenly distributed as they were, North and South, to ponder the legitimacy of opposition was also to calculate the value of the Union. The crisis of 1797–1801 therefore had a double character: it was a test of the possibilities of legitimate opposition and of the durability of American federalism.

Where the problem of silencing or suppressing opposition arises, there are at least three questions the members of a government can put to themselves. They can, of course, ask whether they have a *right* to act in this way. But this is a highly sophisticated and self-restrained question, answered in most political cultures all too easily, if it is ever asked at all. Even in America, with its libertarian and Revolutionary inheritance, it was not as difficult to answer as we might expect. If we may judge by the reactions of leading Federalists to the Alien and Sedition Acts, few of them would have made so bold as to claim a categorical right to do away with opposition. Yet none of them doubted the *right* of the government, in their particular circumstances, to silence newspaper opposition or to police the expression of political opinion by statute (though one, John Marshall, doubted the *expediency* of it).

But there are two other questions which are likely to be asked before the question of right is raised: There is, to begin, the question: Do we have the *power* to suppress opposition? And if this can be answered, however tentatively, in the affirmative, it may be followed by the more circumspect question: Will the *cost* of suppressing opposition be higher, to ourselves or to the whole community, than that of enduring it and even risking its coming to power? On these two counts there were many Federalists, not least of them President Adams, who made careful and rather inhibiting estimations of the situation. In effect they concluded—though this is to condense outrageously, to oversimplify a series of events and a mass of complex sentiments, and to make conscious and calculating what was often arrived at by instinct and training—that the people would not bear the cost of a full-scale foreign war and a domestic hard line; that persistence in foreign war and partisan oppression might break the Union; and that to create an army sufficiently strong to overbear domestic opposition (this was certainly Adams's conclusion) would be to create an instrumentality much more suitable to an ambitious Bonapartist tyrant than to the leaders of a popular government.

From the outset of Adams's administration the Federalists were of two minds about their course of action. The High Federalists, based chiefly in New England (though even there they were usually outnumbered by moderates) and taking their cue mainly from Hamilton, stood for extreme measures, for war and repressive statutes. The moderate Federalists, who rallied in the end behind Adams, recoiled at the very least from the resort to war, and by implication forswore the circumstances under which the suppression of opposition would have been conceivable. An orthodox Federalist of rather temperate disposition, Samuel Lyman, explaining in a letter of 1800 to his constituents what had been dividing his party in the past few years, wrote that he thought it was not split on sentiments or principles but on men and measures: "There is a division as to the degree of hatred and animosity necessary to be used in order to destroy all opposition to Government. A small party, I suppose, sincerely believe that a few bold strokes would silence all opposition; others say no, let it be done by civility and sound argument; so here they are at issue. . . ."[28]

---

[28] Dauer, *The Adams Federalists*, 200. That many High Federalists favored war seems clear enough. Oliver Wolcott: "Nothing but open war can save us. And the more inveterate and deadly it shall be, the better will be our chance for security in the future." General Philip Schuyler, Hamilton's father-in-law: "War with all its calamities would be less injurious to my country than a peace which might be followed . . . with the reintroduction of the destructive principles which prevail

What the High Federalists hoped for, when the reaction to the XYZ affair set in motion a wild frenzy of anti-French feeling, was the following: First, some hoped for a full-scale, all-out war with France, which would end once and for all the question whether our foreign policy was to have a pro-English or a pro-French orientation. A larger number expected that under the conditions either of war or aggravated and prolonged tension with France, their own conviction that the Republicans were seditiously and treasonously pro-French would be shared by an overwhelming majority of the loyal public. And finally, that when the Jeffersonian party had been fully stamped as a French faction, it could be wiped out. Its Irish and French hangers-on could be exiled or imprisoned; but most important, its newspaper editors and public orators could be jailed or driven into silence, much as the Democratic Societies had been

---

in France." George Cabot: "It is impossible to make the people feel or see distinctly that we have much more to fear from peace than war. . . . War, open and declared, would not only deprive our external enemy of his best hopes, but would also extinguish the hopes of internal foes." Theodore Sedgwick: "We ought at once to have put an end to the cooperation of internal and external enemies. This could only have been done by a declaration of war. . . . we should have superseded the necessity of alien and sedition laws—without them we might have hanged traitors and exported Frenchmen." The leading Federalist newspaper, the *Gazette of the United States*, in December, 1798: A declaration of war would "not much alter our relations to France, but it will very materially affect our internal situation; for until that is done, France will not abandon her hopes here; and divisions will be constantly excited and fomented by them. But [war] would take us at once out of our present amphibious situation and crush the French party in this country. . . ." Kurtz, *The Presidency of John Adams* (1957), 311–312, 323; Dauer, *op. cit.*, 198, 224. For an excellent account of this crisis, see Kurtz, chaps. XIII–XV; see also Dauer, chaps. XII–XIV.

But for a learned argument to the effect that many historians have exaggerated the desire for war among High Federalists, see Jacob E. Cooke, "Country above Party: John Adams and the 1799 Mission to France," in Edmund P. Willis, ed., *Fame and the Founding Fathers* (1967), 53–77.

silenced (or so one had reason to think) by Washington's mighty rebuke. When the public frenzy over the XYZ affair began, Theodore Sedgwick, the Federalist whip in the Senate, saw in it great possibilities. "It will afford a glorious opportunity to destroy faction," he said. "Improve it." The impulse to improve it was widespread, though not universal, among High Federalist leaders, and it was this effort to "destroy faction," incarnated in the Alien and Sedition Acts of 1798, which led to "the first instance under the Constitution in which American political leaders faced the problem of defining the role of public criticism in a representative government."[29]

Before launching upon any discussion of the intentions of the High Federalist leaders, I should make it clear that I do not wish to suggest that it was within their power, in this diffuse, divided, loosely structured, untaxable, disorderly, undisciplined, and particularistic country, to impose their will effectively or to suppress opposition. It may indeed be doubted that they could have done so even if they had been in possession of a united party and if, instead of having to cope with the implacable and testy Adams, they had also controlled the President. But what they could have done, indeed might easily have done without Adams's opposition, was to have brought about a crisis severe enough to shatter the Union before it was much more than ten years old.

Federalist leaders made no secret of their hope of destroying opposition. Hamilton predicted that many Republican leaders would be remembered by the people in the same odious light as the Tories. Robert Goodloe Harper of South Carolina, a leading advocate of the Sedition Act in the House, wanted to be sure that "no traitors should be left in the country" to jeopardize its defense. He professed his desire to imitate the internal

---

29 James Morton Smith in *Freedom's Fetters* (1956), 418; for Sedgwick, *ibid.*, 21.

security policies that had been adopted in England, charged the opposition with being "a conspiracy, a faction leagued with a foreign Power to effect a revolution or subjugation of this country, by the arms of that foreign Power," and even proposed that Congressional immunity be circumvented by prosecuting "seditious" Congressmen for criticisms of the government written in letters to their constituents. There was a French party in the country, he said, and the purpose of the sedition law was "to repress the enterprises of this party." Mere partisan allegiance, in the eyes of some, was grounds for prosecution. Representative John Allen of Connecticut seemed to think that the Republican newspaper, the *Aurora*, was vulnerable to prosecution simply because it was the organ of a party. Senator James Lloyd of Maryland, co-author of the Sedition Act, wrote to Washington early in July: "I fear Congress will close the session without a declaration of War, which I look upon as necessary to enable us to lay our hands on traitors. . . ."[30]

The language of the Sedition Act was vague enough to make a man criminally liable for almost any criticism of the government or its leading officers or any effort to combine for such a purpose. It made it possible for the courts to punish *opinion*, arbitrarily defined as seditious or disloyal, even in the absence of any overt act. It drew no definable distinction between criticism and defamation, opposition and subversion. As its leading historian has remarked: "By identifying their administration with the government and the government with the Constitution, the Federalists construed criticism of the administration as opposition to the government and an attempt to subvert the Constitution."[31] Such safeguards as the act introduced to protect defendants, safeguards having to do with the requirement to establish the malicious intentions of writers and

---

[30] Smith, *Freedom's Fetters*, 21, 105–106, 110, 117–118, 120–121, 142.
[31] *Ibid.*, 177.

107

the use of truth as a defense in criminal libel, proved worthless in courts manned by super-ardent Federalist judges.

One may well wonder, in a country where the normal tone of political criticism was uninhibited, not to say scurrilous, and where there were well over threescore of newspapers that were strongly Republican and another fifty or more leaning in that direction, how the opposition press could be smashed. Of course, the most zealous Federalists were counting on a further inflamed public atmosphere to be created by a declaration of war that never came. Besides, it seemed unnecessary to strike at the entire Republican press, if a damper could be put on it by suppressing the small handful of major journals in Philadelphia, New York, Boston, Richmond, and Baltimore from which the others took their cues and indeed a good deal of their news and copy. Timothy Pickering, the Secretary of State, who took charge of prosecution strategy, tried to do just this, and succeeded in getting indictments in the first four of these cities, as well as indicting editors of four of the smaller opposition papers. In all, at least seventeen verifiable indictments were brought in, fourteen under the Sedition Act and three under the common law. Started in the main in 1798 or 1799, most of the cases came to trial in the election year, 1800, when it was hoped to stifle campaign criticism.[32]

At their simplest and most naïve, the prosecutions abandoned all pretensions to respect for the right of opposition. When the distinguished philosopher and controversialist, Thomas Cooper, who wrote in what Abigail Adams called "a mad democratic stile," was indicted for his criticisms of President Adams, Justice Samuel Chase instructed the jury that the relevant publication was "the boldest attempt I have known to poison the minds of the people" and climaxed his charge with the assertion that

---

[32] "Indeed the chief enforcement effort was tied directly to the presidential campaign of 1800." Smith, *op. cit.*, 186; for an evaluation of enforcement, see 76–87.

it was meant "to mislead the ignorant, and inflame their minds against the President, and to influence their votes on the next election"—which last he plainly considered a heinous crime inconsistent with popular government. In the end Cooper got six months in federal prison and a fine of $400.

But the Sedition Act was not conceived in a spirit of realism and it was not efficacious. The opposition was no small or paltry minority. As measured by representation in Congress, it was already at least equal to the administration in numbers. It was better organized, it was growing in strength, it had a stronger potential appeal to the mass of voters, and it was not riven by the fatal and malignant factionalism that set Hamilton against Adams and manned the President's own Cabinet with intriguing opponents. More important perhaps even than this, the country was still thoroughly decentralized, politically and geographically. Government, at the ultimate test, rests on sufficient force, and it was force that would have to be called upon if resistance to the laws became overt. The Virginia and Kentucky resolutions threatened that resistance might indeed reach this point, and at a time when the federal army numbered only about 3,500 men stationed mainly at frontier garrisons as a precaution against Indians, Virginia alone could have easily mustered a militia of twice that number and was indeed planning a force of 5,000. Nothing short of a foreign war would have created the conditions essential to raising a domestic army large enough, as Hamilton put it in one of his brasher moments, to "put Virginia to the test."

And here the demand for an army ran up against two of the deepest American prejudices: the tight-fisted rural reaction to taxes, and the long-standing suspicion (fully shared at this point by President Adams) against a standing army. In the end the proposal for a much enlarged army became another source of intrigue and disaffection among the leading Federalists, stimulated by a popular revulsion from Federalism climaxed by the

Fries rebellion in the very heart of Pennsylvania's rural Federalist stronghold. No doubt it was the question of the army, as John Quincy Adams, reflecting on family tradition, wrote some years afterward,[33] that broke the Federalist party in two. But it was the new taxes required for the army—these even more, I believe, than the reaction to the Alien and Sedition Acts—that forced the Federalists to consider the limitations of their plans, strengthened the moderates among them, and, at last, threw the balance of power to the Republican side. Still, something must be left to the effect of personality, of individual will, of historical accident in this sense. For if we can imagine a determined High Federalist President in the White House seizing upon the most intense moment of anti-French feeling to precipitate a war, we can then imagine a partisan conflict that would have cracked the Union.

And here, ironically, Adams's own anti-party philosophy came to the aid of the evolving two-party system. As a scorner of parties and partisan politics, Adams accepted no sense of obligation to Federalists as a party. This state of mind strengthened his determination not to be pressured, through party considerations, into actions he thought contrary to the national interest. Years later, believing that his insistence upon making peace had avoided a great civil war in the United States, he heaped his reminiscent scorn upon "the pharisaical, jesuitical, machiavelian intrigue and influence of the leading federalists." At the critical moment he had said of these men: "Arrogance shall be made to feel a curb. If anyone entertaining the idea that, because I am a President of three [electoral] votes only, I am in the power of a party, they shall find that I am no more so than the Constitution forces upon me."[34]

The French crisis took the country through an extraordinary cycle of party preponderance. Having begun so auspiciously

---

[33] *Parties in the United States* (ed. 1941), 25–26.
[34] *Works*, IX, 620; Dauer, *Adams Federalists*, 238.

for the Federalists, with its promise of the complete eclipse of their opponents, it fractured their party, lost them vital public support, and brought them to a full stop before the doughty intransigence of their President. The Jeffersonians, having begun as the "French party," stamped with the odium of years of foreign intrigue, had now been transformed into the victims of persecution, the proponents of individual liberties, the foes of military extravagance, standing armies, and unnecessary taxation. But it is now time to look at their own strategic calculations, which carried them through this moment of danger and led them at last toward power.

VI

In considering the problem of the Jeffersonians as an opposition establishing itself, we may find helpful a remark made by Edward Shils concerning the developing oppositions in new states in our time. "Efforts," he says, "to suppress the public existence of an opposition party have hitherto been successful except when the opposition has a particular territorial or regional base or where it has substantial foreign support. . . ."[35] In the American crisis of the 1790's it was a matter of considerable moment that the Republicans had a strong particularist base in Virginia, which, in the event of an outbreak of hostilities might have expected allies in neighboring states. Of course, under the prevailing conditions of transportation and in the face of a federal government so lacking in military means, the idea of open hostilities was hardly more than a whispered possibility—even though Hamilton, in a burst of extravagance, outlined to Jonathan Dayton a scheme by which Virginia could be put down by force and permanently reduced as a factor in the Union.[36] What was quite possible was secession

[35] Shils, "Opposition in the New States of Asia and Africa," 177.

[36] Early in 1799 Hamilton wrote to Dayton, the Speaker of the House, observing that Virginia was now arming, laying new taxes to raise

by Virginia on the ground that the constitutional compact had been fatally breached. After all the difficulties that had been experienced for lack of a strong union, and after all the efforts that had been made to form the present one, this was rightly conceived as a drastic step. It might be sufficient merely to threaten it, or to raise the possibility, and by combining this threat with an appeal to the libertarian views, constitutional scruples, and particularist feelings of the country, to rally enough support against the Alien and Sedition Acts to make secession unnecessary.

The mode of operation, of course, was the Virginia and Kentucky Resolutions. In an important essay on these documents, Adrienne Koch and Harry Ammon describe them not only as statements of a grievance but as an alternative device for attacking the Alien and Sedition Acts—a device other than that of trying to get them repealed in Congress.[37] The resolutions were, above all, party propaganda, but propaganda resting on a regional power base and a particularist appeal to constitutional theory and political sentiment; they represent a temporary resort from parliamentary opposition to particularist resistance. The Jeffersonians understood well that the issue raised by the Alien and Sedition Acts was not merely one of constitutional interpretation or of the status of civil

---

munitions, and reorganizing her militia. He urged vigorous countermeasures: an enlargement of the federal judiciary, the improvement of roads (wretched roads had made movement against the Whiskey rebels unexpectedly difficult), a regular army of 18,000, a bigger navy, a system of federal canals. In the long run he hoped, he said, for "the subdivision of the great states," so that no state would be big enough to "machinate" against the federal government. In another letter he proposed that the contemplated new army move southward on another pretext, and "then let measures be taken to act upon the laws and put Virginia to the test of resistance." *Works*, VIII, 517–518; X, 340–342.

[37] Adrienne Koch and Harry Ammon, "The Virginia and Kentucky Resolutions: An Episode in Jefferson's and Madison's Defense of Civil Liberties," *William and Mary Quarterly*, 5 (1948), 157.

liberties in a narrow legal sense; what was at stake was the very possibility of conducting a legal opposition and sustaining free government. Again, it was Madison who put it best in asserting that the right of opposition, now challenged, was the most fundamental of all rights: The power assumed by the Sedition Act, he said in the Virginia Resolutions, was "a power which more than any other ought to produce universal alarm, because it is levelled against the right of freely examining public characters and measures, and of free communication among the people thereon, which has ever been deemed the only effectual guardian of every other right."[38] The resistance to the attempt of the Federalists to police opinion elicited from some Republican writers statements on the freedom of opinion and the press that marked a new high in libertarian doctrine in this country. But although the Republican pamphleteers were very sharp on the need for a free competition among ideas and its usefulness to society, they did not go so far as to stress the value of opposition *parties* as agencies of criticism.[39]

It is important to add, however, that just as the Federalists were divided over the desirability of war with France and over raising the armed power by which opposition could be suppressed, the Republicans were divided over the precise tactics for pressing their attack and how far to push the implied

---

[38] Cf. also the language of Madison's Virginia Report of 1799–1800, which substantially repeats the phrase. *The Virginia Report of 1799–1800 Touching the Alien and Sedition Laws.* . . . (1850), 23, 227.

[39] For a discussion of this literature, see Leonard Levy, *Legacy of Suppression* (1960), chap. 6. The most elaborate of the Republican tracts, Tunis Wortman's *A Treatise Concerning Political Enquiry and the Liberty of the Press* (1800) is a quite sophisticated statement on the public value of free inquiry, but it does not deal with parties. Neither does George Hay [Hortensius], *An Essay on the Liberty of the Press* (1799), or John Thomson, *An Enquiry Concerning the Liberty and Licentiousness of the Press* (1801). I have not seen James Sullivan's *A Dissertation upon the Press in the United States of America*, which is discussed by Levy.

threat of ultimate secession. A few may have thought that armed conflict was possible and should be prepared for, but they were in a tiny minority.[40] In a situation characteristic of the American party system at many times, and wholly familiar in our own, the center wings, the moderates in both parties, were stronger than the extremists, and together exerted a strong centripetal pull.[41] Jefferson himself occupied a position, in itself basically moderate, which lay between some of his friends like John Taylor, who thought seriously, if only in passing, about the desirability of secession, and others like James Madison, whose nationalism was still stronger than his particularism, and who exerted a strong moderating influence upon his Monticello neighbor.

An exchange of letters between Jefferson and John Taylor of Caroline in June, 1798, while the XYZ mania was raging but before the Alien and Sedition Acts had been introduced, shows that Jefferson had given ripe thought to the problem of opposition in its bearing upon union and secession. It is the closest he seems to have come during this period to accepting the dynamics underlying the two-party system, and it sheds light on the progress of his thought on that subject as well as

---

[40] Some Virginians later claimed to have remembered preparations for armed resistance, but their memories deceived them. D. R. Anderson, *William Branch Giles* (1914), 69–71. Virginians did make arrangements, among other things, to strengthen their militia. They were also building a new armory in Richmond, but both sets of plans were laid before the controversy over the Alien and Sedition Acts. Cf. P. G. Davidson, "Virginia and the Alien and Sedition Laws," *American Historical Review*, 36 (1931), 336–342.

[41] One of the significant facts of this period was the narrow margin between the parties. The Republicans lost strength in the third session of the Fifth Congress (December 1798–March 1799), but even in this session their partisans numbered 43 percent of the Congress as compared with 49 percent for the Federalists and 8 percent nonpartisans. I have here followed Joseph Charles, who set a two-thirds partisan voting record as his criterion of classification. *Origins*, 94.

on his ultimate decision for moderation in pressing the argument of the Virginia and Kentucky Resolutions. Taylor, who was later to be responsible for introducing the Virginia Resolution into the Assembly, had suggested to Jefferson that Virginia and North Carolina escape from the "saddle" of Massachusetts and Connecticut by leaving the Union. Jefferson, arguing for caution, couched his answer in penetrating long-range terms, which show how much he was buoyed up by his confidence in ultimately winning the support of the public. It is true, he agreed, "that we are completely under the saddle of Massachusetts and Connecticut, and that they ride us very hard, cruelly insulting our feelings, as well as exhausting our strength and subsistence."[42] But, he suggested, the present situation was not a natural one. The Federalists had won an artificial preponderance because of the great influence and popularity of Washington, which Hamilton had played upon; this would right itself in time—indeed events were already pushing the pendulum in the opposite direction. There follows a remarkable passage of reflection on the whole phenomenon of party division:

"Be this as it may, in every free and deliberating society, there must, from the nature of man, be opposite parties, and violent dissensions and discords; and one of these, for the most part, must prevail over the other for a longer or shorter time. Perhaps this party division is necessary to induce each to watch and relate to the people the proceedings of the other." Thus far Jefferson had given as brief and clear a statement of the function of parties as any of his contemporaries.[43] It is reminiscent of Madison's papers of 1792.

----

[42] *Writings*, Ford, ed., VIII, 430–433 for the whole letter. For Taylor's interesting answer, which argues that republican governments can do without parties and cites the example of some of the state governments, see "Letters of John Taylor," *John P. Branch Historical Papers*, 2 (1905), 271–276.

[43] An even more striking statement on parties had been made in

"But," Jefferson went on, in a prophetic penetration of the whole problem of opposition under a federal system, "if on a temporary superiority of one party, the other is to resort to a scission of the Union, no federal government can ever exist. If to rid ourselves of the present rule of Massachusetts and Connecticut, we break the Union, will the evil stop there?" If the New England States, for example, were cut off, would there not at once appear a Pennsylvania party and a Virginia party within the southern confederacy? Or would there not on this principle be a split even in a union composed alone of Virginia and North Carolina? This game, he argued, could be played on endlessly until all the confederations were broken down into their "simple units," the individual states. "Seeing, therefore, that an association of men who will not quarrel with one another is a thing which never yet existed, from the greatest confederacy of nations down to a town meeting or a vestry; seeing that we must have somebody to quarrel with, I had rather keep our New England associates for that purpose, than to see our bickering transferred to others."

Congress by the Federalist Robert Goodloe Harper in January, 1798. Out of differences of opinion, he said, opposing parties were bound to arise, which would be "in a perpetual state of conflict." Such a state of affairs not only must exist but even ought to exist. "While opposite parties in the Government struggled for pre-eminence, they were like persons engaged in an exhibition before the public, who are obliged to display superior merit and superior excellence in order to gain the prize. The public is the judge, the two parties are the combatants, and that party which possesses power must employ it properly, must conduct the Government wisely, in order to insure public approbation and retain their power. In this contention, while the two parties draw different ways, a middle course is produced generally conformable to public good." Party spirit could, of course, run to excess and produce mischief, but its characteristic effects, he had no doubt, were beneficial. *Annals of Congress*, Fifth Congress, 2d sess., 873–874 (January 19, 1798). However, a few months later, Harper was prominent among those Federalists who were trying, through the Sedition Act, to suppress partisan opposition.

The New Englanders were geographically circumscribed, he pointed out, and their population limited. Since they were unable to propagate their peculiarly perverse characteristics outside their boundaries, they would in the end constitute a natural minority. "A little patience," he assured Taylor, "and we shall see the reign of witches pass over, their spells dissolved, and the people recovering their true sight, restoring their government to its true principles. It is true that, in the meantime, we are suffering deeply in spirit, . . . but who can say what would be the evils of a scission, and when and where they would end? Better keep together as we are, haul off from Europe as soon as we can, and from all attachments to any portions of it; and if they show their power just sufficiently to hoop us together, it will be the happiest situation in which we can exist. If the game sometimes runs against us at home, we must have patience until luck turns, and then we shall have an opportunity of winning back the *principles* we have lost. For this is a game where principles are the stake."

In another letter to Taylor, written on November 26, 1798, after the Alien and Sedition Acts had been passed, Jefferson wrote that "this disease of the imagination," as he called the current fevers, would soon pass. "Indeed," he shrewdly added, "the doctor is now on his way to cure it in the guise of a tax-gatherer."[44] On no point was his confidence in the public more justified than in this reliance on the tax resistance of the ordinary American, for it was this which seems to have done still more than revulsion from the oppressions of the Alien and Sedition Acts to sink the Federalists.

In his resolution to have patience, Jefferson may have wavered on occasion. But pressure from Madison, the failure of the states to the South to respond to the Virginia and Kentucky resolutions, the negative response of those to the North, the

---

[44] Quoted in Kurtz, *The Presidency of John Adams*, 363–364.

divided condition of Virginia itself (which was about one-third Federalist) must all have added weight to his natural caution. Virginia should make it clear, he agreed with Madison in a letter of August 23, 1799, "that we are willing to view with indulgence, to wait with patience until passions and delusions shall have passed over which the federal government have artfully and successfully excited to cover its own abuses and to conceal its designs; fully confident that the good sense of the American people and their attachment to those very rights which we are now vindicating will, before it shall be too late, rally with us round the true principles of our federal compact." These words of sweet reason directly precede, and therefore considerably soften, the most radical utterance Jefferson made on the subject, for he added: "But determined, were we to be disappointed in this, to sever ourselves from that union we so much value, rather than give up the rights of self-government which we have reserved, and in which alone we see liberty, safety, and happiness." In a subsequent version of the same letter to another correspondent, Wilson Cary Nicholas, for transmission to Kentucky, Jefferson significantly struck out this monitory sentence. And to Nicholas he added that "as we should never think of separation but for repeated and enormous violations, so these, when they occur, will be the cause enough of themselves."[45]

One can see the Virginia leaders sustained through this crisis by certain long-range considerations that they felt to be working in their favor. They were confident that the majority of the people shared their basic political principles, and that certain elements of their program, particularly their insistence upon economy and low taxes, were of profound general appeal.

---

[45] For the whole text and Jefferson's changes, see Koch and Ammon, "The Virginia and Kentucky Resolutions," 165–168, which stresses Madison's influence on Jefferson. See also Koch, *Jefferson and Madison: The Great Collaboration* (1950), chap. 7.

They were aware that their own party organizations among the constituencies were stronger than those of the Federalists and were constantly improving. The balance of strength between the two parties was delicate—the Sedition Act had been passed in the House by a vote of only 44 to 41—and a moderate shift in sentiments would bring the preponderance over to their side. Finally, they could count on the split in Federalist ranks to work for them, and hope that a non-provocative course on their own part would permit the breach to widen. Let nothing be said or done, wrote Jefferson to Madison in November, 1799, "which shall look or lead to force, and give any pretext for keeping up the army. If we find the monarchical party really split into pure Monocrats and Anglomonocrats, we should leave them alone to manage all those points of difference which they may chuse to take between themselves, only arbitrating between them by our votes, but doing nothing which may hoop them together."[46]

Jefferson's native disposition toward caution and moderation reflected, he thought, the public temper. "Firmness on our part, but a passive firmness, is the true course," he wrote to Madison in January, 1799. "Anything rash or threatening might check the favorable dispositions of the middle states, and rally them again around the measures which are ruining us." These are the observations not only of a statesman who thinks he divines a popular preference for moderation but also of a party leader who seeks to strike the right note to build a coalition of opposition interests. Fearing that discontent in Pennsylvania might rise to the point of rebellion (which indeed it did), he wrote the following month to Edmund Pendleton: "Anything like force would check the progress of the public opinion and rally them around the government. This is not the kind of opposition the American people will permit. But

---

[46] Koch, *Jefferson and Madison*, 202–203.

keep away all show of force, and they will bear down the evil propensities of the government, by the constitutional means of election and petition."⁴⁷ These words underline a reality with which the leaders on both sides had to cope—the fact that public loyalties were delicately balanced, and that extreme measures on either side were likely to react against those who adopted them.

Jefferson's sense that a moderate line of action would be best calculated to help the opposition ride out the storm was justified by events. Between them the Jeffersonian leaders on one side and John Adams and his supporters on the other created a situation in which this uncomfortable union could survive, and in which the two parties had to continue the effort to accommodate each other—Adams by eschewing a formal declaration of war, refusing to press war preparations to the ultimate, and eventually seeking peace with France; the Jeffersonians by ruling out separation or force and keeping their protests and threats on a strictly verbal and legal level. But the central actor, after all, was the public itself, which cried out against the new taxes levied in anticipation of war by the Federalists in 1798, resented or suspected efforts at partisan suppression, and refused to provide the recruits for the army the Hamiltonians hoped to raise. It became clear that while the public could be aroused at insults to American "honor" such as that involved in the XYZ affair, it was adamantine when it came to bearing the actual burdens of an avoidable war.

There was another force that had to be weighed in the balance: the machinery of the Jeffersonian party, far better organized than anything the Federalists had to put against it, was worth more than the machinery of legal oppression set in motion to enforce the Sedition Act. Editors and other critics were prosecuted, fined, and jailed, but the Republican press

---

⁴⁷ *Writings*, Ford, ed., VII, 341, 356.

went on; and if the party's campaign in 1800 was seriously hampered by such enforcement, the results of the election do not show it.

The steady progress the Republicans had been making in the organization of an opposition since 1792 continued through the crisis of the XYZ affair and the Sedition laws, and in 1800 the Republicans won the necessary margin to control the presidency and both houses of Congress. Now, since it was *they* who constituted the government, and the Federalists the opposition, they were to have the luxurious chance to find out whether a majority faction in power was as dangerous to the public interest as Madison had argued in *The Federalist*. They were also to have the vexatious problem of coping in their turn with an opposition party. In the next chapter, I will try to show that even their own experience as an opposition, however educative, had not fully reconciled them to the necessity of an opposition, and will attempt to trace their ideas—more benign than those of the High Federalists—about how to get rid of it.

Chapter Four

The Transit of Power

I

JEFFERSON'S IDEAS ABOUT parties were the conventional notions of his age. We have seen that during the crisis of 1798, he had a glimpse of the idea of a two-party system and a moment of remarkable illumination about the problems of opposition under a federal system. But the possession of power impelled him to revert to the orthodox views he had long held, which in fact rather resemble Washington's craving for unanimity. No less than most of his contemporaries he was enthralled by the conviction that the sound citizen who has the public interest at heart is normally above and outside parties and the vices of partisanship.

Probably his first revealing statement about partisan division in America occurred in 1789 when he outlined to a correspondent his view of the new Constitution. "I am not a Federalist," he explained, "because I never submitted the whole system of my opinions to the creed of any party of men whatever in religion, in philosophy, in politics, or in anything else where I was capable of thinking for myself. Such addiction is the last degradation of a free and moral agent. If I could not go to heaven but with a party, I would not go there at all. Therefore I protest to you I am not of the party of federalists."

However, this was not all: "But," Jefferson went on, "I am much farther from that of the Antifederalists." And after explaining that he disliked certain particulars but approved of the Constitution as a whole, he concluded that all this would show that "I was right in saying I am neither federalist nor antifederalist; that I am of neither party, nor yet a trimmer between parties."[1] This last boast suggests that, like Washington, Jefferson preferred to think of himself at this time as having no motives relevant to parties or to party compromises, but as standing, an independent mind, above all party considerations.

As the party battle began to take shape in the 1790's, Jefferson, though himself busy stimulating party animosities, looked upon them with some misgivings. In a letter of 1792, urging Washington to accept a second term, he argued that the President in so doing could prevent "violence or secession," which he feared might be the consequence of some of Hamilton's measures.[2] In the same letter he also stated a notion which was to become all but obsessional in his correspondence for more than a quarter of a century, a notion which indeed colored much Republican thinking about the party battle: that the real aim of the leading Federalists was to restore monarchy on the British model, and that therefore the basic issue between the parties was monarchical versus republican principles.[3]

Two conclusions, both fatal to the acceptance of a continuing party system, seemed to follow from this idea. The first was that the Federalists, since they harbored a goal that ran counter to the convictions of the vast majority and flouted the

[1] Jefferson, *Papers*, Boyd, ed. (1958), XIV, 650–651.

[2] *Works*, Ford ed., VI, 491–493.

[3] For early examples, see *ibid*., VI, 255, 258–259, 298, 315.

explicitly republican covenant of the Constitution, were simply
not a legitimate party at all. And Jefferson's conviction of their
un-Americanism would only have been confirmed if he had
known all the details of Hamilton's uninhibited and near-
treasonous intrigues with James Beckwith and George Hammond. The second, which sustained Jefferson's patient
confidence in his party's ultimate victory, was that since the
hard-core Federalists were monarchists and the American
public was doughtily republican in its sentiments, the final
triumph of his own principles, given a fair chance to assert
them, was secure.

If one imagined that no less fundamental a principle than
monarchy versus republicanism was at stake, one could of
course waive all scruples about a strong partisan allegiance.
And the justice of this course would be trebly confirmed if the
opposition party, by an unmistakable squint toward England,
underlined its essential foreignness. By the time of the Jay
Treaty, when party lines had hardened, Jefferson had no
further use for equivocal men like his fellow Virginian,
Edmund Randolph, whose political conduct, he thought, had
not set him on a lofty perch above parties but rather in the
ignominious position of a trimmer. "Were parties here divided
by a greediness for office, as in England," Jefferson explained,
"to take a part with either would be unworthy of a reasonable
or moral man, but where the principle of difference is as substantial and as strongly pronounced as between the republicans
and Monocrats of our country, I hold it as honorable to take a
firm and decided part, and as immoral to pursue a middle line,
as between the parties of Honest men and Rogues, into which
every country is divided." By early 1796, he was referring to
the Federalists as "a faction" which "has entered in a conspiracy with the enemies of their country to chain down the
legislature at the feet of both." As a conspiratorial, monarchical
faction, the Federalists would have no moral claim to survival,

and one can only concur with Noble Cunningham's conclusion in his careful study of Republican party history that Jefferson "never recognized the validity of the Federalist party either while Adams was in office or as an opposition party during his own administration."[4] In the intensity of his partisan conviction, Jefferson the secularist lapsed into the language of dogma and ecclesiasticism when he spoke of the views of his foes: his letters bristle with heated digs at "apostacy," "sects," "political heresies," "conversions," "bigots," "votaries," and with invocations of "the true faith."[5]

In a series of interesting letters written between 1795 and 1797, while party passions were heating up, Jefferson explained the American party battle to foreign friends in terms which show to what a remarkable degree he saw the events of this period as a continuation of the conflicts of the Revolutionary era. He accounted for the Federalist party in terms partly economic and partly psychological, but always as a congeries of special groups, unreconciled to the Revolution, whose dominance over the larger mass of the people could be ascribed to such factors as their command of the press, their use of Washington's reputation, their wealth, and their strategic concentration in the cities. He generously claimed for the Republicans the entire body of landholders and landless laborers who had not given up their republican principles.

The most elaborate of these letters was written to Professor Christoph Daniel Ebeling in the summer of 1795. Before the Revolution, Jefferson explained, the people believed without question in the eternal superiority of the English constitution. But the Revolution forced them to reconsider, with the result that there was "an universal conversion to republicanism." When the Articles of Confederation proved too weak to sus-

---

[4] *Ibid.*, VIII, 201–203, 232–233; Cunningham, *The Jeffersonian Republicans in Power*, 303.

[5] *Works*, VI, 255, 315, 283 n, 258–259, 260, 298; VIII, 198–199.

tain union of action "as against foreign nations," and the new Constitution had to be framed, those who still yearned for monarchy, the returned refugees of the Revolution, "the old tories and timid whigs who prefer tranquility to freedom" hoped that monarchy would be resorted to as a remedy, "if a state of complete anarchy could be brought on." When the "monocrats" failed to get their principles written into the new Constitution, they still attempted to bring about "the assimilation of all the parts of the new government to the English constitution as nearly as was attainable." And not without some success: the "monarchical features" they hoped for, though much opposed by zealous republicans, were still thinly present; and the first Congress had been peopled by friends of "very strong government" who immediately strengthened everything in it that could be made to resemble the English constitution, "adopting the English forms and principles of administration" and forming, through the funding system, a perpetual public debt. This became "an engine in the hands of the executive branch of the government which, added to the great patronage it possessed in the disposal of public offices, might enable it to assume by degrees a kingly authority." But succeeding elections to Congress, together with the increasing awareness and resistance of the people to this scheme, had caused the numbers of the "anti-republicans" to diminish to the point at which they were now a "weak minority" in the House, and would soon become so in the more slowly rotating Senate. Despite their patronage, then, and their infiltration into the judiciary, the Federalists could be expected to fail in their "plan of sliding us into monarchy."

Jefferson went on to enumerate the composition of the two parties. On the side of the "anti-republicans": the old refugees and tories, British merchants residing in the United States "& composing the main body of our merchants" [a strange estimate], American merchants trading on British capital, speculators and holders in the banks and public funds, officers of the federal government (with some exceptions), office-hunters ("a numerous & noisy tribe"), and finally, "nervous persons, whose languid fibres have more analogy with a passive than active state of things." On the side of the Republicans: almost everyone else, the whole body of farmers and workers, a mass that outnumbers the other party "probably as 500 to one," but whose wealth is relatively small, and who temporarily suffer from their dispersion throughout the country, as against the rich, urban, easily concerted anti-republicans. Later Jefferson wrote (April 1796) that the mass of weight on the republican side was so great "as to leave no danger that force will ever be attempted against us. We have only to awake and snap the Lilliputian cords with which they have been entangling us during the first sleep which succeeded our labors."[6]

Such, then, was Jefferson's view of the Federalists: a small faction creeping into the heart of the government under the mantle of Washington and the perverse guidance of Hamilton, addicted to false principles in politics, animated by a foreign loyalty, and given to conspiratorial schemes aiming at the consolidation of government and the return of monarchy. It was a faction which, though enjoying certain temporary advantages, would ultimately lack the power to impose its will on the great mass of loyal republicans. Here Jefferson's optimism, as always, sustained him: before long the people through their faithful representatives would take over. And at that point it would be the duty of the Republican party to annihilate the opposition—not by harsh and repressive measures like the Sedition Act, but by the more gentle means of conciliation and absorption that were available to a principled majority party.[7]

---

[6] *Ibid.*, VIII, 206–210, 238–241; cf. 281–282, 336–338.

[7] Leonard Levy has emphasized, however, that Jefferson's rejection of seditious libel as a means of silencing opposition was very far from absolute. Although Jefferson did not believe that the federal govern-

Here necessity came to fortify temperament, for the circumstances of Jefferson's election were such as to require a measure of conciliation and appeasement at the very beginning.

II

The election of 1800 was an anomalous election in a double sense: first, in that it was the first election in modern history which, by popular decision, resulted in the quiet and peaceful transition of national power from the hands of one of two embattled parties to another; second, in that it was the first of only two American elections in which, since no candidate had a majority in the Electoral College, the outcome had to be decided in the House of Representatives. The superficial circumstances of the election are quite familiar: the Constitution, written without party tickets in mind, arranged for no separate designation of presidential and vice-presidential candidates before the adoption of the Twelfth Amendment in 1804; in consequence of a lapse in party planning, the two Republican candidates, Jefferson and Burr, turned up with the same number of electoral votes, though it was clearly understood throughout the party that the Virginian was head of the ticket; when the election went to the House, where the states voted as units, the Federalists fell heir to the unhappy luxury of choosing between the two leading Republicans. The resolution of the problem is also a familiar story: how the great majority of the Federalist leaders preferred Burr; how Hamilton repeatedly pleaded that they turn from this dangerous adventurer to the more certain and predictable, as well as endurable, limita-

---

ment could rightly punish such libels, he did not have the same scruples about state prosecutions, and accepted such prosecutions by Republican state officials of Federalist editors. "I have . . . long thought," he wrote to Governor Thomas McKean of Pennsylvania in 1803, "that a few prosecutions of the most prominent offenders would have a wholesome effect in restoring the integrity of the presses." See Levy, *Jefferson and Civil Liberties: the Darker Side* (1963), 59, and chap. 3.

tions of Jefferson; and how, in the end, under the leadership of James A. Bayard of Delaware, who swallowed Jefferson, as he wrote Adams, "so . . . as not to hazard the Constitution," the necessary portion of them abstained from voting and thus accepted Jefferson, only after an understanding, very delicate and proper and quite indirect, about the character of Jefferson's intentions had been arrived at.[8]

Historians have spent so much effort to unravel the details of this complex election, and in particular to evaluate Burr's role and the character of the tenuous understanding or "bargain" upon which Jefferson's election depended, that some aspects of the situation which we may regard as equally significant have not yet had their due. Since the badly needed definitive account of this election remains to be written, it is necessary to proceed with caution, but it is certainly possible to examine in this event the calculations by which the two-party system in the United States took a long and decisive step forward. Here were the Federalists, many of whom, not so many months earlier, had been hoping to finish off the opposition under the pressure of a war with France and through the agency of the Alien and Sedition Acts, now quietly acquiescing in the decision of a few of their fellow partisans to put into office a man whom they had long been portraying as an atheist, a French fanatic, a libertine, a visionary, and a political incompetent. The circumstances give us a rare opportunity to look at the minds of a set of governmental leaders as they faced the loss of power, and at the interplay between the two sides as they groped for an accommodation.

Abstractly speaking, the choices opened to a defeated gov-

---

[8] Morton Borden, *The Federalism of James A. Bayard* (1955), 97; I find this the most illuminating of the accounts of this election. See also Cunningham, *The Jeffersonian Republicans*, 239–248, and John S. Pancake, "Aaron Burr: Would-Be Usurper," *William and Mary Quarterly*, 8 (1951), 204–213.

ernmental party in a new federally organized country where the practice of legitimate opposition is still not wholly certain and where the incoming foes are profoundly suspect are three: *coup d'état*, disunion, or a resigned acceptance of their new oppositional status. Here we may begin by pointing to the central significance of something that did not happen: *violent resistance was never, at any time, discussed.* Neither was disunion discussed as a serious immediate possibility in 1801, though three years later a small but ineffectual faction of New England Federalists would lay abortive plans to bring it about. Something in the character of the American system was at work to unleash violent language but to inhibit violent solutions, and to reconcile the Federalists to the control of the government by a party they suspected of deep hostility to the Constitution. Somehow we must find a way to explain the rapid shift from the Dionysian rhetoric of American politics during the impassioned years 1795 to 1799[9] to the Apollonian political solution of 1800–1801.

What is observable in a wide range of Federalist letters and memoirs is a basic predisposition among the great majority of them to accept a defeat, fairly administered, even in 1800 before that defeat was a certainty. The whole historical experience of America, as well as the temperament of their class, argued against extreme or violent measures. They were conservative men, and extreme responses that might risk what they sometimes called "the public tranquillity" were not to their way of thinking. Even the instrumentalities of force were lacking in the American environment; and a class of intensely

---

[9] And which would be re-echoed by many in 1803 and after. Although Federalists did not discuss violent resistance, some Republicans talked of such action if the Federalists, in plain violation of the popular will, persisted in snatching the prize from Jefferson. I trust it will be clear that the following discussion is not an attempt to praise the Federalists for their restraint but to pose the problem of their adaptation to the transit of power.

political generals, the elite corps of any *coup d'état*, was impressively absent from the American scene.[10] Most Federalists were realistic enough to see that they were not only divided but outvoted; and none of their fulminations against democracy should blind us to the fact that they did not fancy trying to rule without a decent public mandate. Again, the federal system took some of the steam out of their frustration; in New England, where partisan feeling ran strongest among them, the Federalists were, for the time being, still in control of their own affairs at the state level. They had no reason to believe that they would be politically suppressed, and some of them thought that before very long the incompetence of the Republicans would swing the balance back to their side. Finally, the nature of the political parties and of political careers in America took some of the sting out of defeat.

The parties, for all the intensity of their passions and the bombast of their rhetoric, were new, their organization was rudimentary, and in some parts of the country partisan loyalties were thinner and more fragile than they might seem. No one, as Paul Goodman has remarked, had been born a Federalist or a Republican, and time was to show that switches from side to side were by no means unthinkable. Also, for many of the top leaders, politics was far from an exclusive concern. Political

---

10 Madison remarked pointedly upon this. Writing to Jefferson February 28, 1801, he said that he had not thought that the "phalanx" of Federalists in the House would hold out against their fellow partisans in the country at large, "and without any military force to abet usurpation. How fortunate that the latter has been withheld: and what a lesson to America and the world is given by the efficacy of the public will where there is no army to be turned against it." *Writings*, VI, 418. Many years afterward, in 1830, Madison still saw the acquiescence of defeated parties in elections as hinging in good part on the absence of force. "As long as the country shall be exempt from a military force powerful in itself and combined with a powerful faction, liberty and peace will find safeguards in the elective resource and the spirit of the people." *Writings*, IX, 370.

leaders were merchants, planters, lawyers, men of affairs with wide interests and with much capacity for taking pleasure in their private lives. Many of the best of them looked upon politics as a duty and not a livelihood or a pleasure. "To Bayard," his biographer pointedly observes, "the Senate was a job and not a career, a position of dignity and respectability rather than a battleground under observation by the nation." After the first flush of nationalist enthusiasm under Washington, it had become increasingly difficult to find men willing to accept positions of high responsibility and honor. Offices were refused or resigned with astonishing frequency, and Jefferson had to offer the Secretaryship of the Navy on five occasions to four different men before he had an acceptance. Professional politicians were, to be sure, emerging—fewer of them among the Federalists than among their foes—but they were somewhat looked down upon by men of eminence. And professional officeholders were the acknowledged dregs of the political world.[11]

To some degree, the option between Jefferson and Burr distracted the Federalists from facing the full significance of their loss in 1800 and eased them into it by stages. The prevailing Federalist preference for Burr, who was widely regarded as an adventurer without fixed principles and who was even seen by many as being preferable to Jefferson precisely on this count, may certainly argue for a spirit of desperation. But here again the party was divided, and the circumstances of the affair are significant for a reading of Federalist temperature. What the Federalist leaders had to ponder was not simply the

---

[11] On Bayard, see Borden, *op. cit.*, 159; for some shrewd observations upon the nature of the political career and party loyalties, see Paul Goodman, "The First American Party System," in W. N. Chambers and W. D. Burnham, eds., *The American Party Systems: Stages of Development* (1967), especially, 85–89. For some cautions about the significance of partisan rhetoric, see Noble Cunningham, Jr., *The Jeffersonian Republicans*, 227–229.

character of Burr as against that of Jefferson but also whether there was enough left of the spirit of concord or patriotism after the rancor of the preceding years to warrant thinking that they could endure Jefferson's possession of power. While it is an interesting question whether there was a firm, formally concluded "bargain" between the Virginian and some of his enemies—a question answered by most writers in the negative —it is still more interesting to note what particular assurances Hamilton suggested as necessary and that Bayard sought for when Jefferson was subtly and indirectly sounded about his intentions. Hamilton's advice and Bayard's terms shed much light on the practical differences that now separated the parties, and upon the calculations some Federalists were making about the future.

First, as to the terms: Bayard at one point approached a friend of Jefferson suggesting that if certain points of concord could be arrived at, three decisive states would withdraw their opposition to Jefferson's election. The points were enumerated: "First, . . . the subject of the public credit; secondly, the maintenance of the naval system; and, lastly, that subordinate public officers employed only in the execution of details established by law shall not be removed from office on the ground of their political character, nor without complaint against their conduct." These points were later reiterated to another intimate of Jefferson's, General Samuel Smith, who then purported to have won Jefferson's assent to them, and so gained Bayard's consent. On the second occasion the names of some of Bayard's friends were submitted, to give substance as it were, to the point about officeholders, and specific assurances involving them were offered in return. What is perhaps most interesting is that Bayard's conditions, in omitting a neutrality policy, deviate on only one count from those Hamilton proposed that the Federalists seek for: "the maintenance of the present system, especially in the cardinal articles of public credit—a navy, neutrality." Later Hamilton added patronage: "The preservation in office of our friends, except in the great departments, in respect to which and in future appointments he ought to be at liberty to appoint his friends."[12]

One is at first disposed to conclude that despite their public ravings about Monocrats and Jacobins, American politicians were beginning to behave like politicians. The patronage question in particular argues for this point of view. But it should be realized too that for the Federalists in 1801 the question, now raised for the first time in national politics, whether an incoming party would make a wholesale sweep of public offices and install everywhere its own partisans, involved more than solicitude for the jobs and livelihoods of their friends. Jefferson's intentions as to removals and replacements were the object of a good deal of discussion in Federalist letters of 1800–1801, whose tenor suggests that, aside from the concern for loaves and fishes which was not a negligible thing for lesser party figures, the patronage issue had two further points of significance. It was, in the first instance, a symbolic matter of decisive importance: if the Federalist followers were to be swept out of all the lesser offices, the act would be a declaration of partisan warfare suggesting that the two parties were incapable of governing in concert, and that the desire of the Jeffersonians to decide the nation's policies was coupled with a gratuitous desire to retaliate and humiliate. A policy of proscription would put an end to the harmony and balance they considered essential to the republican order. Secondly, one must reckon

---

[12] *Ibid.*, 91; Broadus Mitchell, *Alexander Hamilton*, II, 490, 744. Fisher Ames, urging a Federalist bargain with Burr, wanted a clear understanding: that the country be neither "sold, given or lent to France; peace with England, credit and banks left alone"; and that trade "not be tampered with—nor regulated Madison-wise." Welch, *Sedgwick*, 223.

with the Federalists' conviction that by far the larger portion of honest and able men, competent for the public business, were in their ranks; and that hence a wholesale displacement of such men might, quite aside from differences on policies, reduce the level of civic competence to a point at which the new government, established at so much effort and sacrifice, would be ruined. As Fisher Ames put it: "The success of governments depends on the selection of the men who administer them. It seems as if the ruling system would rob the country of all chance, by excluding the only classes proper to make the selection from."[13]

Some historians have been at pains to establish that there was in fact no explicit understanding and hence no "corrupt" bargain between Jefferson and the Federalists; and certainly the way in which he was sounded out through an intermediary, who took it upon himself to tender the desired assurances after exploring Jefferson's mind, leaves Jefferson in the clear. Yet such efforts to acquit our political heroes seem to me somewhat misplaced; we would probably have reason to think less of them if they had been incapable of arriving at some kind of understanding. After all, Jefferson was morally and constitutionally entitled to the presidency, and it was the part of statesmanship, if not indeed of wisdom and morality, to offer the

---

[13] Gibbs, *Memoirs*, II, 457; cf. also 402; cf. Samuel Stanhope Smith: "Good men will be obliged to retire from public affairs; blockheads and villains will soon hold the rein and scourge over us—may the *patricians* yet be able to save the republic, when the *tribunes* shall have urged it to the brink of ruin!" Walter Fee, *The Transition from Aristocracy to Democracy in New Jersey* (1933), 122–123. Cf. Henry M. Wagstaff, ed., "The Harris Letters," *James Sprunt Historical Publications* 14 (1916), 71; H. R. Warfel, ed., *Letters of Noah Webster* (1953), 244; C. R. King, *Life and Correspondence of Rufus King*, III, 353, 409, 475; Henry M. Wagstaff, ed., *The Papers of John Steele*, I (1924), 215, 445.

Federalists some assurances about his intentions. The survival of the constitutional system was at stake, and it had become necessary for both sides, in the spirit of practical men, to step back from their partisan embroilments, take a larger look at what they were doing, and try once again to make a fresh estimate of each other.

In this respect, Hamilton's appraisal of Jefferson, expressed in the course of his efforts to persuade other Federalists to accept him rather than choose Burr, becomes most illuminating. It was not many months earlier that Hamilton, trying to persuade Governor John Jay to get New York's electoral procedures changed to increase the chances of the Federalists in the forthcoming presidential election, warned Jay once again that the Republican party was a subversive and revolutionary party, and urged that his "scruples of delicacy and propriety" be set aside: "They ought not to hinder the taking of a *legal* and *constitutional step*, to prevent an *atheist* in Religion and a fanatic in politics from getting possession of the helm of the State."[14]

But in January 1801, faced with the alternative of Burr, Hamilton was pushing this atheist and fanatic as a much safer prospective president and portraying him in quite different terms. "I admit," he wrote to Bayard in a remarkable letter, "that his politics are tinctured with fanaticism; that he is too

---

[14] Hamilton to Jay, May 7, 1800, H. P. Johnston, *Correspondence and Public Papers of John Jay* (1893), IV, 271. With some men scruple played a part in these proceedings. What Hamilton was proposing—to have the state legislature change the mode of choosing electors so that the people would choose them by districts—corresponded to what was being done elsewhere to their advantage by the Republicans, but Jay would have none of it. With one eye on his scruples, and possibly the other on the verdict of history, he endorsed this letter, "Proposing a measure for party purposes, which I think it would not become me to adopt," and filed it away among his papers. *Ibid.*, 271 n.

much in earnest with his democracy; that he has been a mischievous enemy to the principal measures of our past administration; that he is crafty and persevering in his objects; that he is not scrupulous about the means of success, nor very mindful of truth, and that he is a contemptible hypocrite—" thus far as damaging an estimate as any Burrite Federalist could have wished. But, Hamilton went on, Jefferson was really not an enemy to the power of the Executive (this would prove all too true) or an advocate of putting all the powers of government in the House of Representatives. Once he found himself by way of inheriting the executive office, he would be "solicitous to come into the possession of a good estate." And then, prefatory to a long and devastating estimate of Burr's character and talents, there occurs the strategic and prophetic appraisal of Jefferson: "Nor is it true that Jefferson is zealot enough to do anything in pursuance of his principles, which will contravene his popularity or his interest. He is as likely as any man I know to temporize; to calculate what will be likely to promote his own reputation and advantage, and the probable result of such a temper is the preservation of systems, though originally opposed, which being once established, could not be overturned without danger to the person who did it. To my mind, a true estimate of Mr. Jefferson's character warrants the expectation of a temporizing, rather than a violent system." Even Jefferson's predilection for France was based more upon the popularity of France in America than upon his own sentiment, and it would cool when that popularity waned. "Add to this, that there is no fair reason to suppose him capable of being corrupted, which is a security that he will not go beyond certain limits." After his scathing dissertation upon Burr, Hamilton reverted to some partisan considerations: if the Republicans got Jefferson, they would be responsible for him; but if the Federalists should install Burr, "they adopt him, and become answerable for him." Moreover, he would doubtless win over many of them, "and the federalists will become a disorganized and contemptible party."[15] Finally, Hamilton repeated to several correspondents his conviction that Burr could not be relied upon to keep any commitment he might make to the Federalists.

In repeated letters to Bayard and others deemed open to his waning influence, Hamilton hammered away at the contrast he had laid down between the temporizing, politic Jefferson, and the dangerous Burr, that "embryo Caesar," "the Catiline of America," the "most unfit man in the United States for the office of President"—a man who, he told Oliver Wolcott in a significant phrase, would call to his side "rogues of all parties, to overrule the good men of all parties."[16] Jefferson would never know how much he owed to Burr for having provided such a chiaroscuro, for throwing him into such high and acceptable relief, if only to a decisive minority of Federalists. But Hamilton's sense of the situation, his implicit recognition that there were, after all, good men on both sides, casts a powerful shaft of light into the roiled and murky bottoms of Federalist rhetoric. There are moments of supreme illumination in history when the depth of men's belief in their own partisan gabble has to be submitted at last to the rigorous test of practical decision. For about eight years the Federalists had been denouncing Jefferson and his party, and in the last few years their accusations had mounted to the point at which the leader of the opposition, the Vice President of the United States, had been charged with Jacobinism, atheism, fanaticism, unscrupulousness, wanton folly, incompetence, personal treachery, and

---

[15] Hamilton to Bayard, January 16, 1801, *Works*, J. C. Hamilton ed., (1851), VI, 419–424; the letter is misdated and out of place here, *ibid.*, VI, 520.

[16] For Hamilton's letters on Burr and Jefferson, *ibid.*, VI, 486, 487–489, 495, 497, 499–501, 520–521.

political treason. Now this atheist in religion and fanatic in politics was to be quietly installed in the new White House, by courtesy of a handful of Federalist Congressmen, and though there was still hardly a man in the Federalist party who trusted him, there was also not a man to raise a hand against him. The Federalists, having failed to install Burr, preferred to risk Jefferson rather than to risk the constitutional system that had been so laboriously built and launched,[17] and the way

---

[17] The contest of 1800–1801 led to a decisive step, in the form of the Twelfth Amendment, toward constitutional recognition of the role played by parties in the federal government. After 1796, when the election left Jefferson as Adams's Vice President, the Federalists had shown some interest, though without effect, in an electoral change that would give separate designation to the presidential and vice-presidential candidates of each party. After the harrowing experience of 1801, the Republicans took up the idea, and now the Federalists opposed it. By 1803 the Republicans had achieved a sufficiently strong majority to win the required two-thirds vote (22 to 10 in the Senate, 83 to 42 in the House) to adopt the Twelfth Amendment and send it to the states. It was quickly ratified by the necessary number and declared in force by September 25, 1804, in time to govern the presidential election of that year. Resistance in Congress from Federalists was strong—only three Representatives from New England voted for it—and the legislatures of Massachusetts, Connecticut, and Delaware refused to ratify it. "The plan of this amendment," said one Federalist manifesto, "is to bury New England in oblivion and put the reins of Government into the hands of Virginia forever. They, the Democrats, have seized on a moment of delirious enthusiasm to make a dangerous inroad on the Constitution and to prostrate the only mound capable of resisting the headlong influence of the great States and preserving the independence and safety of the small ones." Herman V. Ames, *The Proposed Amendments to the Constitution of the United States during the First Century of Its History*, *Annual Report* of the American Historical Association for 1896 (1897), II, 79 n. One of the most interesting arguments against the Twelfth Amendment was made by Senator James Hillhouse of Connecticut, who wanted to assure that the President and Vice President would indeed always be of different parties "to check and preserve in temper the over-heated zeal of party." "If we cannot destroy party," he urged, "we ought to place every check upon it." Lolabel House, *A Study of the Twelfth Amendment of the Constitution of the United*

in which they explained to each other this seeming change of heart deserves some attention.

III

There was, of course, nothing cheerful about Federalist acquiescence in the transit of power. The overwhelming party preference for an acknowledged adventurer like Burr in the face of the clear public mandate for Jefferson was a token of the persistence of the exacerbated party conflict of the past half-dozen years. The Federalists had not softened their view of Jefferson: they expected to have to endure grave evils from a Republican victory, and a few even took a stark apocalyptic view of it. Uriah Tracy of Connecticut, an extreme reactionary, was not long in concluding that the country could not be saved in any way, that with the Jeffersonians in power "a change of Govt. was certain, and to that change we must wade in blood," and the timid Charles Carroll feared that he would be driven into exile and poverty, brooded over a possible war with England, and contemplated a military despotism and the end of property and liberty. William Vans Murray seemed to be giving up on popular government when he wrote that he deeply regretted the election "and wish there had been *none* . . .," while Judge Samuel Sewall was among those who seemed to be willing to risk constitutional irregularity in urging that an election "be wholly prevented." The mercurial Fisher Ames, who, as we shall see, was at times more sanguine, worried about danger to peace abroad and order at home, James McHenry in his gloomier moments thought that only time would tell whether the country was to have a "total revolution," and even in the somewhat calmer climate of North Carolina, W. R. Davie (hardly dreaming that the time would

---

States (1901), 50. A modern study of the origins of the Twelfth Amendment is badly needed.

come when he would accept service under Jefferson), imagined that destruction of the Constitution under the Republicans would be "certain."[18]

But, with all this, the prevailing note among leading Federalists in 1800–1801 was one of short-run resignation and long-run hope, and it was only a few years later that many of them gave way to complete despair. They still had faith in their principles and confident knowledge of their influence among the dominant classes. They were entrenched in the judiciary, strong in the Senate, preponderant in New England, and at competitive strength in other states of the Union. They could hope that their continued opposition would be powerful enough to check some disasters, or, at worst, that if Jefferson did bring an exceptional train of evils, men everywhere would respond by rallying to them and bringing their party back to office, unified and perhaps stronger than ever. Hence their tactical counsel to each other during and shortly after the election and the final balloting in the House of Representatives looked not to extreme responses but to a measured judgment of the situation and to the means by which their interests could be protected and their influence best made felt. Their talk was not that of conspirators planning to react with force, but of politicians, accustomed to power, who must now learn how to play the role of a constructive constitutional opposition. They had lost only by a narrow margin, they were still free to organize opposition, and they expected that they would have an excellent chance to return to power.

---

[18] Richard Welch, *Theodore Sedgwick, Federalist* (1965), 241, 241 n; Kate M. Rowland, *Charles Carroll of Carrollton* (1898), 246; B. C. Steiner, *Life and Correspondence of James McHenry* (1907), 475; Hamilton, *Works*, Hamilton, ed., VI, 467–468; Worthington C. Ford, ed., "Letters of William Vans Murray to John Quincy Adams," *Annual Report*, American Historical Association (1912), 693; Samuel Eliot Morison, *Harrison Gray Otis* (1913), I, 206, 212; C. R. King, *Rufus King*, III, 206, 350; B. P. Robinson, *William R. Davie* (1957), 360.

Even in New England, where suspicion of everything that issued from Virginia was strongest, there was much sentiment of this kind. By now John Adams was no longer so much heeded by other New Englanders; and yet his advice is worth recording. He reflected that the Federalists had paved the way for their own defeat by overrating their influence and popularity, but he still had hope and he urged caution: "We are not yet attainted by act of Congress, and, I hope, shall not fly out into rebellion." Oliver Ellsworth, one of the most respected men in his party, wrote to Rufus King: "You think, as I do, that [Jefferson] dare not run the ship aground, nor essentially deviate from that course which has hitherto rendered her voyage so prosperous. His party *also* must support the government while he administers it; and if others are consistent and do the same, the government may even be consolidated and acquire new confidence." Even Timothy Pickering, later to drift into conspiratorial opposition, was reassuring about Jefferson's probable restraint on the vital issue of removals from office. Oliver Wolcott, another of the Hamiltonian cabal in the Adams Cabinet, anticipating Jefferson's victory, warned against "temporary expedients" that would persuade the public that both parties were equally swayed by "personal and sinister motives" rather than by program and principles. If the Federalists remained firmly attached to the principles of their cause, "we shall remain a party, and in a short time regain our influence." William Plumer of New Hampshire was confident that the Federalists, though unable to carry measures of their own, were strong enough "to prevent the ruling party from doing much mischief." George Cabot showed restrained optimism. Anticipating defeat in July, 1800, he wrote that his own party "is undoubtedly composed of men who will again govern after some vicissitudes" unless foreign events deprived them of their "influence among the people." If Jefferson were elected, the Federalists would still perhaps be powerful enough

142

to "deter him from Jacobin excesses." Considerable time must elapse, and much must be endured, he thought in August, 1801, before the Federalist cause would again have a chance of success.[19]

Caleb Strong, the Governor of Massachusetts, pointed out to the legislature that though the election had disappointed many citizens of the commonwealth, "yet they will reflect that, in republicks, the opinion of the majority must prevail." He voiced his own expectation that the new President would not depart from the essential principles of the government; "and so long as his administration shall be guided by those principles, he will be entitled to the confidence of the people, and their interest requires that he should possess it."[20]

Manasseh Cutler, not long after Jefferson's inaugural, hoped the President would prove " a prudent man" and ventured the thought that he might turn to the Federalists for some of his support. A vigorous opposition would be important, but "it will be on the ground of just principles and fair reasoning, devoid of passion or the spirit of party." Noah Webster, the lexicographer and Federalist editor, concluded in the face of impending defeat: "The evils of our constitution are *radical*, but I hold him to be an enemy who would submit the correction of these evils to the sword." Theophilus Parsons, the conservative jurist, was philosophical about such matters, his son recalled long afterward, believing that there would be "regular stages in the decline and decay" of the system of government, followed by its restoration. He found much hope in the fact

---

[19] Adams, *Works*, IX, 582; W. G. Brown, *The Life of Oliver Ellsworth* (1905), 325; King, *King*, III, 353; George Gibbs, *Memoirs of the Administrations of Washington and John Adams* (1846), II, 404–405; William Plumer, Jr., *Life of William Plumer* (1857), 247; for Cabot see *Rufus King*, III, 279, 292; cf. also 354, 356; and H. C. Lodge, *Life and Letters of George Cabot* (1878), 321.

[20] *Patriotism and Piety: The Speeches of His Excellency Caleb Strong* (1808), 39; cf. the answer of the Massachusetts Senate, 42–43.

that Americans were uniquely free, short of treason or rebellion, to act politically to defend their interests or carry out their civic duties, and was convinced that a decline in political condition would be arrested when personal interests and prosperity were touched or stricken.[21]

For no one was the spectacle of Republican triumph more acutely distasteful than for the acidulous Fisher Ames, yet in the main Ames kept his composure for more than three years before he entirely yielded to his characteristic morbidity in 1803. Even in December 1800 he suggested that public opinion, once fearful of Federalist overgovernment, would be equally and rightly fearful of the new administration, and would swing back; "and it is very possible that we may find ourselves fitter and more united for the work than for sustaining, as heretofore, the men and measures of our choice." A few weeks after Jefferson's inauguration he wrote a remarkable letter to Theodore Dwight which shows how far he had gone in thinking through the potential role of his party as an oppositionist force. Many Federalists, he observed, imagined that nothing could be done, or that it was too soon to do anything, or even that Jefferson would follow Federalist policies and remove the need to act. He disagreed: Virginia had aspirations to govern the whole nation according to her notions, and it would be important to resist by firmer party organization than before. "Party," he wrote, striking an interesting Burkean note, "is an association of honest men for honest purposes, and when the State falls into bad hands, is the only efficient defence; a champion who never flinches, a watchman who never sleeps." Would it not be possible to rally good men and hold Jacobinism within its present limits? And here he went on to outline the ethics of

---

[21] W. P. and J. P. Cutler, *Life, Journals, and Correspondence of Rev. Manasseh Cutler*, II (1898), 44–45; but see 47; Webster, *Letters*, 222; Theophilus Parsons, Jr., *Memoir of Theophilus Parsons* (1859), 116–117, 119.

legitimate opposition: "It would be wrong to assail the new administration with invective. Even when bad measures occur, much temperance will be requisite. To encourage Mr. Jefferson to act right, and to aid him against his violent jacobin adherents, we must make it manifest that we act on principle, and that we are deeply alarmed for the public good; that we are identified with the public. We must speak in the name and with the voice of the good and the wise, the lovers of liberty and the owners of property." Then, after briefly outlining a tactical program, he concluded that he expected good results: "We should, I am sanguine enough to believe, throw upon our antagonists the burdens of supporting and vindicating government, and enjoy their late advantages of finding fault, which popular prejudice is ever prone to listen to. We should soon stand on high ground, and be ready to resume the reins of government with advantage. . . . We are not to revile or abuse magistrates, or lie even for a good cause. We must act as good citizens, using only truth, and argument, and zeal to impress them." Energy and party unity became his rallying cry. He understood full well that the Federalists, with their lack of tight association and unity, had hardly been a party at all, and for a while he anticipated that adversity might forge them into a party strong enough to return and govern. "Perhaps," he wrote philosophically in 1800, "a party, whenever it thinks itself strong, naturally splits; nothing but dread of its rival will bind it firmly enough together."[22] Moments of adversity, with some men, can be a profound stimulus to thought, and so it was with Ames.

As we look southward from New England, we find many leaders of a similar frame of mind. In July 1800, Rufus King wrote to a Federalist friend: "I have no notion that our Government or the security of our property can or will be, in any

---

[22] *Works*, I, 288, 292–295; George Gibbs, *Memoirs*, II, 396.

material degree, affected by any changes that have happened or that in my opinion are likely to happen." If such a grave risk really did exist under the Constitution, it would be useless and criminal conduct to support it. "Presidents, Secretaries, Generals and Ministers—myself among them—may be removed, still the machine will move on!" When Jefferson's election seemed certain to him he wrote to Robert Troup: "Now the event is fixed, we become calm, and without effort convince ourselves that the evils in respect to the great measures of the govt. are not likely to happen." Jefferson's removals from office, Troup wrote to King in like spirit after the inauguration, were not expected to be extreme, and by the fall of the year he reported that public spirit among the Federalists was worn out "and they seem to pant so much for repose that they are ready to submit to any state of things short of Parisian Massacres." The inaugural address, he reported, "has had a wonderful lullaby effect. I do not apprehend the serious mischiefs from [Jefferson's] administration that have been foretold." "Nil desperandum," wrote Gouverneur Morris. "Let the chair of office be filled by whomsoever it may, Opposition will act as an outward conscience, and prevent the abuse of power." "Prudence," he wrote to Hamilton while the issue between Jefferson and Burr was still in doubt, "seems to be more necessary than anything else. . . ." The "democrats," he thought in the fall of 1801, would have their own internal disputes, "and if we have good sense enough not to make too much noise we shall by and by be called in to take the business up in a much better condition than when we were forced (and deservedly, too) to lay it down. . . ." To Hamilton he said he thought the will of the public that Jefferson should be President should be respected and that he had "declared my determination to support the constitutionally-appointed administration, so long as its acts shall not in my judgment be essentially wrong." John Jay shared a preference for moderate ways. "The extent of our country and the temper of our people are favorable to tranquility," he wrote Rufus King. In refusing renomination for the governorship of New York, he preached a temperate spirit. "Time and experience will correct many errors which ought not to have been introduced into public opinions. What the price of that experience may be, cannot be foreseen. . . . It is not to be expected that parties will never be intemperate, but overbearing intemperance or violence in individual leaders ought neither to appal nor inflame good citizens."[23]

James McHenry was among those who foresaw at least a tolerable future. In April 1801, he conjectured that though affairs would not be managed by men of his choice and much too much would be left undone out of the Republicans' regard for economy, "yet they will be generally so conducted as to afford no glaring causes for extraordinary alarm or complaint." Another Marylander, William Pinkney, said in the summer of that year: "I felt no alarm at the idea of Mr. Jefferson's success," and added a few years later: "I have constantly believed that America has nothing to fear from the men now at the head of our affairs." Bayard of Delaware, who played so vital a role in the election, believed with Morris that public opinion must be heeded. Later he avowed, explaining his last-minute intervention for Jefferson: "*I was chiefly influenced by the current of public sentiment*, which I thought it neither safe nor politic to counteract." Reporting the decision of a small crucial bloc of Federalists to yield, abstain, and thus accept Jefferson in the House vote, he said: "The step was not taken until it was admitted on all hands that we must risk the Constitution and a civil war or take Mr. Jefferson."[24] This was

[23] C. R. King, *Rufus King*, III, 269, 381–382, 409, 526, 461, 251; A. C. Morris, *Diary and Letters of Gouverneur Morris*, II, 383, 415; cf. 423; Hamilton, *Works*, Hamilton ed., VI, 494; for Jay see King, *Rufus King*, III, 258 and Johnston, *Jay*, IV, 279–280.

[24] B. C. Steiner, *James McHenry*, 503; Henry Wheaton, *Writings and*

the view which he had urged upon his colleagues in caucus.

Further to the South, Robert Goodloe Harper, despite his intense partisanship and his strong reservations about Jefferson, took a view similar to Bayard's. "Because he is President," he wrote, "I shall be one of the last to oppose, thwart, or embarrass his administration." Directly after the inauguration he issued a warm appeal to Federalists which echoes in some ways the reasoning of Fisher Ames, laying down rules for the guidance of a responsible opposition. Federalists should conduct themselves according to principle, and "should they be compelled ultimately to oppose the administration, . . . they will commence their opposition with reluctance, support it with energy, and conduct it with candour, dignity, and effect," and not resort to "those factious and profligate arts which have been employed against themselves." Federalism was not finished, he insisted, and it would return. In the end Federalist principles would have to be followed because the government could hold together on no others. Another North Carolina Federalist, William R. Davie, even while he expected very subversive things from Jefferson ("every institution must crumble"), still advised that "the true policy of the Federalists is to act an open and manly and decided part, by yielding at once to the public sentiment, with the best possible grace, and placing the painful

---

Speeches of William Pinkney (1826), 37, 40; deposition by Bayard in 1805, reprinted *Congressional Globe*, 33d Cong., 2d sess., 136 (January 31, 1855); Elizabeth Donnan, "Papers of James A. Bayard," *Annual Report*, American Historical Association (1913), II, 127; cf. also 131, 132.

Jefferson himself believed that the Federalists were inhibited by the thought that if Burr were elected "legislative usurpation would be resisted by arms, and a recourse to a convention to re-organize and amend the government." "The very word convention gives them the horrors," he wrote, "as in the present democratical spirit of America, they fear they should lose some of the favorite morsels of the constitution." *Writings*, Ford ed., VII, 491, 494.

responsibility of the *future* where it ought to be, on the succeeding administration."[25]

After the violent and impassioned rhetoric of the preceding years, one is impressed, then, with the readiness of leading Federalists to adapt themselves to evils they considered inevitable, to accept the position of a legitimate opposition, and to disenthrall their practical judgment from the gaudy threats and dire predictions with which their propaganda was so free. One of Rufus King's correspondents, Joseph Hale, put it well in December 1800, when he wrote: "Men of the most judgment with us do not expect those evils to follow the adminn. of Jeff. or Burr which while they were candidates it was thought politic to predict." And what Hale saw as partisan advantage Fish-

---

[25] "Papers of James A. Bayard," 137; Harper, *Speeches* (1824), 325–326; B. P. Robinson, *William R. Davie* (1957), 360–361.

I believe that the findings of David H. Fischer in his learned study of changes in the Federalist party after 1800 suggest that the most important aspect of Federalist response to being out of power was their rapidly growing disposition to adapt by imitating the Jeffersonians in certain tactical matters. For one thing, they were quite articulate in their growing acceptance of party: thus one finds Fisher Ames writing that "Party is an association of honest men for honest purposes." "We must consider," wrote Hamilton in April 1802, "whether it be possible for us to succeed without, in some degree, employing the weapons which have been employed against us." Among these were not only the party and party spirit, but ancillary secret political clubs, such as those Hamilton now began to advocate and which indeed flourished between 1808 and 1815. The Federalists toned down the anti-democratic theme—"We must court popular favor," Ames said, and John Rutledge bluntly urged that "If Jefferson cannot be ousted but by this sort of *cant*, we must have recourse to it"—and after 1805 toned down their Anglophilia also. They made some effort to get closer to the people, and to use party organization more effectively, to organize processions, parades, house-to-house canvassing, tours by candidates, and the like. Fischer, *Revolution*, 33, 59, 110, 140, 180, 192, and passim. The competitive party process, by encouraging the imitation of one party's successful techniques by its opponents, in the end made the parties more like each other in methods, and thus somewhat reduced the distance between them in their philosophical doctrines about party.

er Ames saw too as a form of personal discipline. "While evils are in prospect," he wrote in December 1800, "it is right to aggravate their magnitude and our apprehensions; after they are arrived to make the best of them." And yet, lest this seemed too cheerful, he added: "Bad is best."[26]

IV

It was characteristic of Jefferson that he perceived the keen political conflict of the years just preceding his election not as an opportunity but as a difficulty. Thanks to the efforts both of his detractors and his admirers, his historical reputation has caused us to misread him. In the Federalist tradition, later taken up by so many historians, he was a theorist, a visionary, a radical; and American liberals have praised him for the same qualities the Federalists abhorred. The modern liberal mind has been bemused by his remarks about the value of a little rebellion now and then, or watering the tree of liberty with the blood of tyrants, or having a complete constitutional revision every twenty or thirty years. But Jefferson's more provocative utterances, it has been too little noticed, were in his private correspondence. His public statements and actions were colored by a relative caution and timidity that reveal a circumspect and calculating mind—or, as so many of his contemporary foes believed, a guileful one. He was not enraptured by the drama of unrestrained political conflict; and with the very important exception of some of his views on foreign policy and war, his approach to public policy was far from utopian. He did not look forward to a vigorously innovative administration—he had seen enough of that. The most stunning achievement of his presidential years, the Louisiana Purchase, was an accident, the outcome of the collapse of Napoleon's ambitions for a Caribbean empire—the inadvertent gift of Toussaint L'Ouver-

---

[26] Joseph Hale to Rufus King, December 29, 1800, C. R. King, *Rufus King*, III, 357; Ames, *Works*, I, 286.

ture and the blacks of Haiti to this slaveholding country. Its most stunning disaster was the embargo, and the embargo itself came from Jefferson's penchant, here misapplied, for avoiding conflict. His was, as Hamilton put it in his tardy burst of pragmatic insight, a temporizing and not a violent disposition.

This disposition dictated an initial strategy of conciliation toward the Federalists, which led to a basic acceptance of the Hamiltonian fiscal system, including even the bank, to a patronage policy which Jefferson considered to be fair and compromising and hoped would appease moderate Federalists, and to an early attempt to pursue neutrality and to eschew aggravating signs of that Francophilia and Anglophobia with which the Federalists so obsessively and hyperbolically charged him. But for our concern, it is particularly important to understand that in Jefferson's mind conciliation was not a way of arriving at coexistence or of accommodating a two-party system, but a technique of absorption: he proposed to win over the major part of the amenable Federalists, leaving the intractables an impotent minority faction rather than a full-fledged opposition party. His strategy, which aimed, once again, at a party to end parties, formed another chapter in the quest for unanimity.

"The symptoms of a coalition of parties give me infinite pleasure," wrote Jefferson less than three weeks after delivering his inaugural address. "Setting aside a few only, I have been ever persuaded that the great bulk of both parties had the same principles fundamentally, and that it was only as to our foreign relations there was any division. These I hope can be so managed as to cease to be a subject of division for us. Nothing shall be spared on my part to obliterate the traces of party and consolidate the nation, if it can be done without abandonment of principle."[27] His inaugural address itself had been designed to strike the first conciliatory note, and on the key question

---

[27] Cunningham, *Jeffersonian Republicans in Power*, 8.

of party conflict it was a masterpiece of statesmanlike equivo-
cation. It had a number of grace notes that might be calculated
to appease opposition sensibilities: a prideful reference to
American commerce, a strong hint about sustaining the public
credit, an injunction to "pursue our own Federal and Republican principles," the memorable promise of "peace, commerce,
and honest friendship with all nations, entangling alliances with
none," obeisance to the memory of Washington as "our first
and greatest revolutionary character," modest remarks about
the fallibility of his own judgment, a promise not only to try
to hold the good opinion of his supporters but also "to conciliate that of others by doing them all the good in my power,"
and finally, that *sine qua non* of inaugural addresses, especially
necessary from one widely deemed "an atheist in religion"—an
invocation of divine aid.

But it was in speaking of American conflicts that Jefferson
achieved his finest subtlety. The acerbity of American political
conflict, he suggested, would deceive "strangers unused to
think freely and to speak and to write what they think." But
now that the issue had been decided, Americans would unite
for the common good. "All, too, will bear in mind this sacred
principle, that though the will of the majority is in all cases to
prevail, that will to be rightful must be reasonable; that the
minority possess their equal rights, to violate which could be
oppression." Let us restore harmony and affection to our society, he pleaded, and banish political intolerance as we have
banished religious intolerance. That the agonies and agitations
of Europe should have reached our shores and divided our
opinions over proper measures of national safety is hardly
surprising, but "every difference of opinion is not a difference
of principle. We have called by different names brethren
of the same principle. We are all republicans; we are all
federalists."[28]

---

[28] *Works*, IX, 195. Jefferson also drafted an interesting passage about

In expressing these healing sentiments, which set a fine precedent for other chief executives taking office after acrimonious
campaigns, Jefferson succeeded at a focal moment in reassuring
many Federalists. Hamilton thought the address "virtually a
candid retraction of past misapprehensions, and a pledge to the
community that the new President will not lend himself to dangerous innovations, but in essential points tread in the steps of
his predecessors." It contained some foolish but also many good
ideas, George Cabot judged. "It is so conciliatory that much
hope is derived from it by the Federalists," and he thought it
"better liked by our party than his own." Robert Troup, who
referred to its "wonderful lullaby effect" also thought it dis-
pleasing to the "most violent of the party attached to him,"
as did James A. Bayard. It was well calculated, Robert Goodloe Harper reported to his constituents, "to afford the hope of
such an administration as may conduce to his own glory and
the public good." "A fine opening," said Manasseh Cutler.[29]

Yet the Federalists would have been much deceived if they
had imagined that the striking sentence, "We are all republicans; we are all federalists," implied that Jefferson would put
the principles of the two *parties*, and hence the parties themselves, on a nearly equal footing of legitimacy. The context, as
well as various private utterances, showed that he meant only

parties which he did not use in the address: "Wherever there are men
there will be parties and wherever there are free men they will make
themselves heard. . . . These are the whigs and tories of nature. These
mutual jealousies produce mutual security: and while the laws shall
be obeyed all will be safe. He alone is your enemy who disobeys them.
. . . Let this then be the distinctive mark of an American that in cases
of commotion he enlists under no man's banner, enquires for no man's
name, but repairs to the standard of the laws. Do this and you need never
fear anarchy or tyranny." *Ibid.*, 193 n.

[29] Broadus Mitchell, *Alexander Hamilton*, II, 494. C. R. King, *Rufus
King*, III, 407, 408, 461; Hamilton, *Works*, ed. by J. C. Hamilton,
VI, 522; Harper, *Speeches*, 324; W. P. and J. P. Cutler, *Manasseh Cutler*,
II, 44.

that almost all Americans believed both in the federal union and in the general principles of republican government, and that therefore the two parties stood close enough to be not so much reconciled as *merged*, and merged under his own standard. One can only concur here with Henry Adams's remark that Jefferson "wished to soothe the great body of his opponents, and if possible to win them over; but he had no idea of harmony or affection other than that which was to spring from his own further triumph." Jefferson's letters substantiate this interpretation. He had hardly finished the labors of the inauguration before he was writing letters to John Dickinson, James Monroe, and General Horatio Gates in which his hopes were spelled out with great clarity. Large numbers of his fellow citizens had been "hood-winked" from their principles through an extraordinary combination of circumstances, he argued, but it was now possible to enlighten them. An incorrect idea of his own views had got about, but "I am in hopes my inaugural address will in some measure set this to rights, as it will present the leading objects to be conciliation and adherence to sound principle." The leaders of the "late faction" were, of course, "incurables" and need not be courted, but "with the main body of federalists I believe it very practicable." The XYZ affair had created a political delusion among many people, but the uncertainties of the preceding month arising from the presidential election in the House of Representatives, and the alarm over a possible constitutional crisis had produced "a wonderful effect . . . on the mass of federalists." Many wanted only "a decent excuse for coming back" to a party that represented their own deepest views, and others had come over "rather than risk anarchy." Therefore Jefferson's policies, especially as to patronage, would be prudent, and would be so designed as "to give time for a perfect consolidation." In short: "If we can hit on the true line of conduct which may conciliate the honest part of those who were called federalists, and do justice to those who have so long been excluded from it, I shall hope to be able to obliterate, or rather to unite the names of federalists and republicans. The way to effect it is to preserve principle, but to treat tenderly those who have been estranged from us, and dispose their minds to view our proceedings with candour."[30]

V

Chance plays its part in history. Jefferson's plan of conciliation was favored by a fortunate lull in the European wars, since peace negotiations between France and Great Britain, begun in the month of his inauguration, were concluded a year later in March 1802 when the Treaty of Amiens was at last ratified. For a few years, before war broke out again in May 1803, issues of foreign policy were less exacerbating than they had been at any time since the unwelcome arrival of Citizen Genet. The field was thus left briefly clear for Jefferson's conciliatory strategy on domestic matters to register its effect. The essence of the strategy consisted not in what he did during these first twenty-four months of his administration—for the little he and his party did was provocative enough—but in what he did not do. One could write an alternative scenario for the Jeffersonians, which would call for an all-out attack on the bank charter, a wholesale removal of Federalist officeholders, an inundation of the judiciary with new Republican appointees, an intimate orientation toward France and increasing hostility to England—all things which the most fearful Federalists had reason, by their own lights, to expect. And here some examination of Jefferson's restraint on patronage and the Hamiltonian system is in order.

From the very earliest moment of his administration, Jefferson made it clear to some of his intimates that, however

---

[30] Adams, *History of the United States*, I, 201; Jefferson, *Works*, IX, 201–206; cf. 236–237, 282–283.

strong the Republican clamor for jobs, restraint in removals was a necessary part of his conciliatory plan. In effect, at an early and vital moment in national development, his patronage policy set the principle that to have been a political opponent of an incoming administration did not necessarily mean the loss of one's job in the civil service. That he found an efficient and respectable body of civil servants when he entered office was a tribute to the administrative practices of his predecessors; that he refused to sweep them out wholesale in response to pressure from office-hungry Republicans was a tribute to him. Rather than clean out Federalist officeholders like a petty chieftain in a partisan vendetta, he tried to arrive at a formula for what might be called civil-service coexistence—a formula that would consider both the needs of his partisans for rewards and the sensibilities of the main body of Federalist officeholders.

Jefferson started from the principle that a difference of opinion on politics is not in itself sufficient ground for removal: "Malconduct is a just ground of removal: mere difference of political opinion is not."[31] Of course he would make no *new* appointments of Federalists, but he expected that retirements, resignations, and occasional removals for incompetence or misconduct would gradually create openings for his partisans. Soon, when it became apparent that this process would not go on fast enough and that Republicans were keenly dissatisfied— few incumbents died, Jefferson said plaintively, and none resigned—he retreated to a new principle: removals of a few especially violent and active Federalist partisans would be necessary to give Republicans a fair share of the jobs. Although it was not acceptable to Federalists, this seems an understandable rule if we remember that Jefferson came in with the entire body of federal officeholders staffed by his opponents, and that, under Republican scruples about frugality, not many new

---

[31] *Works*, IX, 225.

posts would be created. But what would a fair share be? Republicans, he thought, ought to be gradually brought in until they had government jobs proportionate to their numbers in the body politic. This proportion, he once suggested, would be about two-thirds or three-quarters—an awkwardly large part if one considers the number of removals it might require, yet not a wholly unreasonable estimate if one measures it by the preponderance soon won by the Republicans in Congress.[32]

In this way, the early American regard for quality and continuity in public service, as well as the widespread sense that public office is a species of property right, proved somewhat inhibiting to party warfare. In his eight years Jefferson removed 109 out of 433 men who held office by presidential appointment; and of these 109, 40 were in a special category, the "midnight appointments" of the Adams administration, whose validity he never conceded.[33]

It would be misleading, of course, to suggest that Jefferson's patronage policies mollified the Federalists as much as he might have hoped. They were unable to respect his rejection of their last-minute appointees, whose posts they considered to be based upon impeccable legal and moral foundations. Many of them could see no justice in any removals whatever below the topmost level of Cabinet and diplomatic positions. And in at least one local situation, an unfortunate Jeffersonian appointment to the collectorship of New Haven, where a competent last-minute Adams man was replaced by a controversial and allegedly incompetent Republican, stimulated strong protest. Word had reached Connecticut that some kind of understand-

---

[32] In the House of Representatives this preponderance varied during Jefferson's eight years from a low of 65 percent (1801–1803) to a high of 83 percent (1807–1809).

[33] Leonard White, *The Jeffersonians*, 379. On patronage policies, see White, chap. 24 and Cunningham, *The Jeffersonian Republicans*, chaps. 2 and 3.

ing had been arrived at over the patronage, and Federalists there considered that Jefferson had violated a firm agreement. In reply to a protest from New Haven merchants, Jefferson pointedly remarked that his own statements about political tolerance, harmony, and affection in social intercourse, and the rights of the minority had been tortured into an inference that the tenure of offices was to be undisturbed. In the preceding administration, only Federalists had been given offices. Now he hardly considered it a violation of the rights of the minority to ask them to share office with the Republican majority who were entitled to "a proportionate share in the direction of public affairs." Some removals were necessary to this end, and he hoped to base them "as much as possible on delinquency, on oppression, on intolerance, on incompetence, on ante-revolutionary adherence to our enemies." Once the imbalance had been corrected, he would be happy to arrive at the point where "the only questions concerning a candidate shall be, is he honest, Is he capable? Is he faithful to the Constitution?" This was not a satisfactory formula to the Federalists, but it was at least consistent with the idea of a bipartisan civil service.[34] In any case, the patronage problem illustrated both the possibilities of conciliation and also its limits.

The Hamiltonian system was a less formidable problem. As issues, funding, and assumption were dead, killed by the very success of Hamilton's system, and it would have been quixotic in Jefferson to revive them, or to try to reanimate an issue with which William Branch Giles had long before failed to rally Republican forces in Congress. "Some things," Jefferson wrote to Dupont de Nemours in January 1802, "may perhaps be left undone from motives of compromise for a time, and not to alarm by too sudden a reformation." As for Hamilton's system,

---

[34] On this affair see Cunningham, *Jeffersonian Republicans in Power*, 19–24; on expectations in Connecticut, S. E. Baldwin, *Life and Letters of Simeon Baldwin* (1919), 434.

though it might have been avoided in the beginning, it could now no longer be thrown off. "We can pay his debts in 15 years: but we can never get rid of his financial system. It mortifies me to be strengthening principles which I deem radically vicious, but this vice is entailed on us by the first error. In other parts of our government, I hope we shall be able by degrees to introduce sound principles and make them habitual." There follows the characteristic sentence: "What is practicable must often control what is pure theory."[35]

Even the Bank, always more objectionable than funding or assumption, would be accepted and retained. Not only was there no attempt to repeal or impair its charter, but under Secretary of the Treasury Gallatin's urgings, its operations were actually extended. To the five banks already existing, the Republicans added three branches, in Washington (1802), Savannah (1802), and New Orleans (1805), the first and last of these on Gallatin's initiative. Jefferson, of course, never gave up his hostility to banks, and he saw in the Bank of the United States, which he still believed to be unconstitutional, a rival political force of great potentiality, one which, "penetrating by its branches every part of the Union, acting by command and in phalanx, may, in a critical moment, upset the government." For the safety of the Constitution, he wrote Gallatin, he was solicitous to "bring this powerful enemy to a perfect subordination under its authorities." And yet he was willing to accept its existence, even its expansion, so long as he could go on grum-

---

[35] *Works*, IX, 344 n. There is an amusing echo of this some years later in a letter of Fisher Ames, of all people, to Josiah Quincy. Laying down tactical principles for the Federalists, Ames wrote: "I confess great prudence and many forbearances are necessary. In almost every case, a popular, or, at least, inoffensive aspect can be given to your argument. . . . The skill of the business is to attempt only what is practicable, and some of the popular tenets are false yet sacred, and therefore respectable." Ames to Josiah Quincy, November 19, 1807, Ames, *Works*, I, 403.

bling and denouncing it. Gallatin kept assuring him that it was useful, and here again what was practicable was allowed to control pure theory, and Jefferson's relatively sophisticated sense of politics overruled his agrarian economics. Madison was to follow him in approving the Bank's continuance—a matter, he said, of "expediency and almost necessity," a thing confirmed by "deliberate and reiterated precedents." In 1811, when the Bank was permitted to die with the expiration of its twenty-year charter, and at a moment when the country was about to need it most, it had many friends among the agrarian Republicans, who were reluctant to see it go.[36]

It was, of course, the state banks, chartered by Republican legislatures, that multiplied and flourished during the first decade of Republican rule, and toward these Jefferson, without relinquishing his anti-bank prejudices, adopted a most politic attitude. "I am decidedly in favor," he wrote Gallatin in July 1803, "of making all the banks Republican by sharing deposits among them in proportion to the dispositions they show; if the law now forbids it, we should not let another session of Congress to pass without amending it. It is material to the safety of Republicanism to detach the mercantile interest from its enemies and incorporate them into the body of its friends."[37] Instead of trying to keep his party purely and dogmatically agrarian—a utopian and surely defeatist course—he was prepared to see it linked to the capitalistic growth of the country, to encourage the development within its ranks of a mercantile-

[36] Bray Hammond, *Banks and Politics in America* (1957), 206, 210; on the Republicans and the Bank see chaps. 5, 8, and 9. Charles A. Beard's *Economic Origins of Jeffersonian Democracy* (1915), 440–450, remains a shrewd appraisal of Jefferson's policies on banking.

[37] *Works*, VIII, 252. "It is certainly for the public good to keep all the banks competitors for our favors by a judicious distribution of them, and thus to engage the individuals who belong to them in support of the reformed order of things or at least in an acquiescence under it." *Ibid.*, VIII, 172.

financial-entrepreneurial segment, and thus to have it develop into a heterogeneous coalition, based not only upon geographical but upon economic diversity as well. In this he and his associates succeeded; but in encouraging the further politicization of the banking of the country, and in committing themselves as much as they did to the state banks, they laid the groundwork for the destructive attack on central banking that came with the Jacksonian era.

VI

It hardly needs to be said that Jefferson's middle course did not succeed in appeasing Federalist leaders. At best it can be said that it avoided goading them into violent responses for the brief period during which he consolidated his influence; and when they awoke from the relative torpor into which they receded in 1801, it was only to find, as many of them promptly concluded, that democracy was so much in the ascendant that all hopes of an early return to power had to be given up. By 1803 most of them had decided that Jefferson was as bad as they had ever expected him to be, and some of them were lamenting that the Constitution was dead. They had been infuriated by the Jeffersonian war on the judiciary, which, beginning with the refusal of some of Adams's midnight appointments, went on early in 1802 to the repeal of the Judiciary Act of 1801, and was climaxed by the impeachments of Justices Pickering and Chase in 1804 and 1805. They were intensely discouraged by the Louisiana Purchase in 1803, which not only seemed to cut off all prospects of war with France but added immense western territories out of which they could foresee the Jeffersonians carving many new agrarian states and thus piling further gains on top of the already substantial Republican majorities. By 1804, when a few maddened New England conspirators tried to use Burr's candidacy for the governorship of New York as a pivot upon which to engineer an independent New England–New York confederacy, they were so far out of touch with reality that even some of the most stoutly parochial New England conservatives, whose support they had to have, hung back in discouragement and disapproval. George Cabot, speaking for Chief Justice Theophilus Parsons, Fisher Ames, and Stephen Higginson as well as himself, warned Timothy Pickering that secession was pointless as long as democracy remained such a general creed that even New England was thoroughly infected with it. The best hope for the Federalists, he thought, would be in the public reaction to a gratuitous war with England.[38]

The assault on the judiciary had been, of course, partisan warfare, pure and simple. The federal judiciary was the only one of the three arms of government in which the Federalists remained entrenched in 1801, and some of the federal judges had been outrageously partisan in the trials arising from the

---

[38] Henry Adams, *History*, II, 164–166. Cabot's warning to Pickering against premature attempts at secession may be profitably compared with Jefferson's letter to John Taylor, written when the Republicans were fretting under the Alien and Sedition Acts. (Chapter 3 above.) The caution about extreme remedies is the same, but where Jefferson's was founded upon a buoyant optimism about the possibility of relieving present evils within the Union, Cabot's was founded upon despair over the proposed remedy because of the condition of New England itself. A separation from the Union, he told Pickering, would do no good because as matters now stood the proposed New England Confederation would itself be infected with democracy; the Federalist party had "no energy" and might lose what little it still had in the state if it acted unwisely. Substantial changes in the form of government could come successfully only after further purgatory, only from "the consequences of great suffering or the immediate effects of violence." Separation could come "when our loyalty to the Union is generally perceived to be the instrument of debasement and impoverishment." "We shall go the way of all governments wholly popular,—from bad to worse,—until the evils, no longer tolerable, shall generate their own remedies." Disunion would break up the Federalist party, but "a war with Great Britain manifestly provoked by our rulers" might bring the people of New England to accept dissolution of the Union.

Sedition Act. Finally, the lame duck Federalists spurred Republican indignation when in February 1801, less than two weeks before leaving office, they enlarged the federal judiciary by adding sixteen circuit court judges and a battery of attendant marshalls, attorneys, and clerks, thus creating what they expected to be a packet of new jobs for their legal corps and digging themselves even more deeply into the enlarged judicial body. Although the needs of the judicial system gave some good grounds for the measure, the Republicans could see it only in its partisan aspect, and its timing was intensely provocative. The Federalists, Jefferson wrote in December 1801, "have retired into the Judiciary as a stronghold. There the remains of Federalism are to be preserved and fed from the Treasury, and from that battery all the works of Republicanism are to be beaten down and erased."[39]

It is easy to understand the Federalist revulsion over the war on the judiciary. Last-minute or not, the judicial commissions which Madison refused to deliver and which led to the case of *Marbury* v. *Madison* had been authorized in a perfectly legal way. The cutback in the size of the judiciary also seemed to the Federalists a way of dismissing supposedly independent judges simply by dismissing their jobs, and the measure was passed by a partisan Republican vote after a high-pitched debate in Congress which rumbled with threats from the minority of secession and civil war. And finally, the impeachments were candidly political proceedings without any pretension that "high crimes and misdemeanors" were involved. But while we may understand why the Federalists saw the assault on the judiciary as a violent and unendurable provocation, we are not obliged to see it the same way. The prescriptions for the judiciary establishment laid down in the Constitution are extremely vague and permissive. Even under the principles of

---

[39] Beveridge, *Marshall*, III, 21.

strict interpretation, it would have been possible for the Jeffersonians to play fast and loose with the Supreme Court by adding judges—to "pack" it, for example, as Grant later did and F.D.R. proposed to do. The Federalists had already set a precedent for changing its size in 1801, when they cut it back from its original six members to five. On this count E. S. Corwin has observed: "When it came to legislation concerning the Supreme Court, the majority of the Republicans again displayed genuine moderation, for, thrusting aside an obvious temptation to swamp that tribunal with additional judges of their own creed, they merely restored it to its original size under the act of 1789."[40]

Federalist historians like Albert J. Beveridge who have charged that a major Republican reason for reducing the judiciary, the desire to save money, was hypocritical, underestimate the tax-mindedness of early agrarian America. In fact, the Republicans may well have been estopped from drastic action on the judiciary more by their penny-pinching than by their political scruples. Pure considerations of partisan warfare might have dictated not a contraction but an expansion of the judiciary in which the Federalist judges would have been drowned. But Jefferson had called above all for a frugal government, and a frugal government there would be.

Moreover, while John Marshall could have been overpowered by packing the Supreme Court, Federalist entrenchment in the lower federal courts could have been undermined at the same time by a constitutional amendment to change the tenure of judges from life to terms of four or six years; and the activity of the Supreme Court could have been further impaired in a number of ways by modifications of the judiciary acts.[41] The preponderance of the Republicans in Congress and the

---

[40] E. S. Corwin, *John Marshall and the Constitution* (1921), 63.

[41] Cf. the judgment of Edward Channing, *The Jeffersonian System* (1906), 22–23.

states after 1802, and certainly after 1804, was such as to make the passage of a constitutional amendment not unduly difficult. Whether their restraint came from scruple, expediency, or ineptitude, the actual response of the Jeffersonians to the Federalist judiciary, when measured against the possibilities open to them, seems relatively moderate—not wholly "temporizing," in Hamilton's language, but certainly not "violent." So far as domestic issues were concerned—patronage, financial policy, and the judicial system—the strain between the two sides was so kept within bounds that it posed no threat to the political order. Once again, as in the 1790's, the acid test was to come with the exacerbations introduced by questions of foreign policy.

As renewed party strife replaced the brief testing period that followed Jefferson's inauguration, his response to the Federalist leaders was as sharp as theirs to him, and while his public stance still invoked the restoration of harmony and affection and left open his bid for the Federalist rank and file, his private correspondence was electric with flashes of impassioned hostility to opposition leaders who would "toll us back to the times when we burnt witches," to the "ravenous crew" of his foes, the "monocrats" who "wish to sap the republic by fraud," "incurables to be taken care of in a mad house," and "heroes of Billingsgate." "I wish nothing but their eternal hatred," he flared out in one of his letters. He could find nothing legitimate or useful in the Federalist opposition. "A respectable minority," he explained to Joel Barlow in May 1802, "is useful as censors," but the present minority did not qualify because it was "not respectable, being the bitterest cup of the remains of Federalism rendered desperate and furious with despair."[42] They would not, they should not, survive at all.

If Jefferson was winning over precious few of the Federalist

---

[42] *Works*, IX, 241, 242, 268, 284, 290; X, 145; IX, 370.

leaders, he had the pleasure at least of taking away much of their following and mobilizing his own to the point of nearly total party victory. To this degree his political optimism was quite justified: he had gauged public sentiment correctly and he was giving the people what they wanted—frugal government, low taxes, fiscal retrenchment, a small army and navy, peace, and the warm sentiments of democratic republicanism. And he had behind him a party far more popular and efficient than anything the Federalists could mobilize against him. He had not been in the White House as much as a year before he was reporting to Dupont de Nemours his immense satisfaction with his efforts at conciliation and unity—by which he meant Republican preponderance. If a presidential election were held a year hence, he ventured on January 18, 1802, solely on grounds of political principle and uncomplicated by personal likes or dislikes, "the federal candidate would not get the vote of a single elector in the U. S." And indeed the Congressional elections of 1802 yielded an overwhelming Republican majority, which, though somewhat weakened later by reactions to the embargo and to the War of 1812, was never substantially endangered. In May Jefferson exulted that Republican advances had reached the point at which "candid federalists acknowledge that their party can never more raise its head." In 1804 he was re-elected with the votes of all New England except Connecticut, and given a party preponderance of four to one in the Senate and five to one in the House. In his second inaugural address he congratulated the country on "the union of sentiment now manifested so generally" and anticipated among the people an "entire union of opinion." In 1807, when the Massachusetts Federalists lost even their governorship, he saw the Federalists as "completely vanquished, and never more to take the field under their own banners."[43] The old dream of national unanimity seemed to be coming true.

---

[43] *Works*, IX, 343 n, 371; X, 135–136, 421.

As Federalism dwindled away toward virtual impotence, Jefferson seemed to fall victim to a certain inconsistency between his passion for unanimity on one side and on the other to his long-standing philosophical conviction that free men will differ and that differences will engender parties. But he was perhaps less inconsistent than he seemed: to him achieving unanimity meant not establishing a dead level of uniform thought but simply getting rid of the deep and impassioned differences which had arisen only because the extreme Federalists had foisted upon their party a preference for England and for monarchy. Unanimity did not require eliminating various low-keyed and negotiable differences of opinion between different schools of honest republicans. The chief limit to unity now indeed seemed to stem from divisions appearing in the Republican ranks in Congress and from such intrastate factionalism as disturbed the party in Pennsylvania. But none of this worried him unduly. He understood that a party which had no opposition to fight with would develop a centrifugal tendency: "We shall now be so strong that we shall split again; for freemen thinking differently and speaking and acting as they think, will form into classes of sentiment, but it must be under another name, that of federalism is to become so scouted that no party can rise under it."[44]

On this count we can find him prophetic. Partisan victory

---

[44] The new party division, he thought, would be into "whig and tory, as in England formerly," a division founded in the nature of man. *Works*, IX, 371. The understanding that a party enjoying overwhelming preponderance would split was not peculiar to Jefferson. We have seen it in Fisher Ames (p. 145), and in the summer of 1801, Thomas McKean, the Republican governor of Pennsylvania, who would have his own difficulties with party division, had written to Jefferson: "When ever any party are notoriously predominant they will split; this is in nature; it has been the case time immemorial, and will be so until mankind become wiser and better. The Outs envy the Inns. The struggle in such a situation is only for the loaves and the fishes." Cunningham, *Jeffersonian Republicans in Power*, 203.

seems finally to have brought him back to his original understanding that party differences are founded in human nature.
For him the goal of unanimity was satisfied by the elimination
of Federalism, the disappearance of fundamental issues; and
it may not be too fanciful to see in this some likeness to Burke's
satisfaction in the disappearance of "the great parties" which
was the very thing Burke thought laid a foundation for moderate party differences and justifiable party loyalties. Jefferson
once observed that with "the entire prostration of federalism"
the remaining Federalists might form a coalition with the
Republican minority; but in this he saw no danger so long as
the Republican dissidents were not—here the party obsession
raises its head once again—flirting with monarchy. "I had always expected," he wrote to Thomas Cooper in 1807, "that
when the republicans should have put down all things under
their feet, they would schismatize among themselves. I always expected, too, that whatever names the parties might bear,
the real division would be into moderate and ardent republicanism. In this division there is no great evil,—not even if the
minority obtain the ascendency by the accession of federal
votes to their candidate; because this gives us one shade only,
instead of another, of republicanism."[45] The notion that the
animating principle behind Federalism had been a passion for
monarchy, however delusive it had been, led to the comfort-
ing conclusion that the last nail had now been driven into the
coffin of the hereditary principle, and hence that the country
had reached a unanimity deep enough. But in 1807 neither
Thomas Jefferson nor George Cabot could possibly have
imagined what would come in the next few years: that Jefferson would leave the presidency with a sense of failure and
with diminished popularity; that Federalism, for all this, would

---

[45] *Works*, X, 451; he had expressed the same view to Gallatin in 1803,
ibid., IX, 456.

undergo only a modest resurgence; that a war with Great Britain would finally come under the Republicans, and that, though conducted with consummate incompetence, it would lead to the complete triumph of Republicanism and the final disappearance of the Federalist party.

Chapter Five

The Quest for Unanimity

I

THERE IS A FETCHING irony in the fact that after all the efforts of Federalists and Republicans to dispose of opposition by partisan strategy, by schemes and plans that were founded on the premise of party effectiveness, opposition should have been at last done in at a moment of unusual fecklessness in the party in power. The quest for unanimity that runs like a red thread through discussions of party from Washington to Monroe was at last rewarded under the Republicans not because of the brilliance with which they handled public problems but because of the Federalists' default. From Jefferson's first election onward one can see a steady breakdown of opposition in Congress, momentarily but never decisively reversed, which was climaxed by the total collapse of Federalism as a national force after the War of 1812. It is impossible now to say to what extent the political ineptitude of the crisis years after 1805 can be attributed to the absence of an effective and responsible opposition; but it is possible to suggest that the decline of opposition in Congress removed some of the brakes of discretion, gave reign to an increasingly mediocre and passive political personnel, shut off the flow of information and criticism from the country to Washington, deprived the governing group of a good intellectual sounding board, and, not least, immobilized the moderate center which had been so effective in swinging the balance during the crisis of 1797–1798.[1] Here one must reckon with the fundamental change in the environment of the party battle brought about by the persistent international crisis that led to the War of 1812; and in order to comprehend later changes in the idea of party we must pause to consider a few issues of policy.

In a world that is changing rapidly, a close and furious immersion in the controversies of yesterday and today may prove one of the poorest preparations for the events of tomorrow. It is chastening to think how little the embroilments of the 1790's prepared the generation that experienced them to anticipate the course of American politics in the first fifteen years of the nineteenth century. Although many Federalists had hoped that tensions with France, perhaps climaxed by a Franco-American war, would finally crush the Republicans, they were to be mocked by time: war indeed came in the end, but it was a war against England, and under Republican leadership; and even though the war was disastrously conducted, it was the Federalist party itself that was crushed. The Federalists might have expected that the Republicans would one day bring the country to war with England, but they could hardly have imagined that their enemies, supposedly maddened with Anglophobia, could have dallied so long and could have responded so feebly for so many years to the challenge of English

---

[1] For an instructive statement on the value of opposition in a crisis situation, see Eric L. McKitrick, "Party Politics and the Union and Confederate War Efforts," in W. N. Chambers and W. D. Burnham, eds., *The American Party Systems* (1967), 117–151.

maritime policies. They might have expected, as few Republicans could, that Jefferson, the high priest of political anticentralism and the supposed foe of presidential power, would use the presidency to make the central government an engine of oppression through the instrumentality of his embargo—and of an oppression more keenly felt than any act of government since Parliament's Coercive Acts of 1774. But it is doubtful that they would have expected to find themselves, with all this provocation at work to stir up new recruits for their side, incapable of rousing enough support to restore themselves as an effective opposition.

Republicans, for their part, might have expected war with England. But few would have been optimistic enough to predict that if it should be conducted with disastrous incompetence and grave humiliation it would not bring about a formidable revival of Federalism. Some Republicans were shrewd enough to see that a war would result in departures from Republican policies—from economy, from the minimal army and navy, from opposition to aggrandized federal power —but few could have expected that it would go so far as to make the Republican party the exponent of a kind of neo-Federalism, in which almost the whole range of Hamiltonian policies, including even the Bank, should be included. Presumably none would have expected to find a substantial body of old Federalists standing in stout opposition to these measures. Neither side was at all prepared for the country it lived in after 1814: a country self-confident and strikingly unified, but led largely by politicians whose minds were still fixated on obsolescent antagonisms.

Jefferson's years in power were haunted by constant foreign provocations, for which the absence of strong and coherent domestic opponents proved no adequate compensation. As we have seen, Jefferson had been fortunate enough to begin his administration during a lull in the European wars marked by the peace negotiations of 1801 and concluded in March 1802 with the ratification of the Treaty of Amiens. But the peace was brief: in May 1803 war began again, and by 1805 Jefferson was faced once more with the familiar vexing problems—the seizure of ships, the impressment of seamen, the defense of trade, the choice between England and France. One could still hope for peace, but to be altogether neutral was impossible.

So far as domestic opposition was concerned, Jefferson faced the problems of foreign policy with a relatively free hand. After the Congressional elections of 1802, the Federalists in Congress were a negligible voting force, outnumbered by 25 to 9 in the Senate and 102 to 39 in the House. In the presidential election of 1804 the Republicans successfully invaded New England itself. Jefferson carried the electoral votes of every state but Connecticut and Delaware—even Massachusetts fell—and the Federalists now shrank to a fourth of the Senate and little more than a fifth of the House. Helpless, bitter, and increasingly withdrawn, a few zealous Northern Federalists toyed with secession schemes in 1804; but they rested their hopes on Aaron Burr's conquest of the governorship of New York, and Burr not only disappointed them there but promptly thereafter cut down the leading intelligence of Federalism on the duelling ground at Weehawken. Henceforth there was no time—not even during the revivals of Federalism that followed the enactment of Jefferson's embargo and the outbreak of war—when the Federalists held more than 30 percent of the Senate (in 1815–17) or more than 37 percent of the House (in 1813–15).[2]

As Jefferson had foreseen, the overwhelming preponderance

---

[2] James S. Young, in his brilliant study of *The Washington Community, 1800–1828* (1966), 111, has reminded us that party affiliations in Congress were not formally declared, and that figures may be less definite than they seem. But he too operates on the assumption that party affiliations were usually known. For example, *ibid.*, 115.

of the Republicans did lead to fissions in their ranks, but neither the dissident Republicans in Virginia, the schismatic ones in New York and Pennsylvania, nor the corporal's guard of Federalists in Congress constituted an effective or consistently responsible opposition. Federalists and a few Republican heretics subjected administration policies to a stream of criticism, sometimes shrewd, often merely pettish, but the President had little reason to fear that opposition elements could combine into an effective force either in Congress or at the polls. One administration measure, the Yazoo compromise, was blocked by Congressional opposition, and two others, the appropriation of two million dollars for the purchase of Florida and the Nonimportation Act of 1806, were embarrassed, but such opposition was occasional and short-lived. In their basic political values, the Republican dissidents or Quids in Congress stood even further than the mainstream Republicans from the Federalists, and in the end they alienated even the sympathetically disposed conservative wing of their own party. Under the waspish guidance of John Randolph, whose gift for leadership never approached his gift for invective, the strength of the Quids was decidedly self-limiting. Once the Jeffersonian floor leader in the House, Randolph quickly went into eclipse after going into open and shrill opposition in April 1806, and by the autumn of the following year even the sympathetic John Taylor pronounced "poor Randolph . . . lost and his party . . . vanished."[3] Firm in control of the majority of the party, Jefferson was left free to indulge himself in his most experimental no-

_____

[3] Norman K. Risjord, *The Old Republicans: Southern Conservatism in the Age of Jefferson* (1965), 82. "Upon all trying questions," Jefferson exulted on May 4, 1806, "exclusive of the federalists, the minority of republicans voting with him [Randolph] has been from 4 to 6 to 8, against from 90 to 100." *Writings*, VIII, 447. On the Quids and other schismatic tendencies, see Cunningham, *The Jeffersonian Republicans in Power*, chaps. IV and IX, and Risjord, chaps. III and IV.

tions: in the field of military and foreign policy these were as bizarre and venturesome as his domestic policies were circumspect.

Although Jefferson hated war, he was no pacifist. In 1811, as his party drifted toward war, he wrote: "When peace becomes more losing than war, we may prefer the latter on principles of pecuniary calculation."[4] However, experiences dating from the non-importation agreements of 1774 had profoundly impressed upon his mind, unfortunately more profoundly than the facts warranted, the idea that economic sanctions might be an adequate way of defending the national interest, an adequate substitute for offensive armaments and for war. Along with many of his party, he thought that a navy was particularly expendable. A navy strong enough to protect American commerce on the high seas, would be expensive and hence inconsistent with that frugal government he had promised. It would also, he believed, afford occasions for maritime clashes that would increase the likelihood of war. Somehow he had been led to overestimate vastly the vulnerability of England to American commercial retaliation. Moreover, in the course of defending American commercial interests against the Tripolitanian corsairs, he had conceived one of his less admirable enthusiasms: the idea that small, lightly armed gunboats were an adequate naval arm for the coastal defense of the United States. Accordingly, the Navy was deprived of some of its frigates and provided instead with well over 200 fifty-foot gunboats, incapable of action against a coastal blockade and useless as a bargaining counter on the tables of international diplomacy. Yet only nineteen Federalists and Quids out of a House of Representatives numbering 142 opposed Jefferson's gunboat bill in December 1807.

Jefferson's embargo policy, which took shape in his mind at

---

[4] Quoted by Bradford Perkins, *Prologue to War* (1961), 41.

the same time, was consonant with this commitment to a passive coastal defense. As he saw it, greater regard for American maritime rights could be won through economic coercion, and the basic goals of foreign policy could be achieved not only without war but even without the extravagance of strong naval armaments. This view of foreign policy ran counter to the ideas of some Republicans and of almost all Federalists, who would have built a strong naval arm usable in bargaining with the two great European powers and, should diplomacy fail, usable in carrying naval warfare to the enemy at a distance (as Jefferson himself had done in Tripoli). As one looks at Republican party behavior in the years from 1801 to about 1820, one finds an apparent reversal of the normal maxims of politics. Arm to parley, and if parley fails you will be prepared to fight —this is the usual prescription of *Realpolitik*. The Republicans —and it should be clear that they did so with strong popular backing—chose instead to remain substantially unarmed at first; being unarmed, parleyed ineffectively; then, still unarmed, drifted into war; and finally after waging an unsuccessful war, at last gave serious attention to the permanent problems of national defense.[5] This attitude toward an ocean-going navy was intended, of course, to reduce the risks of war. But having a negligible navy, the Republicans were weakened in their efforts to achieve the diplomatic gains that would make war unnecessary. In the end, oddly enough, going to war became, for them, the *alternative* to developing a navy.

However, in his embargo policy Jefferson did at least give the Republicans a theory of national defense and a device for its execution which was meant to combine the pursuit of national interests with the quest for peace. Jefferson's embargo brings

---

[5] The government spent $1.9 million on the Navy Department and $2.0 million on the War Department in 1811, when war was a virtual certainty; it spent $14.7 million and $8.6 million respectively in 1815, when the war was over.

to mind Herbert Hoover's famous characterization of Prohibition as "an experiment noble in motive," for the embargo was attended by some of the same grave difficulties: the effort to force the normal course of human activities into rigidly preconceived channels; the conversion of thousands upon thousands of ordinary citizens into lawbreakers; the conversion of their own government into an enforcement agency directed against them.

Historians have written much about the lack of discipline in the Republican party, but the striking thing about the congressional situation, which underlines the absence of a capable, organized opposition, was the dispatch with which the Embargo Act was passed and the tenacity with which it was maintained over so many months. This fateful law, with its profound consequences for peace and war, and for commerce, and with its threat of invasion of the lives and liberties of American citizens, was passed by the Senate (22–6) after less than one day's discussion and by the House (82–44) after less than three. With some justice, Jefferson took satisfaction in the degree of party discipline reflected in the vote on so drastic a measure. The opposition, he wrote, "consisted of one-half Federalists, ¼ of the little band [of Quids], the other fourth of republicans happening to take up mistaken views on the subject."[6]

Much has also been said by historians about the grave costs of the embargo, its failure to attain its objectives, its ruinous economic effects. Jefferson himself admitted in the end that in cash terms it had been far more costly than a war. More can still be said about its effect on Jefferson's party. The embargo unseated the wits of Republicanism, brought out its starkest internal contradictions, caused it to turn against its own principles, and tainted the shining image of its moral and intellectual leader. It turned the libertarian and legalist Jeffer-

---

[6] Risjord, *The Old Republicans*, 83.

son into a tyrant grasping for power, ignoring elementary procedural principles, and making decisions without consulting many of his chosen intimates. It turned the strict constructionist who had choked on the Bank into a brash advocate of loose construction who could swallow the idea that power to regulate commerce became the power to prohibit it, and the foe of aggrandized federal government and strong presidential powers into a President assuming for his office and for the national government powers beyond anything the Federalists had dared to contemplate.[7]

And yet, although the embargo was a self-confessed failure, a fourteen-month disaster that sent Jefferson out of the presidency smarting with a sense of defeat, bereft of his grasp of leadership, and shorn of much of his prestige, its effect in reviving opposition was notably limited. That it brought some resurgence of Federalist strength has often been observed. David H. Fischer has written a brilliant book showing how Federalists began to reconsider the need for a strong party organization and to realize how much their anti-popular stance had cost them in their pursuit of power.[8] But the astonishing thing—especially when one thinks of the way some other failures in statecraft have brought reprisal at the polls—is how slight the Federalist resurgence was, and how far it still left their party from the status of an effective opposition. In the election of 1808, which occurred after embargo hardships had made themselves felt, Madison was still easily elected as Jef-

---

[7] The account of the embargo and its enforcement in Henry Adams' famous *History* is still essential. See also Bradford Perkins, *Prologue to War*, chap. 5; Leonard Levy, *Jefferson and Civil Liberties*, chaps. 5 and 6; and Leonard White, *The Jeffersonians* (1951), chaps. XXIX–XXX. For contrary views see Louis M. Sears, *Jefferson and the Embargo* (1927), and Marshal Smelser, *The Democratic Republic* (1968), 163–180.

[8] *The Revolution of American Conservatism* (1965).

ferson's successor. Not only did he win an electoral majority in all but five of the seventeen states, but the Federalists gained not a single seat in the Senate. They did double their representation in the House, but this impressive-sounding gain must be measured against the low base from which they had started: with all their new seats, they still had only a third of it. And then, rather than increasing their gains, they lost half of them in the elections of 1810. The disaster of the embargo was probably intensified by the arbitrariness of one-party government, but it was a disaster that did not bring its own remedy. True, the Federalist opposition mounted a strong presidential challenge in 1812 by supporting DeWitt Clinton on a fusion ticket, and Clinton lacked only the votes of Pennsylvania to swing the election. But this did not materially affect the balance of forces in Congress. Parliamentary opposition was still hardly more than negligible, and again the most articulate form of opposition was regional: New England took over the regionalism of the Republicans, who now found themselves assailed by legislative protests that sounded hauntingly like the Virginia and Kentucky Resolutions.

By the second decade of the century the Republicans were beginning to falter over a basic dilemma confronting advocates of an agrarian society. They had begun as a party of agrarian principles fearful of national centralization as a threat to agrarian interests and republican freedom. They were now fast becoming a party of nationalism, deferring for the sake of national honor and advancement to the centralizing measures they had once seen as anathema. The more fully they controlled the central government, and the more free they were in the face of enfeebled opposition to shape its ways, the more reconciled they became to the exercise of powers that had alarmed them when they had themselves been the party of opposition. Despite their increasing heterogeneity, they were still an agrarian party, and agrarianism had its own internal

179

contradictions which they could not escape. They wanted a frugal, decentralized, almost anarchic agrarian order that would preserve as intact as possible the original American Eden. At the same time the nation whose political leadership they now almost monopolized was a trading society, and its substantial farmers and planters, only slightly less than its merchants, were a trading people, dependent upon domestic transportation to move their products and upon foreign markets to vend them. Their constituents wanted certain goals— free navigation of the Mississippi, the right of deposit at New Orleans, expansion into Florida, an end to impressment, trading privileges, the integrity of their cargoes—which had to be won through the conventional means of national self-assertion. But the aggressive pursuit of these goals demanded certain unwelcome instrumentalities—a navy, an army, taxation, a national bank, an effective central government—and it involved the high risk of war. This reality they had not anticipated and some of them never fully acknowledged. They had railed at the Federalists, for example, for accepting in the Jay Treaty the unfavorable terms that a weak nation had to settle for; but then they had also resolutely opposed the construction of a navy large enough to make it strong.

As time went on, and particularly during the first years after the failure of the embargo, more and more Republicans were driven to the conclusion that the young nation was unlikely ever to be heeded by the tigers and sharks of Europe until it committed at least one forcible act of self-assertion. National self-respect—a highly intangible thing, to be sure, but a massive reality when it is deeply wounded—was at stake, and with it the future of their party and perhaps even of all republican government. There had always been in their ranks an intense and unquestionably sincere concern for the future of republicanism, of which they regarded themselves as the world's trustees. For the Republican party to fail in the United States would mean that republicanism had failed the world over: there was, after all, no avant-garde republican experiment anywhere else like the American one, and there was no other American party that would or could uphold the republican standard. Their incessantly repeated fears about monarchy and what they had called "consolidation" were only the negative side of this concern; its positive side was now manifest in their sense of custodianship of the honor and morale of the world's only popular republic. Party honor became identified with the national honor. As Jefferson put it in 1811, appealing to William Duane in behalf of party unity, the nation would be undone if the party went to pieces. "For the republicans are the *nation*. . . . The last hope of human liberty in this world rests on us." Monroe used a different but perhaps an equally expressive rhetoric when he said in his first inaugural address: "National honor is national property of the highest value." I believe that Roger Brown is right in emphasizing the importance of the conviction, so often expressed by Monroe's contemporaries, that the Republic itself and the fate of republican government had come to rest on the ability of the Republican party to take a forceful stand against foreign incursions on American rights.[9] And so in the end, unprepared as they were, the Republicans drifted into war, almost for sheer lack of a morally tolerable alternative. It is hard to guess how much a formidable and constructive partisan opposition might have done to chasten the policies of Republican leaders, but nothing could have enabled them to find a happy solution to the agrarian dilemma. Their custodianship of national honor, and with it of world republicanism, proved inconsistent with their insular, pacific, economy-minded republican principles. When the Republicans at last reluctantly took hold of one

---

[9] Jefferson, *Works*, XI, 193; cf. Roger Brown, *The Republic in Peril: 1812* (1964).

horn of the dilemma and went to war, they set in motion a train of events that soon transformed their identity and principles. But they also quite unpredictably killed off the Federalists altogether. This was one of several ironies that lay hidden in the quest for national unanimity.

II

If one is lucky enough, it is better to be lucky than clever. Bearing in mind that in 1812 the United States blundered unprepared into a war with one of the world's two greatest powers and was still waging it at a time when England became free to divert major energies to this hemisphere, the damage was relatively slight. While there were no immediate gains, neither were there losses of territory or rights. And the news of Andrew Jackson's smashing victory at New Orleans, which came too late to affect peace negotiations but just at the right moment to convince Americans that they had brought the war to a victorious end, made the results far from unhappy for the public morale. The end of the war, its supposed success, and the taint of treason that now hung over New England Federalists and supporters of the Hartford Convention sent the Federalists, if not Federalism, into complete eclipse, and moved the country more rapidly from the party-and-a-half system under which it had in fact been functioning to the one-party system which lasted until 1828. That unanimity for which Washington had so passionately yearned now seemed at last to be possible under Republican leadership. Jefferson, who never ceased to denounce the Federalists in language reminiscent of the 1790's, celebrated their postwar eclipse, as a signal result of the nation's victory. The proofs the war had given, he wrote to LaFayette in 1817, "that our government is solid, can stand the shock of war, and is superior even to civil schism, are precious facts to us." But, he added, the "best effect" of the war "has been the complete suppression of party." All the truly

American Federalists were being cordially taken into Republican ranks, and the election of Monroe would establish republican forms and principles beyond the danger of change. "The evanition of party dissentions has harmonized intercourse and sweetened society beyond imagination. The war then has done us all this good, and the further one of assuring the world, that although attached to peace from a sense of its blessings, we will meet war when it is made necessary."[10]

Each party now found itself in a peculiar position. The problem of the Republicans was that though they had taken over political leadership, had also assumed a pivotal position in Washington and most state capitols, and had substantially put the Federalists out of business, they now had to defend themselves against the charge of having surrendered their program and their identity. Yet many Federalists were unable to take the pleasure they might have expected from seeing much of their program appropriated. They found themselves, above all, without offices, without positions of leadership, suffering the humiliation of proscription.

Although the Republicans never had to answer to any sense of failure stemming from the War of 1812, they did have to reckon with the charge, made by some of their own dissidents as well as by Federalists, that they had turned their back on their old program and lost their character as a consequence of the war. The phenomenon of party amalgamation in the Era of Good Feelings raised the question in many minds on both sides whether the new unanimity was being achieved on Republican or on Federalist terms. Under Madison the Republicans, impelled by what they had learned about finance during the war, chartered a new Bank of the United States

---

[10] *Works*, XII, 62–63. An early token of the trend was the great popularity of Mathew Carey's, *The Olive Branch* (1814), an appeal, as its subtitle put it, "on the Necessity of Mutual Forgiveness and Harmony."

and embraced a moderately protective tariff. In his Seventh Annual Message (December, 1815) Madison not only recommended the national bank that was in fact created in the following year, but also a program of internal improvements, which he suggested could be sanctified by a constitutional amendment. He also suggested the maintenance of an adequate military and naval force, a program of harbor defenses, a system of direct internal taxation, higher salaries for public officials, a national university, and a tariff to encourage manufacturers. That year the Federalist governor of Connecticut, John Cotton Smith, remarked: "The Administration have fought themselves completely on to federal ground."[11]

If the Republicans were to swallow the national bank, which had been the most objectionable of the major Hamiltonian measures nearly a quarter of a century earlier, and which only in 1811 they had refused to recharter, one might well have wondered what meaning the old party lines could still have. Intransigent Republicans like John Randolph, who could sniff Federalism in every breeze and who had accused Jefferson of bowing to it even in 1806, had understood before the war began that the very preparations for it were a step back toward Federalist policies and a liquidation of the Jeffersonian system. "This war for honour," John Taylor of Caroline had predicted, "like that of the Greeks against Troy, may terminate in the destruction of the last experiment in . . . free government. . . ." Taylor, of course, was very alert to the slightest hint of Federalism, and had been critical even of Jefferson's compromises. "Federalism, indeed," he had written to Monroe in 1810, "having been defeated, has gained a new footing by being taken into partnership with republicanism. It was this project which divided the republican party."[12] The paradox

[11] Shaw Livermore, *The Twilight of Federalism* (1962), 15.

[12] For Taylor, see Risjord, *The Old Republicans*, 145, 25; cf. 49, 135–145.

of fighting a war with the Republican *bête noire*, Great Britain, only to move a hundred and eighty degrees closer to Hamiltonianism was not lost on Republicans of his breed.

Madison, who was quite sensitive to the charge that "the Republicans have abandoned their cause, and gone over to the policy of their opponents," offered an articulate answer in a letter of 1823 to William Eustis, the newly elected Republican governor of Massachusetts. He argued that it mattered greatly what the timing of measures was, and in what spirit they had been adopted. "It is true," he said, "that under a great change of foreign circumstances, and with a doubled population, and more than doubled resources, the Republican party has been reconciled to certain measures and arrangements which may be as proper now as they were premature and suspicious when urged by the champions of federalism. But they overlooked the overbearing and vindictive spirit, the apocryphal doctrines, and rash projects, which stamped on federalism its distinctive character; and which are so much in contrast with the unassuming and unavenging spirit which has marked the Republican ascendency."[13]

We should, I think, resist the temptation to smile at the notion that a tariff or bank which was suspicious in 1791 became proper a quarter of a century later because the country was bigger and richer, or that the impeachment of judges was unavenging, or the enforcement of the embargo unassuming. There is, still, a certain reasoning behind this apologia that cannot be altogether dismissed: it *does* matter when and by whom a measure is adopted, and there are certain kinds of proposals whose place in the political order becomes settled only after they have been accepted and sanctified by their original opponents. (Our own generation has seen a diplomatic settlement in Korea, made by a general, a national hero, and a

---

[13] *Writings*, IX, 136.

Republican President, quietly accepted and even applauded by the same public that would have indignantly condemned even a somewhat less unfavorable settlement had it been contracted by his Democratic predecessor.) At least one shrewd Boston Federalist contemporary, who welcomed the Republican drift toward Federalist programs, saw it that way. "It was much better," he said, "that the party which had displaced it [the Federalist party], and which had the popular prejudice in its favor, should gradually assume its principles, which were the original principles of our government. It was well enough for the Republicans to have strengthened the navy, since the same policy carried out by the Federalists would have inspired suspicions in every step."[14]

Federalist responses to the new drift of Republican policies were understandably mixed. Many Federalists were able to take consolation in the victory of their policies, others showed irritation at the righteousness with which the Republicans had denounced their motives and then appropriated their program, while some, in response to changing local interests or perhaps even partisan pique, no longer found it possible to vote for the measures, under alien sponsorship, upon which their party had once been built.

Most important of all, if the Republicans, to a marked degree, capitulated to Federal*ism*, they did not capitulate to the Federalists. In continuing the proscription of Federalists from office the Republican policy-makers, even in the so-called Era of Good Feelings, repeatedly jangled an exposed nerve of the Federalist class. The Federalist stalwarts had always imagined that they had a near monopoly of the ability to govern. John Quincy Adams, who had had plenty of opportunity to observe them closely, found them "honest in the belief that all of the

---

[14] Livermore, *The Twilight of Federalism*, 56.

wisdom of the nation is in their heads, and all of its virtues in their hearts. They have erected their whole political system upon the perverted axiom that the part is greater than the whole."[15] Moreover, one can hardly doubt that the desire for office was already a powerful craving in the United States, and yet among the Federalists, who were still so largely recruited from the ranks of men of substance, the passion for office was more than a passion for the spoils as an end in itself. To be shut out of office—and that by men who had run off with so much of their program—was galling to the Federalist elite, not least because in the American social system political honor was such a signal evidence of acceptance and recognition. Looking back, Edward Everett, who had been raised among the Massachusetts Federalists, shrewdly observed in 1828: "In this country, . . . office is more important than in England. In England where families are hereditary, the hereditary family politics are of vast consideration. . . . Besides this, mere Rank is of vast consequence there, and fills the utmost ambition of many persons in a larger class of Society. Here it is unknown. Prodigious accumulations of fortune exist there, conferring of themselves very extensive influence and power, and making mere office a small thing with its possessors. The outgrown naval and military establishments open a career in which the ambitious find scope for their talents. In place of all these, we have nothing to which the ambitious can aspire, but office. I say nothing, because all the private walks of life are as wide open in England as here, and afford, in that country as well as this, occupation for much of the active talent of the Community. But office here is family, rank, hereditary fortune, in short, Everything, out of the range of private life. This links its possession with innate principles of our Nature; and truly

---

[15] *Writings*, VI, 138.

incredible are the efforts men are willing to make, the humiliations they will endure, to get it."[16]

On one count the three leaders of the Virginia dynasty agreed completely and stood consistently: however far they might go toward accepting old Federalist *measures*, they had no intention of accepting Federalist *men*. They did not mind adopting a Federalist policy now and then, or bidding for the votes of the former Federalist rank and file, but they were intensely concerned not to haul aboard, along with this inert cargo, any live vipers. For them the essence of Federalism lay not in the various elements of its program but in the perverted principles and intransigent spirit of its longtime leaders. "Their object is power," Madison wrote of these leaders in 1814. "If they could obtain it by menaces, their efforts would stop there. These failing, they are ready to go to every length for which they can train their followers."[17] However, he thought that revolts and secessionism by them would really depend upon foreign collaboration, and that they presented no threat without it.

III

As to Monroe, who requires our extended attention here, he had always been an ardent party man with ardent anti-party convictions. No one represented more stoutly than he the conviction that the Federalist party, as a threat to Republican institutions, ought to be extinguished, and no one was more confident that the American system, whatever one might say of other systems, could be managed without a partisan opposition. He had always been an intense and convinced party warrior. In 1801, during a brief moment of partial conciliation, he had taken it upon himself to confirm Jefferson's partisan

[16] Massachusetts Historical Society *Proceedings*, 3d series, I (1907–1908), 376.

[17] *Writings*, VIII, 319.

prejudices, warning him strongly against accommodating the Federalists ("Royalists," as he called them), expressing the belief that they would sink of their own weight if not temporized with, and that they should be watched for their tendency to intrigue with foreign powers. "The opposing parties can never be united, I mean the leaders of them; because their views are as opposite as light and darkness." So long as the Republicans were kept together, he thought, "the overthrow of the opposite party is as final as it is complete . . . adversaries who are without power and character."[18]

In 1808, when the question of Jefferson's successor was posed to the party, Monroe threatened briefly to become a party schismatic, but not out of lack of devotion to republican principles or to the Republican organization. He was put forth as an alternative to Madison by a few Republicans who followed John Randolph on what could be called anti-administration grounds. But the main body of his supporters endorsed him not as an anti-administration figure but because they regarded him as a purer Republican and as more likely to be an effective President than Madison. John Beckley, the ubiquitous party organizer, expressed these concerns in a letter to Monroe in the summer of 1806: "Madison is deemed by many too timid and indecisive as a statesman, and too liable to a conduct of forbearance to the federal party, which may endanger our harmony and political safety. It is believed that in you, with equal knowledge of and talent to direct our foreign relations, the known energy and decision of your character would effectually put down all federal views of disuniting us, and ruling themselves."[19] Monroe allowed his name to be used, but his role was relatively passive, and he left the door open to a complete reconciliation with Jefferson and

[18] Monroe, *Writings*, ed. by S. M. Hamilton, III, 262–263, 270.
[19] Cunningham, *The Jeffersonian Republicans in Power*, 232.

Madison. By 1810, firmly within the fold again, he took it upon himself to defend the growing nationalism of his party against certain Virginia dissidents. In that year he entered into a long correspondence with John Taylor of Caroline, expounding his opposition to splitting the party, even when he disagreed with the majority, and explaining his philosophy of party loyalty. In these letters Monroe endorsed at least one basic postulate of party organization that flew boldly in the face of the anti-party doctrine of the 18th century—here he accepted the Burkean proposition that a party is of such nature that individual opinions must on occasion be sacrificed to the views dominant among one's regular associates. This was the essence of Monroe's answer to the factionalism that had emerged during Jefferson's administration.

These letters clarify Monroe's role not only as the arch-spokesman of party loyalty but also as the most enthusiastic celebrant of the emergent one-party system.[20] Here Monroe used the old Republican myth that the Federalist leaders were nothing but a pack of subversive monarchists as the primary ground for suppressing the relatively minor and modest differences among honest Republicans and sustaining the measure of party unity necessary to "annihilate" the Federalists. And if Monroe had any reservation about the recently ended administration of Jefferson, it was only that Jefferson had not gone far enough toward this annihilation.

Looking back on the events of the recent past, Monroe warned Taylor against any steps that could be considered an attack upon the administration. "A systematic republican opposition to a republican administration," he thought, would be more likely to give it "an artificial and unmerited strength than to weaken it." But should such opposition actually succeed in

---

20 For these letters, which are the source of quotations in the following paragraphs, see *Writings*, V, 142–157; cf. a similar letter to L. W. Tazewell, *ibid.*, 167 n–168 n, and also 176–177.

overthrowing the administration, "there would be great danger of involving in the same ruin the whole republican party, if not the cause itself." There were only two ways, he thought, in which party majorities could be made to change their policy —one by force, the other by consent. Of force he had seen quite enough in France, where successive suppressions of minorities caused the Revolution to consume itself and ultimately restored "monarchy." Only consent deserved consideration, and consent must be voluntary, the result of reflection and conciliation, of a process of persuasion in which the passions are kept in check.

He went on to lay down rules by which a party minority should operate. "For minorities to become majorities, even where they are in the right, the character of a distinct party in each must cease, and that change may be essentially promoted by the moderation and forbearance of the minority. It is in this mood only that the minority may become the majority. The whole party must be brought together again, in which state the members of the minority will be seen voting in the majority, for the collision being at an end, good sense will prevail." Should a minority beat down or turn out or score any victories against the majority that would discredit it, "it seems probable that the rival, or federal, party alone would profit by it." The Federalists would then make use of the Republican split, and the people themselves might weary of the internal contention the Republican party showed and "seek repose in an effort to rid themselves of it by opening the door to the federalists." Monroe thought it possible to bring about a change of measures through internal party discussion, without necessarily having a change of men. It was probable that the party majority would, "under the pressure of circumstances, turn completely round, and even adopt the measures of the minority without affecting materially the strength or credit of either party."

191

The status of opposition, Monroe insisted, is different in the United States from that in England. "In England an opposition to the government is almost in all cases popular, while it can hardly ever be so under our constitution." In England there is always some tension or opposition of interests between the king and the people, and a politician, throwing his weight against the Crown, gains public favor. "But under our constitution that difference of interests between the People and their Chief Magistrate either does not, or is believed not, to exist." In a situation in which every branch of the government is elected, and not least the President, an opposition to a Republican President by a Republican representative "can scarcely ever be popular. In general it is considered by their constituents as a species of insubordination, or disobedience to themselves. . . ." A representative differing from a Republican President and putting himself in apparent agreement with an anti-republican rival party, would incur a special displeasure.

This did not mean, Monroe explained, that a representative should become "the tool and instrument" of the President, and obey orders from him with servile submission. It would not be necessary to vote for measures running against one's own judgment and conscience. But, "divided as we are into parties, a Representative should keep within the limit of his party. I mean in the great outline of his conduct. The party should constitute the nation to him, except under particular circumstances only. If he fixes himself permanently out of that limit, he destroys the means which he might otherwise have of being useful. If he is a man of great ability, acts with prudence, and enjoys the confidence of his party, he will rarely find himself reduced to the necessity of separating from it, or from the administration, and when those instances occur ample excuses will be made for him."

Monroe closed with a renewed warning against the consequences of Republican division. "There can be but two permanent parties among us, one of which is friendly to free government, the other to monarchy, in which latter I never did include many persons. Every other division should cease with the cause which produced it." The government had already changed its unwise policy in relation to the embargo, and it now behooved the minority not to boast of its victory, but to hold the lines of solidarity.

When Taylor persisted in holding that Monroe should pursue a firm independent course, Monroe returned to the subject with further arguments. No one knew better than Taylor, he reminded him, of the existence of party and the dangerous designs of the Federalists, and he called upon Taylor to remember a time when the Republicans were happy to get any help, however small, and when they well understood the necessity of humoring the weaknesses of one's friends in order to keep the party together. When Jefferson took over, he, Monroe, had hoped "that all distinction of parties would have been firmly levelled by the wisdom and success of his administration; that we should all (with a few incurable exceptions only) have become republicans." Jefferson's inaugural address showed that he too accepted this ideal, but Monroe criticized his removals policy as having failed in its purposes. Jefferson should have removed from office only the leading members of the Federalist party who were suspected (rightly in some cases) of entertaining "principles unfriendly to free government," and thus separating these leaders from the honest body of their following. However, by making removals of some lesser figures, and by continuing with such removals over a period of time, and thus giving repeated occasions of excitement over patronage, he had stimulated Federalist resistance. His policy "overwhelmed the federalists, but it did not annihilate them." And now, with the provocation of the embargo, the Federalists had appeared once again in what Monroe thought to be menacing force, and revived fears of their possible return to power. "I am one of those," he went on, "who think that the safety of free government depends on the existence and exertions of the republican party. If it is broken whither shall we be driven, and where shall we terminate our course? Will not the federal party come again into power? And in the present state of the world, not another republick in it, how long would our unprotected system last?" No, "there never was greater reason (one gloomy period excepted) for the preservation of the republican party than at this time." The interior was not yet settled. The struggle in New England produced by the embargo had thrown the Republicans there on the defensive in a contest for their life, and had even threatened a breakup of the union, and after that "every other species of national calamity." The movement in that direction was not yet over. If the Federalist party did not still exist or some of its leaders did not "entertain principles unfriendly to liberty," there would be no need to keep the Republican party in existence. It would be a happy circumstance if that state of things had come about, because then the government would rest on its true principles and the President would "cease to be the head of a party, an event which, with you, I anxiously wish to see. . . ." But so long as the present situation continued, the maintenance of the Republican party was vital to the existence of republican government.

IV

It fell to Monroe as President to carry on with the process of party consolidation that Jefferson and Madison had initiated. But he made it clear, sensitive as he was to charges that Republicanism had been Federalized already under Madison, that this process could not be carried out on too conciliatory a basis, and that party considerations could not be sacrificed to it. Conciliation would be achieved on firm Republican terms.

The issue arose in a concrete form between his election and inauguration when he received a letter from Andrew Jackson recommending the appointment of the South Carolina Federalist, General William Drayton, as Secretary of War and urging Monroe to submerge party feeling by rewarding Federalists who had been loyal during the war.[21] The proposal that at least one Federalist be included in his Cabinet as a token of party reconciliation had been made by others.

Monroe's reply to Jackson is illuminating. It is ironic, when one thinks of the identities of the sender and the recipient of the letter, that the President-elect should have begun by agreeing "decidedly in the principle that the Chief Magistrate of the Country ought not be the head of a party, but of the nation itself."[22] He agreed too that those Federalists who had served the country in the war should receive signs that their patriotism and attachment to free government were understood and appreciated. But the Federalists had been unfriendly to "our system of government," and the struggle with them, as witness the opposition of so many during the recent war, was not yet over. To compromise too indulgently with them would tend to mitigate the shame of the Hartford Convention and offer them the hope of a party revival. "To give effect to free government, and secure it from future danger, ought not its decided friends, who stood firm in the day of trial, to be principally relied upon?" Monroe feared that the inclusion of any of their opponents in the administration would wound the feelings of such men and thus damage the republican cause. "My impression is that the Administration should rest strongly on the Republican party, indulging toward the other a spirit

---

[21] On this situation and Monroe's strategy, see Harry Ammon, "James Monroe and the Era of Good Feelings," *Virginia Magazine of History and Biography*, 66 (1958), 387–398.

[22] See *Writings*, V, 342–347.

of moderation, and evincing a desire to discriminate between its members, and to bring the whole into the republican fold as quick as possible."

Many distinguished men, Monroe went on in a curious passage, "are of the opinion that the existence of the federal party is necessary to keep union and order in the republican ranks, that is that free government cannot exist without parties. This is not my opinion." In this anti-party faith he went even further than Jefferson since he did not accept the idea, recurrent in Jefferson's writings, that party divisions have a basis in human nature. To him, their foundation was in the defects of government, from which the United States was free. It was true that the ancient republics were always divided into parties and that the English government is maintained by a party in opposition to the ministry. "But I think that the cause of these divisions is to be found in certain defects of those governments, rather than in human nature; and that we have happily avoided those defects in our system." The object for the future was to maintain the morale of the Republican party, and to prevent the reorganization and revival of the Federalists, an end which would not be impracticable "if my hypothesis is true, that the existence of parties is not necessary to free government. To accomplish both objects, and thereby exterminate all party divisions in our country, and give new strength and stability to our government, is a great undertaking, not easily executed." The main difference between Monroe and Jackson was simply over how the generous spirit to be shown to the amenable Federalists should be expressed. It was clear that Monroe regarded moderation toward the Federalists as a fine thing, but that there was more than one way to show it, and he was in favor of doing so very gradually. One notes too here how the increasingly self-conscious defense of the one-party system is linked to a persistent utopian note: party divisions arise in defective states, but American republicanism is, at least in principle, perfect, and has no need of them.

This idea of American exceptionalism was made quite explicit in Monroe's first inaugural address, in which he expressed great satisfaction over "the increased harmony of opinion which pervades our Union." "Discord," he went on, "does not belong to our system. . . . The American people have encountered together great dangers and sustained severe trials with success. They constitute one great family with a common interest." "Never did a government commence under auspices so favorable, nor ever was success so complete. If we look to the history of other nations, ancient or modern, we find no example of a growth so rapid, so gigantic, of a people so prosperous and happy. In contemplating what we have still to perform, the heart of every citizen must expand with joy when he reflects how near our Government has approached to perfection; that in respect to it *we have no essential improvement to make. . . .*"[23]

In his second inaugural address Monroe struck this theme once again in tones that seem perilously close to *hubris*: "In our whole system, national and State, we have shunned all the defects which unceasingly preyed on the vitals and destroyed the ancient Republics. In them there were distinct orders, a nobility and a people, or the people governed in one assembly. Thus, in the one instance there was a perpetual conflict between the orders in society for the ascendency, in which the victory of either terminated in the overthrow of the government and the ruin of the state; in the other, in which the people governed in a body, and whose dominions seldom exceeded the dimension of a county in one of our States, a tumultuous and disorderly movement permitted only a transitory existence."

---

[23] *Ibid.*, VI, 13–14; italics added.

America was altogether different from these predecessors. "In this great nation there is but one order, that of the people, whose power, by a peculiarly happy improvement of the representative principle, is transferred from them, without impairing in the slightest degree their sovereignty, to bodies of their own creation, and to persons elected by themselves, in the full extent necessary for all the purposes of free, enlightened, and efficient government. The whole system is elective, the complete sovereignty being in the people, and every officer in every department deriving his authority from and responsible to them for his conduct."

Although perfection had not been incarnated in American institutions at the outset, either in the national or state governments, many of the defects demonstrated by experience had already been remedied. "By steadily pursuing this course in this spirit there is every reason to believe that our system will soon attain the highest degree of perfection of which human institutions are capable, and that the movement in all its branches will exhibit such a degree of order and harmony as to command the admiration and respect of the civilized world." This sense of American exceptionalism and near perfection was to continue to be the pivot of Monroe's theory of the function of party. An oppositional system was good enough for the defective states of the Old World, but it was rendered unnecessary by the popular harmony of the New.

V

Monroe's letter to Andrew Jackson reminds us that the leaders of the Virginia dynasty were largely agreed in wanting to continue the quest for unanimity, and that their main difference was over the terms on which it could be secured. Monroe's strategy was not to give jobs to leading Federalists but rather to give them a series of ceremonial occasions to confirm their loyalty and celebrate their readoption into the

Union. His famous Northern visit of 1817 marked the first time that an American President had undertaken what might be called a good-will trip in his own country, and its success proved astonishing. One is struck by the disproportion between Monroe's pleasant gesture and the enthusiastic response it evoked. Federalists and Republicans alike turned out to pay fealty to the President of the United States—an act which, on the part of the Federalists, was rightly termed by Abigail Adams an "expiation." The occasion marked the return of a degree of social comity among men who had ceased to speak to each other. The Boston *Chronicle and Patriot* remarked: "The visit of the President seems to have allayed the storms of party. People now meet in the same room who would before scarcely pass the same street—and move in concert, where before the most jarring discord was the consequence of an accidental rencounter. . . ." The *Centinel* asserted that the visit had above all made us *one people*: for we have the sweet consolation . . . to rest assured that the president will be president, not of a party, but of a great and powerful nation." "The most distinguished in the opposition," Monroe reported to Madison, ". . . seemed to seize the opportunity which my journey afforded them, to remove by the most explicit and solemn declarations, impressions of that kind [i.e., their lack of attachment to republicanism], which they know existed, and to get back into the great family of the union."[24]

---

[24] For the press, W. P. Cresson, *James Monroe* (1946), 288; Ammon, "James Monroe and the Era of Good Feelings," 395.

In congratulating Monroe on the success of his tour, Madison observed that "an opportunity has been given and seized for a return to the national family of the prodigal part which had been seduced from it and for such commitment of the seducers themselves that they can not resume their opposition to the Government without a public demonstration that their conversion was inspired by the mere hope of sharing in the loaves and fishes." To Monroe, August 22, 1817, Madison papers, Library of Congress.

Monroe continued to show especial courtesy to Federalist Congressmen in public, and in private to rejoice at the further waning of partisan opposition. Before long it was clear that party warfare was dying out altogether, as the Federalists continued to dwindle both in states and nation. In New York and Pennsylvania they were reduced to coalescing with Republican factions. In New England, where by 1819 they held only Massachusetts, their power still waned. In the same year they lost Maryland, and by 1824 Delaware was the only Federalist-controlled state left in the Union.[25] In the Congress elected in 1818 Federalists were outnumbered 35 to 7 in the Senate and 156 to 27 in the House. Monroe himself was unopposed for the presidency in 1820, and he found that the chief brake on his policy of conciliation was the continuing feeling among a few Republican partisans that he had carried it too far.

Monroe wrote to Madison in 1822 that the American political system had reached a "new epoch" of nonpartisan government. "Surely our government may go on and prosper without the existence of parties. I have always considered their existence as the curse of the country, of which we had sufficient proof, more especially, in the late war." As to keeping parties alive he did not see how it was possible: "We have no distinct orders. No allurement has been offered to the federalists to calm them down into a state of tranquillity. None of them have been appointed to high office, and very few to the lowest." It was the war and their wartime misconduct that had done them in, he went on, and he himself deserved very little credit for it. "Parties have now cooled down, or rather have disappeared from this great theatre, and we are about to make the experiment whether there is sufficient virtue in the people to support our free republican system of government."[26]

---

[25] Livermore, *The Twilight of Federalism*, chap. IV.
[26] *Writings*, VI, 289–291.

The issue that disturbed most Southern Republicans during this period, and particularly the leaders of the Virginia dynasty, was the Missouri problem, which threatened to break the unity of their party over the slavery-extension question. For them Federalism could never be dead enough. They shared the widespread Republican belief that the whole matter was a conspiracy to revive the Federalist party. Jefferson thought, for example, that "the Missouri question is a mere party trick," having no relation to the morals of slavery but intended to give "the leaders of federalism" a new lease on life by bringing about "a division of parties by a geographical line." Jefferson's correspondence of the early 1820's is haunted by this fear. Even after the Missouri question was compromised on terms acceptable to the South and resolved on the strength of Southern votes, he considered that the issue had "given resurrection to the Hartford Convention men." In 1822 he was still concerned that the amalgamation that had taken place between the parties was one of name and not of principle, and that the old Federalist passion for centralization was beginning to find new ground. "All indeed call themselves by the name of Republican because that of Federalists was extinguished in the battle of New Orleans. But the truth is that finding that monarchy is a desperate wish in this country, they rally to the point which they think next best, a consolidated government." Hence there were new Republicans in the Congress preaching the old doctrines of the Federalists and questioning the rights reserved to the states. Presumably the Federalists would fail again in this new phase, but the threat was there. "I scarcely know myself which is most to be deprecated, a consolidation, or dissolution of the states. The horrors of both are beyond the reach of human foresight."[27]

---

[27] *Works*, XII, 165, 179–180, 187–188, 251, 252–253 n, 262–263, 264–265, 300, 303; cf. Livermore, *The Twilight of Federalism*, 102; Glover Moore, *The Missouri Controversy*, 253–255. Cf. Dangerfield, *The*

Madison too was alarmed by the potential of the Missouri agitation for the revival of Federalism. Even the adoption by the Republicans, he said, of measures that had been "prematurely" urged by the Federalists, had not rubbed out the essential difference between the two parties—which was nothing less than a disagreement over the capacity of the people to govern themselves. But looking at the matter from the long range, he cut much closer to the heart of the problem and sent a shaft many decades forward into American history. With remarkable clarity he saw the unifying function of intersectional parties, and expressed his fear of their dissolution. "Parties," he wrote to Robert Walsh in 1819, "under some denominations or other must always be expected in a Government as free as ours. When the individuals belonging to them are intermingled in every part of the Country, they strengthen the Union of the Whole, while they divide every part. Should a state of parties arise, founded on geographical boundaries and other physical and permanent distinctions which happen to coincide with them, what is to control these great repulsive Masses from awful shocks against each other?" The real object of the Missouri agitation, he wrote not long afterward to President Monroe, was "to form a new state of parties founded on local instead of political distinctions; thereby dividing the Republicans of the North from those of the South, and making the former instrumental in giving to the opponents of both an ascendancy over the whole."[28] He saw in this a good reason

---

Awakening of American Nationalism, 123. To many Republicans the former Federalists could do no right: if they stuck to their guns, it proved that they were the same old devils; if they tried to be conciliatory, it was obvious that they were only boring from within.

[28] *Writings*, IX, 12, 21–22; cf. letter to C. J. Ingersoll, November 17, 1827, Madison papers, Library of Congress; Livermore, *The Twilight of Federalism*, 103. "A Government like ours," he wrote to Lafayette in November, 1820, "has so many safety-valves giving vent to overheated passions that it carries within itself a relief against the infirmities

for being conciliatory over the counterbalancing admission of Maine.

Monroe agreed with his friends that the Missouri question had been raised with the sole object of acquiring power and that it had had some success in arousing sympathy in many sectors of the North, but his basic optimism was unshaken. The bond of union was too strong for the schemers, he wrote Jefferson in February 1820.[29] His passive conception of the presidential function permitted him to remain largely aloof from the struggle in Congress, but he favored compromise on principle. The particular device incorporated in the Missouri Compromise, the exclusion of slavery from part of the territories, was in his view a measure of doubtful constitutionality; he actually drafted a veto measure, which of course was never delivered. His final decision to accept the Compromise was consonant with his optimism about the American system, and in the short run at least, that optimism proved justified.

VI

In their closing days, as their generation gradually passed from the scene, Jefferson, Madison, and Monroe ventured to express from time to time views on government and parties which show them still perplexed by the problems they had inherited from eighteenth-century political thought. Monroe in his post-presidential retirement even began work in 1829 upon a political tract, *The People the Sovereigns*, in which he elaborated on the idea of American exceptionalism that had been set forth in his inaugural addresses. Unlike Jefferson and Madison, Monroe refused to see conflict and parties as the inevitable result of human nature or of the plurality of interests in society. Rather parties were, in his view, the result of defective social

---

from which the best of human Institutions cannot be exempted." *Writings*, IX, 36.

[29] *Writings*, VI, 114.

and political systems, characterized by the existence of priv-
ileged orders and a conflict of classes. The United States, he
thought, was free of the defects that had wrecked all previous
republics, ancient and modern, because it had no social orders
set off against each other and had a perfectly designed state,
embodying popular sovereignty, a separation of powers, and a
system of balanced government. This archaic tract,[30] a piece
of eighteenth-century political speculation in which Monroe
took issue with Aristotle's classification of types of government
and tediously compared the government of the United States
with those of the republics of Athens, Lacedaemonia, and
Carthage, was left unfinished, and appeared long after his death
in 1867, at a time when the fate of the American political system had already made a mockery of his utopian expectations
and when it could have commanded interest only as a curiosity.

Jefferson continued to repeat from time to time the inconsistencies about parties which stemmed on one side from his
persistence in classical eighteenth-century anti-party views and
on the other from his occasional shrewd remarks founded on
the realities of the American system. In 1811 he casually suggested in one of his letters that parties might offer an alternative
method of expressing opposition, that would be superior to the
threats of division and the particularist aspirations that had so
often prevailed in the United States. "The purity of government," he suggested, might be preserved "by the censorship
which these parties habitually exercise over each other." This
echoes the views he had expressed to John Taylor in 1798, but
he never saw fit to develop at any length the insight it embodies.
He returned to this view once again near the end of his life.
"I am no believer in the amalgamation of parties," he rather

---

[30] Published as *The People the Sovereigns, being a Comparison of the
Government of the United States with those of the Republics which
Have Existed Before, with the Causes of their Decadence and Fall*, ed.
by S. L. Gouverneur (1867).

startlingly announced to a friend in 1824, "nor do I consider it either desirable or useful to the public. . . ."[31]

There is, I believe, no use in trying to find a more consistent pattern in such observations than they actually had, and certainly none in trying to argue that Jefferson had at last discovered with finality the functional merits of the two-party system. He had always had, from time to time, glimpses of it; he did cling to the psychological conception of the origins of parties that he had long before espoused, the idea that there is a "natural" human tendency to divide into "whigs and tories, republicans and federalists, aristocrats and democrats, or by whatever name you please,"[32] and that the basic difference between the two sides was always the degree to which one's fear of the people or one's "cherishment" of them was uppermost. This view, though perhaps superior to Monroe's notion that America was a perfect state in which the classic reasons for parties could be avoided, had less reality and specificity than Madison's sociological approach to parties, and indeed less realism than some of Jefferson's own occasional observations about party conflict.

It was one thing for a sage old man to accept party differences as eternal and quite another to understand the range of the positive functions parties might play. Abstractly, Jefferson accepted the idea of political division and the reality that opposition would be embodied in the form of parties; but concretely he could never see the legitimacy of any particular opposition in his own country. Certainly the idea of an even balance between the parties had no attraction for him. He could remember, after all, the brief period of the late 1790's, when for the only time in the history of their rivalry the Republicans and Federalists were more or less equal in strength, as

---

[31] *Works*, XI, 188; cf. *ibid.*, 12, 374.
[32] *Ibid.*, XII, 375.

a nightmarish period; and he seems to have concluded that the gravity of the situation had been due not to the transitional character of the period itself but rather to the parity between the parties themselves. "In Mr. Adams' time and mine," he wrote to Gallatin in 1817, "parties were so nearly balanced as to make the struggle fearful for our peace."[33]

The most interesting and receptive mind among the three men continued to be that of Madison. In 1824 Madison had occasion to write to Henry Lee, who proposed to found a new literary journal, to warn him not to exercise too much "remedial power" in the press over the spirit of party. Parties, he continued to warn, had a permanent foundation in the variety of political opinions in free states and of occupations and interests in all advanced states. In the United States, the Constitution itself would provide an additional and "unfailing source of party distinctions." The division of power between state and federal governments in the United States was another peculiarity which would always encourage party. However, he thought there was scope for holding the spirit of party in check "in efforts to divert it from the more noxious channels; to moderate its violence, especially in the ascendant party; to elucidate the policy which harmonizes jealous interests; and particularly to give to the Constitution that just construction, which, with the aid of time and habit, may put an end to the more dangerous schisms otherwise growing out of it." In this connection he urged a return to the original sense of the Constitution and warned against an excessive flexibility in the language of interpretation.[34]

In his closing years Madison was deeply alarmed by the nullification struggle, and by the anti-majoritarian rationale which, with Calhoun as its leading spokesman, was then emerging. This crisis elicited from Madison one of the clearest departures

---

[33] *Ibid.*, XII, 74.
[34] *Writings*, IX, 190–191.

from the conception he had expounded in *The Federalist* that the primary objective of a well-designed government was to check a majority coalition. In 1833 Madison wrote an unsent letter to an unspecified recipient, which may indeed have been intended simply as a memorandum for himself or for post-humous use, in which he expressed a view of majorities different from the view he had expressed in *The Federalist*. There he had argued that in a pluralistic society under a well-designed constitution, oppressive majorities cannot coalesce. Pluralism was still a central concept in the later memorandum, but the emphasis had become significantly different. Now, in 1833, Madison argued that the majorities that do coalesce will not, in a pluralistic society, *become* oppressive. The opening words do not sound like *The Federalist*:[35] "You justly take alarm at the new doctrine [*sic*] that a majority Government is of all other governments the most oppressive. The doctrine strikes at the root of Republicanism, and if pursued into its consequences, must terminate in absolute monarchy, with a standing military force; such alone being impartial between its subjects, and alone capable of overpowering majorities as well as minorities." Madison was now particularly concerned to refute the notion that a government with power centered in the states was a sufficient answer to the threat of majorities in the Union as a whole. He argued forcefully that "every friend to Republican Government ought to raise his voice against the sweeping denunciation of majority Governments as the most tyrannical and intolerable of all governments." He strongly insisted that any abuse by a majority that was possible within the federal Union was also possible inside the borders of a single state. Indeed, he asserted, it was likely to be worse there, because inside a single state there would be less variety of in-

---

[35] For this document, see *Writings*, IX, 520–528. But for an illustration of his continual concern for the protection of minority rights, see *ibid.*, 232–233.

terests and hence less balance in the interests represented. Those who think that majority governments are the worst of governments, he contended, cannot be republicans. "They must either join the avowed disciples of aristocracy, oligarchy, or monarchy, or look for a Utopia exhibiting a perfect homogeneousness of interests, opinions and feelings nowhere yet found in civilized communities." In *The Federalist* Madison had been particularly concerned about the fallibility of majority decisions and about the necessity of checking "the superior force of an interested and overbearing majority." Now, after more than forty years of additional experience with Republican government, and in the face of the threat of nullifiication, he continued to develop the contrary insight into the merits of majority decision, which he had begun to express in his essays of 1792. "If," he said near the end of this document, "the will of a majority cannot be trusted where there be diversified and conflicting interests, it can be trusted nowhere. . . ." As he now put it, "the vital principle of republican government is the *lex majoris partis*, the will of the majority." The final step from this conception to a full sense of the relation between party structures and the plurality of interests was one that Madison never made.

VII

At first glance it might appear that the political leaders of the young republic had moved hardly at all, after more than thirty years of political experience, from the anti-party ideas and aspirations they had inherited from the mid-eighteenth century. But this seems true only because we have had our eyes fixed firmly on members of the passing generation who showed a characteristically human desire to cling to old and seemingly well-grounded ideas and to modify them at best very slowly. But this was, after all, the *passing* generation; and the second generation of leaders who began to appear at the time of the

War of 1812, came on the scene as the beneficiaries of these thirty years of trial, from which they were bound to draw some new conclusions. Even in 1792 Madison, trying for the first time to find a historical as well as a moral foundation for forming a national opposition, had reverted to the previous twenty years of experience to find precedents for two-party behavior over major issues since the early days of Revolutionary agitation. When the second American party system emerged out of the intervening chaos after 1824, a whole generation of politicians found the travail of Madison's contemporaries instantly available to them as a body of usable experience.

Moreover, this generation found itself faced with the need to devise practices suitable to a whole new political environment.[36] With the admission of Maine and new tiers of states in the West and Southwest, the Union had grown from sixteen states in 1800 to twenty-four in 1824. In this larger nation, the need for instrumentalities of cohesion was even greater than before, and the parties found it necessary to extend themselves to improve the machinery of communication, cohesion, and publicity. Internal changes were also important. No factor was more decisive in creating the national parties than the contest for the presidency, and a significant change in the method of presidential election gave greater scope to party organization. In 1800 presidential electors were chosen in most states by the legislatures, and only in two by a popular vote. By 1824 only six states still adhered to the original method, and very soon afterward all but one of these dropped it in favor of the now dominant mode of popular election. Now that it was necessary almost everywhere to mobilize a popular vote for presidential contests, the authority of legislative caucuses was undermined and the need became acute to develop party machinery

---

[36] On this count see Richard P. McCormick, *The Second American Party System* (1966), chapter II.

throughout each state. With the decline of the caucus, the presidential election became more central than before as a feature of national politics, and the participation of voters in presidential elections began to rise, and more often to overshadow participation in local contests.

The proportion of eligible popular voters was also growing. In these years the states of the eastern seaboard were liberalizing their suffrage requirements to a point that allowed virtual universal manhood suffrage, and the new states of the West were entering with minimal limitations. By 1824 nearly all adult white males could vote in presidential elections outside of Virginia, Rhode Island, and Louisiana. Voter apathy had prevailed in non-competitive states during the interval between party systems and in the ill-contested presidential election of 1816 and the non-contested one of 1820. But the renewal of keen personal rivalries in 1824 persuaded politicians that there was an increasing potential electorate, available to be won by well-organized parties. The return of party competition, once set in motion, began to feed upon itself, as strenuous efforts to reach the enlarged electorate began to pay off.

On all sides, politicians had learned a lesson from Federalist experience that would not be forgotten: in party competition, survival demanded that one should not assume a haughty antipopular stance, that one should not scorn the arts of party organization and management, or fail to keep up with any new technique of popular suasion that might become available. Discipline must be matched with discipline, hard work with hard work, demagogy with demagogy, and if need be, as the election of 1828 showed, slander with slander.

Finally, new political conditions diminished the power of the old elites. The new efforts to reach broad electorates, the increasing use of political "staging"—that is, of national and state conventions, huge rallies, campaign tours, and direct contact with voters—required more and more time and devotion, and a greater willingness to approach the common man on his own terms. It therefore put a premium on the efforts of men who were willing to devote all, or almost all, of their time to politics, and who did not expect leadership to fall to them as a matter of deference, celebrity, or wealth. Where political leadership in the time of Hamilton and Jefferson was a thing that almost automatically fell to the gentry, it now fell increasingly to men who were prepared to make a vocation of politics, and one now saw the emergence of that generation of political managers and professionals to which men like Martin Van Buren and Thurlow Weed belonged. It was not surprising that such men should have, in addition to their new problems and new agencies, a different feeling about political life, and that they should develop new ideas about the role of the party.

Chapter Six

Toward a Party System

I

THE MODERN IDEA of the political party, and with it a fully matured conception of the function of legitimate opposition, flowered first among the second generation of American political leaders—that is, among men who were in the main still children when the Federalist and Republican parties were founded. Where the Federalists and Republicans, still enchanted with eighteenth-century visions of political harmony, had schemed to devour, absorb, or annihilate each other, many Republicans raised on the one-party politics of the misnamed Era of Good Feelings, began to see clearly and consistently what such predecessors as Madison and Jefferson had seen only dimly and fitfully—the merits of the party organization as a positive principle, and of two-party competition as an asset to the public interest. The men of the second generation built firmly upon the foundations of early Jeffersonian experience with the organization of the party, but in both theory and practice they went well beyond their predecessors.

Here I propose to look at the history of the Republican party in New York State, to take the men of the so-called Albany Regency as archetypes of the new advocates of party, and to focus upon their leader Martin Van Buren, an intelligent and seasoned exponent of the emerging partisan creed, and the first representative of the new generation and mentality to become President. In settling upon New York as the archetype of these changes, I do not suggest that they were taking place only there: quite the contrary, what makes New York significant is that it was only the first political center—first surely in point of importance and articulateness, and perhaps also in point of time—to manifest clearly the new valuation of party. Along with Pennsylvania, New York had long been a leading state in developing a politics that approximated a consistent two-party rivalry, and it was natural that it should take the lead in the party revival.

The new apologia for partisan politics was in some considerable measure the work of a generation and a type. Its leading exponents were men who, in the main, were born during the years of the early party battles or who, like Van Buren himself, came of age during Jefferson's presidency and took the first Republican President as their model of a political hero. As children they were raised on hero tales of the Revolution. As youths they saw an established two-party competition in action, then in decline. As young men making their own places in the civic order under different conditions, they could look back upon the years from 1790 to about 1812 with a new perspective and with at least a trace of detachment; and, for all their firm Republican loyalties, they could see merit in some items of the Hamiltonian program which their own party had in fact begun to appropriate. They were considerably more interested than their predecessors in organization, considerably less fixed in their view of issues, considerably less ideological. They were less thoroughly imbued with eighteenth-century anti-party doctrines, and hence more capable of finding clues to a novel political outlook in the cumulative experience of a quarter century of political life under the Constitution.

These men provided a new type of political leader—new not in the sense that men of their kind had not long been present in American political life but rather that such men were now for the first time moving toward a place at the center of the stage. Late eighteenth-century political life in the American states had been dominated by interlocking elites and led by men of wealth and aristocratic background. Political power fell to men of status because their fellows deferred to them as the "natural" leaders of the political order. This was particularly true of continental and inter-colonial (later inter-state) affairs. But during the Revolution, the ferment of the times and the upsurge of republican faith, brought to the fore a kind of middle- or lower middle-class citizen, previously overshadowed in the establishment politics of the colonial era, who began to assume a much more forceful role in government, quite evident in the composition of the assemblies, in the new post-Revolutionary states.[1] To a degree, the adoption of the Constitution and the domination of the early Republic by Federalist leaders marked a setback for men of this sort in national politics. But it was not more than temporary; they came surging back with the developing Republican party, and became increasingly visible not only in the state legislatures but also in Congress, especially as Jeffersonian democracy waxed strong in the Northern states after 1800. Van Buren and the Regency leaders, though hardly the first generation of men of this type, went further than their predecessors.

II

In considering the career and mind of Martin Van Buren, I intend to discuss briefly the formative facts of his early life and then to define his ideas of party and of good political practice by counterposing him to the three men against whom he

---

[1] See Jackson T. Main, "Government by the People: The American Revolution and the Democratization of the Legislatures," *William and Mary Quarterly*, 23 (1966), 391–407.

most sharply reacted. It will help to look at him first in his state setting by taking note of the early political antagonism to DeWitt Clinton that shaped and hardened his convictions about party, and then in the national setting by seeing how these convictions animated his response to the leadership of two successive Republican Presidents, James Monroe and John Quincy Adams.

Born in 1782, in Kinderhook, Columbia County, Van Buren was old enough to work for Jefferson's campaign in 1800, and came of age when his hero was President. He was proud that he rose to his many honors "without the aid of powerful family connexions."[2] His father, who had been a tavernkeeper—a fact Van Buren seems not to have been proud of, since it is not mentioned in his autobiography—was admittedly a man of very "moderate" circumstances, which became so pressingly moderate that he found it difficult to educate his children, and Van Buren's education ended with the village academy, after which (at about fifteen) he was put to work in a lawyer's office. In 1803, after several years of clerking in more than one office, Van Buren was admitted to the bar, and it is important to remember not only that his role in national politics was shaped by many years of experience in state politics but also that his political conduct was to some extent shaped by the experience of a quarter of a century of adversary pleading at the bar. A man without aristocratic antecedents or the habit of command, without impressive stature or personal elegance, with keen intelligence but no notable intellectual brilliance or edge of wit, he adopted a mode of address that relied upon friendly and rational persuasion, a feeling for the strengths and weakenesses of others, a spirit of mutual accommodation, and a certain relish for the comedy of human encounters of the sort one sees daily in the county courthouse or the country tavern.

Van Buren emerges, in this respect, as one of the first notable

---

[2] *Autobiography* (1919), 7.

examples we have of a personal type which is quite common and I suppose even dominant in modern American politics, but which was still making its mark in the first decades of the nineteenth century—the type of the placatory professional politician, whose leadership comes in large part out of his taste for political association, his liking for people, and his sportsmanlike ability to experience political conflict without taking it as ground for personal rancor. When one thinks of the towering rages, the petty spites and sulks, the partisan depressions, the almost paranoid suspicions, and the fierce vendettas of men like Hamilton, Jefferson, Burr, Randolph, Fisher Ames, and John Taylor, one realizes how much the passing generation had waged its politics in the code of proud and jealous notables. Van Buren typified the spirit of the amiable county courthouse lawyer translated to politics, the lawyer who may enjoy over a period of many years a series of animated courtroom duels with an antagonist, but who sustains outside the courtroom the mutual respect, often the genial fellowship, of the co-professional.[3]

---

[3] Characteristic here was Van Buren's relationship with the brilliant Federalist lawyer Elisha Williams, with whom he tangled at the bar of Columbia County innumerable times over many years. Van Buren recalled: "We were at the same time prominent leaders in our respective political parties, and both warm partisans. To the danger of imbibing personal prejudice from these prolific sources was added that which threatened the discharge of adverse duties in cases embittered by the strong personal antipathies of the parties to the litigation; and yet, with a constant indulgence in what is called loose and means liberal practice, we never had, to my recollection, a motion before the Court for relief against what is called technical or formal advantages taken on either side. I invariably encountered him with more apprehension at the Circuits than any of the great men I have named. . . . On closing our last professional concern after my retirement he expressed to me by letter his great satisfaction that in a practice so peculiarly exciting as ours had been we had never any cause for personal complaint in our professional proceedings and tendered me assurances of his respect and esteem, feelings which were very cordially reciprocated on my part." *Autobiography*, 21–22.

Perhaps something of Van Buren's style came from his father, whom he remembered as "an unassuming amiable man who was never known to have an enemy," but for those who want to understand his breed of politician it is of more sociological importance that he was one of those professionals who take a friendly adversary relationship in stride as part of their daily business. This conception he carried over almost compulsively into politics. As one reads his remarkable *Autobiography*, one sees that to Van Buren one could make enemies in politics as well as friends; but the enmities (to be avoided where possible) as well as the friendships were both truly personal and not necessarily linked to political alignments. Van Buren spoke countless times of his "personal and political friends"—a repeated specification which shows that he labored under no illusion that the two were necessarily to be considered identical. But, above all, political foes might still be personal friends of a sort. Party loyalty was a sacred principle, but so sacred that it was also impersonal. Repeatedly Van Buren would assure an opponent that he held him in high esteem, and he associated on amiable terms with many Federalists. By the same token, when one suffered defeat, one expected to lose a number of perquisites and spoils to one's opponents as a part of the game—and no hard feelings.[4]

Looking back on this aspect of his career with great pride Van Buren wrote: "My political opponents, at every stage of my public life, have with great unanimity, and with no more than justice, conceded to me a rare exemption from that personal ill will which party differences are apt to engender, nor is my breast now the abiding place of those morbid feelings and adhesive prejudices so often cherished by public men who have been thwarted in their career."[5]

It was characteristic of Van Buren's reputation that upon

---

[4] On his father, *ibid.*, 10; on spoils, 93.
[5] *Ibid.*, 34.

the death of DeWitt Clinton in 1828 it fell to him to deliver an address of eulogy in the Senate, and also that he should have been able to respond handsomely. The following spring, John Quincy Adams, who had just been displaced from the White House by the Jackson administration, recorded that Van Buren, as the new Secretary of State, had just paid him a morning visit. "Of the new Administration he is the only person who has shown me this mark of common civility." Running down a list of administration members, once on friendly terms but now spurning him, Adams added acutely: "Van Buren, by far the ablest man of them all, but wasting most of his ability upon mere personal intrigues, retains the forms of civility, and pursues enmity as if he thought it might be one day his interest to seek friendship."[6]

Van Buren found his image of principled statecraft in Thomas Jefferson, and in the national conflict between Jeffersonians and Federalists. But he saw his model of practical politics in New York State, where he was politically active for so many years before he went to Washington as a Senator. His admiration of Thomas Jefferson was deep and genuine, his Republican adherence highly principled: he resisted considerable personal pressure to become a Federalist in a county where the Federalists were strong and influential. In this respect he was one of the many thousands of Northerners who in the late 1790's and the early years of Jefferson's administration were being recruited to the Jeffersonian party because they liked its democratic spirit, its passion for frugal government, its insistence upon the decentralization of power, and the avenues it opened for political success to men of talents but modest means.

In New York the Republicans were soon becoming all too

_____

[6] On the Clinton eulogy, Robert V. Remini, *Martin Van Buren and the Making of the Democratic Party* (1959), 168–169; Adams, *Diary*, ed. by Allan Nevins (1928), 394–395.

preponderant. They split into factions, and Van Buren had soon had a surfeit of the shifting factionalism of his state which, when compared with the grand struggles over principles and programs that had been waged between the great national parties, looked hazardous, drab, and disorganized. He had picked his own way surefootedly through the mazes of New York politics, holding a series of offices, from Surrogate of Columbia County (1808) to State Senator (1813) to Attorney General (1816). He was reared, oddly enough, largely in the Clintonian faction where he must had learned most of what he knew about the use of the spoils,[7] and even as late as 1812 he was still willing, with whatever misgivings, to support Clinton's bid for the presidency. But the following year he broke with him, and quickly became his leading political rival in the state. After many ups and downs, and after a few distinctly unprofessional mistakes, he and his followers finally established themselves as the successors to Clinton and succeeded in bringing about a substantial measure of unity and harmony in the New York party.

III

DeWitt Clinton was not only the foe but a personal model of the kind of leadership which Van Buren and his followers opposed. A transitional figure between the old politics of personal factionalism of the magnates and notables, and the new popular politics of the professionals, Clinton belonged much more to the old order than the new. He came into politics as a Jeffersonian of sorts, with a fine Revolutionary heritage and broadly republican principles; he shared Jefferson's views about limiting the role of the federal government; and, like the new professionals, he had a keen sense for the importance of patronage in politics and a masterful way of using it. But un-

---

[7] See Howard Lee McBain, *DeWitt Clinton and the Origin of the Spoils System in New York* (1907).

like his professional opponents, he did not come up through the ranks or arrive at his success by the careful cultivation of rank-and-file party practitioners. He came from a family of prominence: his father, who held several public offices and owned an estate in Orange County, had been a major-general at the end of the Revolutionary War. More important, his uncle, George Clinton, revolutionary Governor of the state, held control of New York in 1788, when he made DeWitt Clinton, still some months short of his majority, his secretary. For a time after 1795, the Clinton faction went into eclipse, but by 1803, at thirty-three, DeWitt Clinton became Mayor of New York, an appointment then held on commission from the Governor and prized as a source of tremendous patronage and substantial fees. Clinton, unlike Van Buren, entered politics at the top.

A tall handsome figure, versatile in interests and accomplishments, Clinton was dubbed Magnus Apollo in his early years, a term his foes took up in a spirit of mocking resentment. He led partly through the force of competence, manifest in his promotion of the Erie Canal, and partly through personal magnetism and brilliance, but never by party good-fellowship, and he was more admired than popular. "The charge of a cold repulsive manner," a correspondent bluntly told him, "is not the most trifling charge that your political enemies have brought against you—you have not the jovial, social, Democratical-Republican-how-do-you-do Suavity . . . ."[8] Tactless and often overbearing, Clinton could grant a favor but somehow leave the recipient feeling as though he had been spurned.

But most important, Clinton was not a good party regular in the Jeffersonian fashion. His style of leadership was rooted in the era of intense personal factionalism when the Republican

[8] Dixon Ryan Fox, *The Decline of Aristocracy in the Politics of New York* (1919), 200.

party in New York was divided among the Clinton and Livingston clans and the Burrites, and he looked upon his political following with a proprietary eye. Although the Virginia–New York alliance made him Vice-President upon Thomas Jefferson's re-election in 1804, he was tainted by party unorthodoxy. He was unenthusiastic about the embargo, and later took a dim view of entering so ill-prepared into war in 1812. Passed over for the presidential succession, he finally broke with the party in 1812, refused to accept the decision of the party caucus, accepted the nomination of a group of New York Republican followers, and challenged Madison in the presidential election. Even though he declined to come out in flat opposition to the war (it was his view that it should be more efficiently conducted), he made a formidable showing, in large part because of support from Federalists to whom he represented the lesser evil. For a long time his conservative pronouncements, his promotional activities, and his easy association with the prominent men of the state had convinced the Federalists of his basic soundness.

To good party men like Van Buren, Clinton appeared henceforth as a disguised Federalist and a party-wrecker. His opposition in 1812 was the last straw to the party loyalists centered in Tammany Hall, who now took it upon themselves to destroy his power. Although in 1815 he was turned out of the mayor's office, which he had held most of the time since 1803, he was elected Governor in 1817 with the help of many Federalists. For long years an unremitting struggle was waged against him by the Van Buren men. They came within a few hundred votes of unseating him in 1820 and mounted such an opposition that he decided not to run for re-election in 1822. Two years later the Tammany Bucktails made the dreadfully unprofessional mistake of removing him from his unsalaried post as canal commissioner, an inappropriate and vindictive act that set a wave of public sentiment in motion for him and resulted in his election once again. He survived another close election in 1826, and thus remained unvanquished at his death early in 1828, which at last left the field clear for the Bucktails.

Despite his almost impeccable earlier record as a partisan, Clinton enjoyed during his governorship a quasi-coalition status which made the posture of the anti-partisan statesman congenial to his purposes. Accordingly, he began to talk about the evils of party and partisanship in classical eighteenth-century accents, posing a philosophical as well as practical opposition to the partisan solidarity the Tammany men were trying to build. He began to criticize the caucus and party discipline and to argue for the merits of the independent citizen. A tract written by him or one of his aides, lamenting the bygone days of George Clinton, declared in 1819: "All our part and lot in the election is to be appointed on a ward committee, and to do a duty at the polls and to scour around through the cellars and groceries to buy up votes, and for what? to elect a set of young men, of whom I know but little and care less." "Hereafter," he concluded, "I will none of your committees, or caucuses, or tricks, or legerdemains, or mysterious committeemen . . . as to your regular mode, and all that makes us drill soldiers. . . . If I can find the old Republicans again I'll join them; if I cannot, why I'll be independent and vote as I please."[9]

Although he still held to the idea that under republican freedom differences of opinion would give rise to parties, he was also concerned about the grave dangers of party: "When these contentions spread over society, they form parties; and mingling sometimes with private views and local interests, degenerate into faction, which seeks its gratification in violation of morality, and at the expense of the general good." Parties often reached the point, he said, at which even in the absence of significant differences on measures of government, efforts were

---

[9] Clinton, *The Martling Man* (1819), 5–6, 8.

made to whip up the remnants of past controversy "by appealing to the vindictive feelings of disappointment, or exciting the cravings of ambition and cupidity." He began to urge a more direct relationship between the people and their leaders, particularly with the Governor, that would circumvent the party regulars. The effort to maintain old party names and antagonisms he thought merely distracting and self-interested: "It is easy to see that the difference is nominal—that the whole controversy is about office, and that the country is constantly assailed by ambitious demagogues for the purpose of gratifying their cupidity. It is a melancholy, but true reflection on human nature, that the smaller the difference the greater the animosity."[10]

It became the fixed purpose of the Republicans both to defeat Clinton in the arena of practical politics and to devise an intellectual and institutional answer to his old-fashioned moralizing view of party spirit. The ethos of the party system, which was so clearly articulated by Van Buren and the other spokesmen of the Albany Regency group between 1817 and 1824 may be taken as an effort to systematize the imperatives of their developing organization and to devise an answer to Clinton's posture of the independent old-style statesman and his standard eighteenth-century ideas on party.

During his battle with Clinton and his first years in Washington in the early 1820's, Van Buren appears to have arrived at a coherent view of party politics. Formulated only in a fragmentary way in this busy period, these views have to be pieced together out of occasional expressions. But after 1848, with his retirement from active politics, he began writing his *Autobiography*, in the course of which he became so concerned with vindicating his idea of party that he also produced a long

---

[10] C. Z. Lincoln, ed., *Messages from the Governors of New York State*, II, 1018, 1020–1021; D. T. Lynch, *An Epoch and a Man: Martin Van Buren and His Times* (1929), 240.

treatise on the history of American parties, finally published posthumously in 1867.[11] Although written afterwards, these documents are, I believe, authentic sources on the philosophy of party that he formulated during his active years. If his occasional utterances in the thick of battle are supplemented by these later elaborations, one can distinguish a reasonably full and cogent conception of party, adequate to the purposes of a working politician.

Van Buren did not deny that party spirit can be abused, but he considered parties not only inevitable but fundamentally a good thing for the public interest, when properly harnessed. "The substitution of motives of selfish advantage," he wrote in his *Autobiography*, "for those of fairness and right is the characteristic of soulless corporations of all kinds, and political parties are very liable to become similarly demoralized." The answer to this lay in the high character and mutual confidence of those who conducted party affairs. The indiscriminate condemnation of parties was utterly pointless. Van Buren spoke of his "repugnance to a species of cant against Parties in which too many are apt to indulge when their own side is out of power and to forget when they come in." "I have not, I think, been considered even by opponents as particularly rancorous in my party prejudices, and might not perhaps have anything to apprehend from a comparison in this respect with my contemporaries. But knowing, as all men of sense know, that political parties are inseparable from free governments, and that in many and material respects they are highly useful to the country, I could never bring myself for party purposes to

---

[11] *Inquiry into the Origin and Course of Political Parties in the United States* (1867). On Van Buren's thought see also Max M. Mintz, "The Political Ideas of Martin Van Buren," *New York History*, 30 (1949), 422–448. Van Buren's ideas on party were fully expressed as early as February 1828, and it seems safe to say that his later elaborations were not afterthoughts. Remini, *Van Buren*, 186–187.

deprecate their existence. Doubtless excesses frequently attend them and produce many evils, but not so many as are prevented by the maintenance of their organization and vigilance. The disposition to abuse power, so deeply planted in the human heart, can by no other means be more effectually checked; and it has always therefore struck me as more honorable and manly and more in harmony with the character of our People and of our Institutions to deal with the subject of Political Parties in a sincerer and wiser spirit—to recognize their necessity, to give them the credit they deserve, and to devote ourselves to improve and to elevate the principles and objects of our own and to support it ingenuously and faithfully."[12]

Sound and useful party contests, of course, should be based on general principles and not on personal factionalism. Party life itself would serve as a kind of moral discipline, putting a high premium upon loyalty, fidelity, patriotism, and self-restraint. Moreover, controversies were most conducive to the general interest if they were waged between *two* parties, in what could even then already be called the national tradition. Even though the Federalists by 1814 were branded guilty of disloyalty, a retrospective view of American history showed that most of such losing causes had something to offer to the general fund of public policy and public belief.[13]

As one recognized the legitimacy of party, so one accepted the agencies necessary to its existence—the patronage, for example, as a legitimate instrument of party cohesion and reward, and the caucus, as a necessary instrument of party decision. It was important that party members subordinate personal fancies and ambitions to the dictates of the caucus. Personal relations—both in the interest of human civility and in the public interest—should not be soured or spoiled by party an-

---

[12] *Autobiography*, 73, 125.

[13] For Van Buren's views on the legitimacy of the bipartisan tradition, see *Parties*, 52 ff.; on Federalism and disloyalty, *Autobiography*, 50–51.

tagonisms. In the ethos of the professional politician, the party became a means not merely of institutionalizing strife within manageable limits but also of cementing civic loyalty and creating a decent and livable atmosphere. Similarly, parties, if they were national and not sectional, could become valuable instruments of intersectional cohesion. Finally, Van Buren believed in the value of opposition itself as a cohesive force. It was partly on this count that he favored keeping all Federalists out of the Republican party rather than trying to incorporate them. Restore the Republican party on its clear principles, he urged, and let the Federalists carry on with theirs. Naturally, he was sure that in such a competition, the Republicans, as the more popular party, would dominate most of the time. He plainly preferred such a prospect to what he had seen in New York, where a split within the Republican ranks had given the Federalists a chance to gain leverage out of proportion to their numbers by throwing their support to one faction or another. But here, for all his desire to be a sound Republican in the Jeffersonian tradition, Van Buren was a heretic on one vital count: he accepted, he even welcomed, the idea of a permanent opposition. And this in turn marked the longest single stride toward the idea of a party system.

IV

For a politician like Van Buren, engaged in a keen struggle to form a disciplined party in his own state, it was painful to watch the collapse of the presidency and the disintegration of the national party under Monroe and Adams. Elected to the Senate in 1820, Van Buren promptly set himself up in unequivocal opposition to what he later called "Monroe's fusion policy."[14] He thought that this policy of conciliation, by destroying the open party contest, was permitting Federalists to

---

[14] Remini, *Van Buren*, 24.

infiltrate the Republican party and undermine the integrity of its organization. Monroe thus became the first President against whom Van Buren found it necessary to define and assert himself.

Van Buren was convinced that he represented the true inheritance of the tradition of Jefferson and Madison, and that Monroe had sponsored a fatal heresy that carried the party away from their purposes and methods. When he left for Washington, he told one of his New York friends that it was his purpose "to revive the old contest between federals and anti-federals and build up a party for himself on that." Years later, explaining his role, he wrote: "Jefferson and Madison were brought forward by caucus nominations; they, throughout, recognized and adhered to the political party that elected them; and they left it united and powerful. . . ." Under Monroe, however, despite the absence of any "very disturbing public questions," the whole thing had gone to smash: "The Republican party, so long in the ascendant, and apparently so omnipotent, was literally shattered into fragments, and we had no fewer than five Republican Presidential candidates in the field." Worse than this: "In the place of two great parties arrayed against each other in a fair and open contest for the establishment of principles in the administration of Government which they respectively believed most conducive to the public interest, the country was overrun with personal factions. These, having few higher motives for the selection of their candidates or stronger incentives to action than individual preferences or antipathies, moved the bitter waters of political agitation to their lowest depths."[15]

What had gone wrong? Not even Van Buren could argue that Monroe was appointing many Federalists to office. But Van Buren was in fact witness to a striking disintegration in

---

[15] Remini, *Van Buren*, 15; Van Buren, *Parties*, 3–4.

the presidency, the national party, and indeed the tone and fibre of national politics—all of which he saw fit to lay at Monroe's door. Popular interest and participation in national politics was declining to a very low point—despite the potential excitement in such national problems as the Missouri question and the panic of 1819, as well as other important issues like the tariff and the sponsorship of internal improvements. The centripetal forces had so completely taken over that not one of the leading politicians had a national organization. The presidency, already losing influence under Madison, seemed to be robbed of its remaining force by Monroe. Others could see what Van Buren saw. In 1818 Justice Story concluded that the House of Representatives had absorbed all the effective power in the country; and two years later Henry Clay told John Quincy Adams that Monroe "had not the slightest influence on Congress. . . . Henceforth there would not be a man in the United States possessing less *personal* influence over them than the President."[16]

What Van Buren found particularly objectionable was that Monroe had failed to hold the national party together through a firm reliance on the party caucus as the instrument of the presidential succession and party unity. Without a clearly designated successor and a disciplined caucus to ratify the choice, he believed, the contenders would—as they soon did—break the party into fragments. And to Van Buren the general breakdown of the national party must have been distastefully reminiscent of the factional disunity of the New York Republican party. The caucus had fallen into disrepute and uncertain use, the national party convention had not yet been devised to replace it, and in the absence of firm leadership and an acknowledged center of party consensus, every presidential aspirant

---

[16] James S. Young, *The Washington Community*, 188; cf. chap. 9 on the decline of the presidency.

was free to rally a factional following. Who could tell what opportunities would be opened to the Federalists by these chinks in the partisan armor?

Here it became evident that the party had lost ground not because of the presence of a strong rival party but because of its absence: without external pressure toward solidarity, internal disintegration was unchecked. The lesson was clear: the divisive and agitating effects of personal factions were far more serious, and far more to be condemned, than the open principled conflict of two great parties. Monroe, Van Buren explained, might have avoided the discreditable personal factionalism of the 1820's if he had followed Jefferson and Madison in the "steady adherence on the part of the Republican party to the caucus system." It was a striking fact of our political history, Van Buren thought, that the Federalist party gained by casting disrepute on "every usage or plan designed to secure party unity." He suggested that the Federalist party, with its sharply defined program and its more limited and homogeneous constituency, had a smaller need of partisan unity than the more heterogeneous Republican party.[17]

Although these reflections were written some years afterward during Van Buren's retirement, they are consistent with his contemporary actions and statements. "The disjointed state of parties here," he wrote, as the election of 1824 approached, "the distractions which are produced by the approaching contest for president, and the general conviction in the minds of honest and prudent men, that a *radical reform* in the political feelings of this place has become necessary, render this the proper moment to commence the work of a *general resuscitation* of the *old democratic party*."[18] Convinced that old Federalists were infiltrating the party, Van Buren proposed to

---

[17] Van Buren, *Parties*, 5–6.
[18] Remini, *Van Buren*, 23.

carry the fight to them—a fight similar to that which had been waged in New York against Clinton—to make them accept and avow their identity, and restore the open two-party contest.

The significant episodes of Monroe's second term showed the determination of the Van Buren men to fight their battle on every front. In 1821 they blocked the re-election of John W. Taylor as Speaker of the House of Representatives, despite his current affirmations of party loyalty, because this fellow New Yorker had once helped some Clintonians in their race for the New York legislature. The New Yorkers caucused, reported their determination to vote for someone else, and succeeded in recruiting enough support to bring about Taylor's defeat. A second encounter occurred when Monroe's Postmaster General named the New York Congressman, General Solomon Van Rensselaer, a former Federalist, to the position of Postmaster of Albany. Van Buren promptly announced his opposition on the ground that the General had consorted in the past with Federalists and Clintonians. This one appointment took on such importance that Van Buren called a Republican caucus over it, from which he emerged with a request, signed by its majority, that Monroe block the appointment. Indeed a Cabinet meeting had to be called over the question, after which Monroe resolved to uphold his Postmaster General, and the Van Buren faction was forced to accept defeat.[19]

Van Buren never ceased to believe that the primary responsibility for the breakdown of the two-party system lay with Monroe's "fusion policy." The party no doubt suffered from the diffuseness, the factionalism, and the personal rivalries that prevailed throughout the country. By failing to settle upon a single successor and promote him in a party caucus, Monroe also gave full scope to the centrifugal forces, and could thus be charged with some responsibility for the breakup of the

---

[19] See Leonard White, *The Jeffersonians*, 323–325.

party into the four separate factions which were visible by the election of 1824. For the Albany Regency the national experience, which they were now seeing through Van Buren's eyes, seemed a perfect confirmation of those principles of party discipline and coherence that they had been preaching with increasing self-consciousness in their own state since about 1817. Van Buren hoped to unite the party by refashioning the old New York–Virginia alliance that had elected Jefferson, and to throw both parts behind William H. Crawford of Georgia. But he was checked not only by the paralytic stroke that overtook Crawford before the presidential year began, but also by the final breakdown of the national party caucus. In 1824 he could do little but stand by and watch as John Quincy Adams, whose Republicanism he profoundly suspected, was elected to the presidency.

V

John Quincy Adams was no better as a party man than his father. He was never a good Federalist, and after his conversion he never became a good Republican. Avoiding the black arts of political maneuver became for him almost a kind of puritan trial of virtue, a political hair shirt of his own devising. One finds in him a throwback to eighteenth-century views of party, which suited the headstrong independence of his temperament. Thinking of himself not as a party politician but as the custodian and spokesman of the whole nation, he never saw any way of reconciling these two roles.[20] His very

[20] Adams's first act when elected to the Massachusetts Senate in 1802 was to break party lines by proposing to the Federalist caucus that two or three of the Governor's Council be "of opposite politics to our own, by way of conciliatory procedure," and he was soon labelled as hopeless in partisan affairs. Nevertheless, the legislature sent him to Washington as Senator early in 1803, and it was not very long before he turned out to be the only Federalist member from New England in either house of Congress who supported the purchase of Louisiana.

presence in the Republican ranks testified to a self-castigating inexpediency, for he had chosen the embargo issue as the occasion to leave the Federalists and support Jefferson—a decision which promised nothing but isolation and execration in the Massachusetts of 1807, and which soon impelled him to resign. But Adams, whose experience in diplomacy had begun in his adolescence, proved a strong diplomatic asset to his new party. After successive missions which took him to the court of the Tsars, to the leadership of the American peace delegation at Ghent, and then to London, he became Monroe's Secretary of State, and in that office he was the moving spirit behind the Monroe Doctrine. He had won his way to the top of the Republican ranks through competence and expertise, and not through political management; and from the time of his resignation from the Senate in 1808 to his campaign for the presidency, he held only appointive and not elective offices. But on the eve of the election of 1824, he enjoyed the solid respect of his section as well as the distinct advantage of having been out of the country during the rancorous factional disputes of the so-called Era of Good Feelings. Pre-eminently suited to be an administrator or a diplomat, he had few qualifications for presidential leadership. "No man," his biographer has written of him, "has ever been better fitted, as a professional public servant, for the Presidency. No man has had less aptitude or inclination for the organization and command of political cohorts."[21]

Although Adams was capable, with the great prize almost in his grasp, of arriving at the necessary statesmanlike understanding with Henry Clay, he had done almost nothing for years

---

Samuel Flagg Bemis, *John Quincy Adams and the Foundations of American Foreign Policy* (1956), 113, 119–120; *Dictionary of American Biography*, I, 84.

[21] Bemis, *John Quincy Adams and the Foundations of American Foreign Policy*, 11.

before this to advance his own cause. He refused to take any action to unite the various groups throughout the country which favored him or to offer them any leadership. He would not pursue the presidency. He would not ask, he said, "for that which of all others ought to be most freely and spontaneously bestowed." "If my country wants my services, she must ask for them." After his election, he usually refused, as he put it, to "exhibit himself" to the public, showing, in contrast to Monroe, an unwise but intensely sincere aversion to the dawning ceremonial aspects of the presidency.[22]

Early in 1825, when the choice of president was still uncertain, Adams was approached by those who feared that he would exclude Federalists from office. On more than one occasion he made it clear that he had no such intention. "I shall exclude no person for political opinions or for personal opposition to me," he told one visitor. "My great object will be to break up the remnant of old party distinctions and bring the whole people together in sentiment as much as possible." But though this might seem politic enough for one whose support could be expected to be strong in old Federalist sections of the country, Adams on one occasion seems almost to have tried to throw away what advantage it might give him by saying that his desire to harmonize the country was a motive which he believed that either Jackson or Crawford would pursue in the same way.[23]

It was a token of the importance of the anti-party theme in Adams's mind that he chose to devote almost half of his inaugural address to rejoicing over the decline of internal dissensions in the country and to repudiating the spirit of party. Looking back over the generation that had passed, he was both placatory and optimistic: "From the experience of the past we derive instructive lessons for the future. Of the two great

[22] *Ibid.*, 18–20, 99.
[23] *Ibid.*, 44–45.

political parties which have divided the opinions and feelings of our country, the candid and the just will now admit that both have contributed splendid talents, spotless integrity, ardent patriotism, and disinterested sacrifices to the formation and administration of this Government, and that both have required a liberal indulgence for a portion of human infirmity and error." The revolutionary wars of Europe, Adams went on, launched the United States upon a time of trial that lasted twenty-five years. But now that era was over: "With the catastrophy in which the wars of the French Revolution terminated, and our own subsequent peace with Great Britain, this baneful weed of party strife was uprooted." Now no basic difference of principle connected either with the theory of government or foreign relations existed to give rise to more than "wholesome animation" to public sentiment or legislative debate. All Americans were now agreed upon the basic elements of the national political creed. "Ten years of peace, at home and abroad, have assuaged the animosities of political contention and blended into harmony the most discordant elements of public opinion. There still remains one effort of magnanimity, one sacrifice of prejudice and passion, to be made by the individuals throughout the nation who have heretofore followed the standards of political parties. It is that of discarding every remnant of rancor against each other, of embracing as countrymen and friends, and of yielding to talent and virtue alone that confidence which in times of contention for principles was bestowed only upon those who bore the badge of party communion." Adams rejoiced at the return of comity to the nation's councils in Washington: "Here the distinguished men from every section of our country, while meeting to deliberate upon the great interests of those by whom they are deputed, learn to estimate the talents and do justice to the virtues of each other. The harmony of the nation is promoted and the whole Union is knit together by the sentiments of mutual respect, the habits of social intercourse, and the ties of personal friendship formed between the representatives of its several parts in the perform-ance of their service at this metropolis."

Since parties no longer existed, it was hardly necessary for Adams to urge their abolition, but the whole spirit of his ad-dress, with its deep overtones of satisfaction with non-partisan harmony, clearly suggested that the old parties, despite all the "splendid talents, spotless integrity, and ardent patriotism," they had admittedly produced, ought not to be encouraged to revive. Adams implicitly assumed that since both historic parties had had their good men and measures, they need no longer continue to contend against each other. Van Buren and his followers believed just the opposite—that if the men and the measures of the two historic parties had been, each in their way, meritorious, and if their strife had somehow served the country, then the parties and the strife should continue.

Adams's subsequent conduct gave his critics reason to say that he was the ideal man to unite the country—against himself. His first annual message to Congress was one of the most wholly impolitic documents in the history of American gov-ernment. After outlining a program of federal activity that was utterly unacceptable in most sections of the country, Adams went on to urge Congressmen in considering these proposals not to be deterred by their unpopularity—or, as he put it, not to be "palsied by the will of our constituents."

Adams followed his refusal to court other politicians or the public by refusing to use the patronage to build a machine that would keep him in office. In his four years he made only twelve removals from office, he refused to favor his friends and sup-porters for new posts, resented pressure over offices, refused in one case to remove a Cabinet member (Postmaster General John McLean) who was intriguing against him, and gave a postmaster's appointment in the election year 1828 to a Jackson supporter. Even after his inevitable defeat in 1828, he refused to juggle old party labels in order to fight for continuing leadership. "I have no wish," he wrote to Henry Clay in April 1829, "to fortify myself by the support of any party whatever."[24]

Adams had made himself a personal caricature of the anti-party creed. This "Republican with Federalist sympathies," as one Van Buren man in New York called him, outraged the New York Republicans by offering the position of Minister to England to DeWitt Clinton (who, however rejected it) and a district judgeship in New York to a prominent Clintonian. It was not long before Van Buren, concluding that Adams was still promoting "Monroe's fusion policy," prepared to destroy the administration. It would have taken less marksmanship than Van Buren had to harpoon a whale that rose so benignly to the surface and exposed its belly. After his first major attack on the administration over Adams's proposed mission to the Panama Congress, Van Buren became the leading anti-administration man in the Senate, fighting Adams on internal improvements, courting Calhoun as a possible opposition leader, casting about for a good candidate for 1828, and finally settling upon Andrew Jackson.

Under Adams, Van Buren reverted to a plan he had conceived during Monroe's administration of cementing a union between the Albany Regency and the Richmond Junto in Virginia. In a letter written to the Virginian Thomas Ritchie in January 1827 Van Buren outlined his plan to revive the Republican party as an alliance between Southern planters and Northern republicans.[25] He conceded that a general convention might now be a superior instrument to a Congressional caucus, since a convention would concentrate the party vote behind Jackson and bring about "what is still of greater im-

---

[24] *Ibid.*, 135–140; cf. Leonard White, *The Jeffersonians*, 380–381.
[25] On this letter, see Remini, *Van Buren*, 130–131.

portance, the substantial reorganization of the old Republican party." Adams could be defeated if one could find a way of mobilizing both Jackson's personal popularity and the remaining "old party feeling." Van Buren argued that his plan would advance the interests of Republicans in the northern and middle states by "substituting party principle for personal preference as one of the leading points in the contest."

Always intensely aware of the possibilities of the political party as an agency for surmounting sectional rivalry, Van Buren pointed out that party interests would subordinate sectional conflict: "Instead of the question being between a northern and a Southern man, it would be whether or not the ties, which have hitherto bound together a great political party should be severed." Throughout the country, he thought, the divisions between Republicans and Federalists were still alive, and should be kept alive. Party distinctions should always be kept up, "and the old ones are the best of which the nature of the case admits. Political combinations between the inhabitants of the different states are unavoidable, and the most natural and beneficial to the country is that between the planters of the South and the plain Republicans of the North. The country has once flourished under a party thus constituted and may again."

Van Buren did not fail to emphasize that the party system was the surest way of combating the mutual antagonism between the free and the slave states. "It would take longer than our lives," he suggested, "(even if it were practicable) to create new party feelings to keep those masses together. If the old ones are suppressed, geographical divisions founded on local interests or what is more, prejudices between free and slave-holding states, will inevitably take their place." In the past, attacks upon Southern Republicans had been looked upon by those in the North as assaults upon their political allies. "This all powerful sympathy has been much weakened, if not destroyed, by the amalgamating policy of Mr. Monroe." A new party, he was plainly trying to convince his Southern correspondent, would be an anchor for the South, a security against sectional agitation.

In the end, Van Buren, by settling upon Andrew Jackson as his candidate, and, as he had planned, "adding his personal popularity to the yet remaining force of old party feeling,"[26] succeeded in creating a new national party as the presumptive heir to old Republican principles, in restoring party rivalries, and in forging a national party organization of monumental durability. There were, of course, some elements in this achievement that marred its perfect partisan symmetry: De-Witt Clinton too would have chosen Jackson, and as it turned out, Jackson appointed more former Federalists to office than all his Republican predecessors combined. But Clinton did not survive to contend for influence in the Jackson administration; and Jackson's use of the patronage (like Jefferson's of the presidency) seemed more acceptable to Van Buren as insider than it had in anticipation, and it hardly did harm to the newly emerging party.

There were, of course, other important Jackson managers in other parts of the country. But Van Buren, by playing a vital role in Jackson's campaign of 1828, had succeeded in bringing the strong partisan spirit of the Bucktails and the Albany Regency to the national scene, and in making the New York organization and its doctrines an object of national attention. What was soon known to many politicians as "the New York philosophy" had reached a strikingly mature articulation in the political culture from which Van Buren had emerged, and it will now be pertinent to look more closely at the conception of party politics that had developed among the members of the Albany Regency.

[26] Van Buren's aspirations, as expressed to a member of the Richmond Junto in November 1826, Remini, *Van Buren*, 120.

VI

The group of men who led Van Buren's Bucktail faction, and then, with increasing power, became designated as the Albany Regency, are more interesting as a collectivity than as individuals, and except for Van Buren their names are forgotten by all but professional historians. At the top of this group—there was also a large middle stratum of lieutenants whose names flit in and out of New York history—were Van Buren himself and his colleague William L. Marcy, who is chiefly remembered for his candor about the spoils system, but who was elected to the Senate, served three terms as Governor of New York, and later became Secretary of War and Secretary of State. Van Buren put much stock in the advice of his law partner, Benjamin F. Butler,[27] a leading figure at the bar who was more interested in private practice than public office, but who became Jackson's Attorney General and also served several years as a United States district attorney. Enos Throop, Congressman, judge, Lieutenant Governor, and Governor, was a representative figure from Western New York; but the two party wheelhorses who exerted greatest influence behind Van Buren and Marcy were probably Azariah C. Flagg, who spent years as an assemblyman, as New York's Secretary of State, and as Comptroller, and Silas Wright, who followed Van Buren and Marcy to the United States Senate and the governorship. Among the younger members of the group were Edwin Croswell, who after 1823 took over the editorship of the Albany *Argus*, one of the most influential newspapers in the country, and John A. Dix, Secretary of State in New York for six years and United States Senator, who went on to a brilliant career in the Civil War era.

---

[27] Not to be confused with Benjamin F. ("Beast") Butler, the Union general, controversial military governor of New Orleans, and later Governor of Massachusetts.

John A. Garraty's characterization of Silas Wright goes far to characterize the group as a whole: "He was a hard-headed practical politician, honest and industrious, but limited in his outlook by the small agricultural world in which he had been raised. He was intelligent but not brilliant, well meaning but not idealistic, [an] example of the new type of public official that could be seen at that time rising up in every state of the Union." Chronologically and socially, these were new men, born in the fifteen years between 1782 and 1797, and still preponderantly young when they began to make themselves felt in New York politics soon after the peace of Ghent. When Van Buren, for example, was elected to the United States Senate in 1820, he was not yet forty, and yet he already had over twenty years of experience in state politics. Marcy went into politics in his early twenties, and had had a long history of minor officeholding before he received his first important job, the New York comptrollership, which involved, among other things, managing the Erie Canal. When he at last arrived in the United States Senate early in 1831, it was as a politician thoroughly seasoned in the ways of New York politics, of which he was to be such a well-remembered apologist. The Regency men were, in the illuminating language of contemporary political sociology, locals rather than cosmopolitans, whose interest was fixed first on gaining and holding control of New York, and then in seeing to it that New York had its full share of influence in national affairs. "Love the State," Wright wrote to Flagg in 1827, "and let the nation save itself."[28]

In origin the Regency men were middle class or lower middle class, often self-made men or the sons of self-made men,

---

[28] John A. Garraty, *Silas Wright* (1949), 32, 31; on the increasing importance of locals as against cosmopolitans in the Jacksonian officeholding elite, see Sidney H. Aronson, *Status and Kinship in the Higher Civil Service* (1964), 75–76.

moderately prosperous and respected, but (with the exception of Dix) not rich during their early years, and not connected to the leading families of the state. Three of them—Croswell and Butler besides Van Buren—were the sons of tavernkeepers, and the others characteristically went from farms to small-town law offices. Few Regency men had advanced formal education, although among the leaders Dix, the son of a well-to-do and imaginative New Hampshire merchant, had been provided with an unusual and solid education, and Marcy and Wright managed to put themselves through college by teaching school. Lawyers, often without enough practice to keep their minds and energies fully occupied, they were also the friends and associates of small-town businessmen and small-scale bankers. They came from a social class for which the perquisites and connections, the marginal advantages and limited prominence of small offices were much esteemed as means of making one's way toward the top. What they had was, by and large, hard earned, and there was a distinct edge of class resentment in their attitude toward patrician politicians who assumed that office was a prerogative of social rank that could be claimed without the expenditure of years of work in party-building and without the exacting discipline of party loyalty. Long afterward, Van Buren could remember vividly their dislike of such men, "Federalists from their birth," who hoped that with Clinton's help they could now move easily into the "democratic ranks": "Most of these gentlemen had from early manhood enjoyed high and influential position in what was called good society, and the supposition that they expected to occupy, on that account, greater consideration in the democratic organization was not acceptable in that quarter."[29]

For men of the Regency breed, Thomas Jefferson was a hero of towering stature, the leading national figure of their early

---

[29] *Autobiography*, 105.

days; and his party, in which they were raised, most of them from childhood, was a sacred repository of political energy and wisdom. Their loyalty to the party survived the stress of the war of 1812 in a state in which opposition to the war was widespread, and for many of them this test of their loyalty became a kind of equivalent to what the Revolution had been for their fathers. Although they did not tend to be crusading democrats, having the temperament of men of affairs rather than reformers, they belong to a type for which the democratic promise of the Jeffersonian creed had a strong and genuine appeal. They were, after all, outside and somewhat at odds with the older aristocratic leaders, estranged from political leadership by inherited wealth and position or personal brilliance and glamour. They thought that negotiation and the management of opinion were better than leadership through deference. Coming out of the ranks of the people, they spoke with an authentically demotic voice, and found the little ceremonies of politics by which one sought for the votes of the common man not at all distasteful.

They were, in short, modern political professionals who loved the bonhomie of political gatherings, a coterie of more-or-less equals who relied for success not on the authority of a brilliant charismatic leader but on their solidarity, patience, and discipline. Their party gave them a creed, a vocation, and a congenial social world all in one. It is hardly surprising that they should have developed a firm and self-conscious awareness of the imperatives of party organization, and have laid down a comprehensive set of canons for its management.

It was appropriate that the members of the Albany Regency, as men raised in political parties, should be among the first to formulate a full justification for modern party life. What they were justifying, of course, was not the old type of political party, the familiar personal clique, but rather the new one that they themselves were constructing—popular in its base and more democratically run. The New York Republican party had been little more than a coalition of family factions, and it had been these factions, not the party as a whole, which had retained the loyalty of the working members. DeWitt Clinton's style of leadership stood clearly within the traditional standards of the factional proprietary party. In order to find grounds for departing from him, his opponents needed a set of new criteria for party organization, and such criteria they developed between about 1817 and 1825 with marvelous articulateness and system.[30] In many ways their ideas stem from the need of breaking with the patrician idea of the party as an aristocratic clique and also of going outside parliamentary bodies and small groups of politicians to form popular parties with broad roots in the electorate. Much of the organizational work of this sort had, of course, been done by the Jeffersonians before them; but it fell to the Regency to develop the implications of political organization and the idea of the party system.

In the teeth of the aristocratic tradition of the proprietary factions, the Regency spokesmen applied democratic principles to the parties themselves. The parties ought to be democratic associations run by and for their active members, and not for a proprietary leader. There was to be a chain of command, but its orders would issue from the members in conclave, and not from a leading notable and his clique. Parties were not to be personal factions. As their leading newspaper, the Albany *Argus*, put it: "On one side is arrayed the old Republican party, and on the other the followers of a man." The personal faction would only serve the interests of its aristocratic leader. But the

---

[30] The party theme in the thought of the Albany Regency is amply and sensitively documented by Michael Wallace, "Changing Concepts of Party in the United States: New York 1815–1828," *American Historical Review*, 74 (1969), 453–491. Quotations in the following paragraphs, except where otherwise indicated, are from this essay, 459 ff., and I have followed Wallace's analysis closely.

popular party would underwrite a series of careers open to talents: it would create opportunities for nominations, patronage, careers, in return for the loyalty it demanded of its members. Its leaders were not the owners of the organization but its agents, who earned their way upward in its ranks through faithful service. Van Buren himself fitted this model perfectly. "We speak of him with pride," said a mass meeting of Albany Republicans, "because without the influence of fortune, or the factitious aid of a family name, he has, by his entire devotion to the republican cause, raised himself to the first grade as a statesman and a patriot."

As a combat organization, the party would demand discipline of an almost military severity. "Tell them," said Wright in issuing the word to loyal party men in 1825, "they are safe if they fear the enemy, but that the first man we see *step to the rear*, we *cut down*. . . . they *must* not falter, or they perish."[31] In their claims for loyalty and discipline and for the subordination of personal opinion to group decisions, the spokesmen of the Albany Regency went beyond what Burke had reached in his canons for the party member. Burke had assumed that a civil man active in politics ought to be able to find a corps of men with whom he could agree nine-tenths of the time, but he was not clear about the extent to which individual judgment ought to be subordinated to the will of the group. The Regency spokesmen demanded not merely voluntary concurrence but thoroughgoing subordination. "We hold it a principle," said an upstate paper in 1824, "that every man should sacrifice his own private opinions and feelings to the good of his party—and the man who will not do it is unworthy to be supported by a party, for any post of honor or profit." Such canons of subordination were meant, among other things, to strengthen the party caucus. Day in and day out, the Regency men preached

---

[31] Garraty, *Wright*, 40.

loyalty to the caucus, and one of their most fundamental criticisms of the Clinton men and other factionalists stemmed from the Clintonians' "bad faith" in not adhering to caucus decisions after they were made.

Personal careers, like personal views, were to be sacrificed to the common interest.[32] The politician was expected to pursue his personal advancement, but not aggressively, and certainly not outside the pattern settled by his political associates. Humility, Van Buren later suggested in the course of some asperities on Calhoun, ought to be the governing rule: "It has been those who . . . refrained the most from suffering their personal behavior from being inflamed by their political rivalries and were most willing to leave the question of their individual advancement to the quiet and friendly arbitrament of their political associates [who] have in the end been the most successful."[33] Such demands for loyalty extended not only to the legislator in his parliamentary conduct but also to the editor of the party paper, whose business it was to serve party views with fidelity. The code embraced scrupulous loyalty to party nominees. "An opposition," wrote William L. Marcy significantly to Azariah C. Flagg in 1825, "to a candidate which is abstractly right may be politically wrong. . . . The example of opposing a candidate nominated by political friends is bad not only as to its effect on the pending election but as to others that are to succeed it. An opposition upon the ground of principle will be used to authorize an opposition on the ground of caprice."

The central value of party unity to an organization of men

---

[32] A dramatic example was the case of the "infamous seventeen," who followed an unpopular party decision in voting down the electoral bill of 1824 which would have allowed voters to choose their presidential electors on a general ticket. Each of the seventeen knowingly risked the ruin of his career.

[33] *Autobiography*, 519 n.

of their origins seems to have been quite clear to the Regency spokesmen. Party unity was the democrat's answer to the aristocrat's wealth, prestige, and connections. In these they could never match him, but by presenting a united front in party affairs, they could give democracy a more than compensating foundation of strength.

In the repetitive demands for the subservience, loyalty, and diligence that were necessary to any combat organization, the New York Republicans tended to make of the party an end in itself, and as time went on the code of party loyalty became more important than issues. "Most of their political advertisements," writes Michael Wallace, "were in fact apolitical; they were calls to the colors, exhortations to keep the organizational faith. . . . Republicans were enjoined to ignore objections to particular Regency policies, as they were simply threats to the safety of the organization."

This observation deserves emphasis: to a considerable degree the newly emerging party, even though founded on a commitment to republican principles, became an anti-ideological force. The Regency way of developing the party, which was to become in effect the American way, brought with it that lack of consistency and clarity on ideas and issues that is so often the despair of critics of the American party system. It is true, of course, that Van Buren and his cohorts always argued, with a sincerity that need not be questioned, for parties that were constituted on great leading principles. The central principle, on which they showed the highest degree of consistency, was simply the old Republican antipathy to Federal centralization and loose construction of the Constitution. This guiding principle was agreeable to their localist bias; it was also, after New York had its profitable canal, consonant with the interests of those in the state who could see no reason to expend their substance on federally aided internal improvements that might help their competitors. The Regency spokesmen never seem to have shown much anxiety over the possibility that forging a strong national party and putting a strong President at the head of it might open the door to centralization.

But for all their well-meant statements about principles, the very concern of the new politicians for the party as a structure, and for the mechanisms and maneuvers that would strengthen it, tended to displace ideological, and even at times programmatic commitments. These men were moved by a new passion that would have seemed strange, possibly even sinister to their predecessors—the passion for organization. Marcy, writing to Flagg, "When party is strong almost anything that is done is right," was laying down a principle that would have been unacceptable to Jefferson and Madison, incomprehensible to Monroe, and little short of satanic to Washington and the two Adamses. More and more the old passions gave way to the new one. The distaste for Federalists and their principles became more important as a device than as a conviction. The Bucktails, though freely crying "Federalist" as an epithet whenever a reversion to the vendettist spirit seemed useful, would not refuse to unite with certain chosen old Federalists at points where it was opportune. They called for the advance of democracy, and it is quite likely that their party was more democratically managed than those of the past; but their position on the political advance of the common man—on the suffrage, for example—was not always more friendly than that of their opponents, nor always closer to the popular will.[34] Even when one descends from principles to program, one finds a certain agile flexibility: the Regency men would be equivocal or inconsistent on state or national issues when it seemed necessary. Van Buren recalled—almost, it seems, with a kind of pride —his performance at a New York state tariff convention of 1827, after which two interested auditors agreed that it was

[34] Kass argues this case, *Politics in New York State*, chap. 5 and passim; for Marcy, *ibid.*, 29.

"a very able speech" but were unable to determine which side it was on. This conversation, Van Buren blandly remarked, "would seem to indicate that directness on all points had not been its most prominent feature," and even those who later had the opportunity to read it, he reports, used it in the South to prove him a protectionist and in the North to prove him an anti-protectionist.[35]

But for all their emphasis on discipline and their disposition to bypass ideology, the most decisive new departure taken by the Regency politicians lay in their break with the old ideal of national unanimity, or of a consensus transcending party, and in their acceptance of the idea that a sustained opposition has value in its own right. They saw the necessity of giving up the ancient ideal of social harmony that had haunted men from Bolingbroke to Washington and Monroe, and accepted the useful, the constructive contributions of political competition and conflict. To do this meant at last to accept opposition as a permanent fact. "Their goal," as Wallace puts it, "was not to destroy, overwhelm, or eliminate their opponents; they were not ideologues bent on the destruction of evil doers. They were able, therefore, to realize that the continued existence of an opposition was necessary, from the perspective of perpetuating their own party; opposition was highly useful, a constant spur to their own party's discipline." This they might well have learned from observing the factional condition of the Republican party during the period of Federalist decline in New York, or from observing at a distance the rapid dissolution of the national Republican party in the period of one-party politics. They followed, in short, the practical implica-

---

[35] *Autobiography*, 171–172; Van Buren explained that he had in fact changed his mind on the tariff, but (characteristically) had chosen his own way of undermining it because he believed it had "a hold on the public mind which could only be loosened by degrees and by means which would not rouse the prejudice of its supporters." *Ibid.*, 171.

tions of an idea Jefferson had stated much earlier but had been content to leave as a purely theoretical observation—that a party possessed of an excessively clear domination of the field, tends to "schismatize."[36] Thus we find Van Buren remarking as early as 1819 that his party was already quite strong enough in the New York Senate: "We will stand as strong as we could possibly wish, more might endanger our harmony." The party, said the Albany *Argus*, was "most in jeopardy when an opposition is not sufficiently defined." There is, said another, "such a thing as a party being too strong; a small and firm majority is more to be relied upon than an overwhelming and loose one."

Now, most imperatively, the two-party system began to acquire the sanction of history. Said the *Argus* in 1824: "From the first organization of the government . . . this country has been divided into two great parties. . . . Neither party has yielded to the other in the zeal with which it has sought to procure concert among its members, or to give ascendency to its principles, and although we may lament the occasional inconsistencies and the dangerous excesses into which both have unavoidably been betrayed, . . . we cannot for a minute admit that the majority of either have been actuated by any other than the purest, the most patriotic, and the most disinterested motives."

In the 1820's the New York Republicans significantly began to speak with a certain complaisance about opposition as a settled fact in politics. The code of opposition required certain canons of sportsmanlike decency. Republicans, one newspaper remarked, should "exercise a liberal and tolerant spirit toward political opponents, and . . . treat them with a moderation and courtesy which shall leave them no reason for complaint." "It is right," said another, "that the Clintonians should have their meetings. . . . . To interfere with the meetings of the

---

[36] See above, pp. 167, 168.

opposing party, is blackguardism; it betrays a little, mean spirit, that an intelligent, high minded man would disown." Sooner or later, power would be alternated with the opposition, and it was understood among Regency politicians that when such a political change takes place the spoils of office rightly go with the victorious party. It was, of course, a Regency man who made the first well-remembered national proclamation of this principle when William L. Marcy, defending Van Buren's appointment to be Minister to England in January 1832, made his famous assertion, "To the victor belong the spoils." "It may be," said Marcy to the Senate, "that the politicians of the United States are not so fastidious as some gentlemen are, as to disclosing the principles on which they act. They boldly preach what they practice. When they are contending for victory, they avow their intention of enjoying the fruits of it. If they are defeated, they expect to retire from office. If they are successful, they claim, as a matter of right, the advantages of success. They see nothing wrong in the rule, that to the victor belong the spoils of the enemy."[37]

Having rejected the idea of party amalgamation favored by Monroe, the Regency men opposed it as consistently in theory as in practice. Amalgamation would open the party to Federalist infiltration, they argued. The old parties had never really dissolved, and the forces at work to express them should have clear and separate identities. It was foolish to expect free men

---

[37] I. D. Spencer, *The Victor and the Spoils: A Life of William L. Marcy* (1959), 59–60. In fact this forthright statement was more direct and brutal than the actual policies of the Regency, which recognized the need of bureaucratic continuity in lower offices and the impracticability and injustice of a wholesale sweep of jobs. The idea was, of course, not absolutely new in American politics. In a biography of Elbridge Gerry, which Marcy appears to have read, James T. Austin, a Massachusetts politician, had said: "But, after all, what is the worth of a victory if the enemy are allowed to possess the spoils?" *The Life of Elbridge Gerry* (1828–1829), II, 322; cf. Spencer, *Victor*, 61.

to exist in politics without contention, and it was best that contending forces stand clear and apart. The existence of parties must be understood not merely in the old way as a sign that freedom existed but as a guarantee that it would continue to exist. The maintenance of parties, said the Albany *Argus* in 1824, was "necessary to the just exercise of the powers of free government." But most remarkable, and most novel, in the Regency defense of parties against the amalgamation philosophy was their forthright commitment to the idea, heretofore set forward only fleetingly, that permanent competition between parties is of positive social value. "The spirit of party," one member said, was "the vigilant watchman over the conduct of those in power." Hardened partisans would "expose the crimes, and even the failings, of competitors for the people's confidence. Competitors of this description *force* into notice facts . . . which the people at large could never have derived from the ordinary commerce of thought." "Those party divisions," declared Governor Enos Throop in 1829, "which are based upon conflicting opinions in regard to the constitution of the government, or the measures of the administration of it, interest every citizen, and tend, inevitably, in the spirit of emulation and proselytism, to reduce the many shades of opinion into two opposing parties. . . . Organized parties watch and scan each other's doings, the public mind is instructed by ample discussions of public measures, and acts of violence are restrained by the convictions of the people, that the prevailing measures are the results of enlightened reason."

Active party competition would thus inform the people, cure apathy, check dishonesty and corruption, and become conducive to the larger social peace. When prevailing honest differences of opinion were discussed, Van Buren said in 1814, "and the principles of contending parties are supported with candor, fairness, and moderation, the very discord which is thus produced may in a government like ours, be conducive to the public good."[38] This was an arresting view of party spirit that could even reconcile Americans in their past battles. "The old divisions," said Benjamin F. Butler in 1824, "are virtues which we . . . cherish. The contests which grew out of them are salutary and needful efforts for the preservation of the community."

The various utterances of Albany Regency men between 1817 and 1825, even though never cast into a single magisterial statement or even a memorable document, provide a complete, articulate, quite sophisticated, quite modern defense of the political party. This rationale for the party appears not to have been derived from theoretical writings but rather from an awareness of past American experience with party conflict and from efforts to cope with contemporary realities. It was one of those pragmatic American innovations, based upon experience and experiment, which one usually finds keyed closely to changing institutional necessities. After more than a generation of party-building by anti-party thinkers, there had at last evolved a rationale for parties which made it unnecessary for politicians to apologize for doing what the necessities of their trade plainly required them to do, and which now made it possible for them to say why forming and managing parties were acts of service to the liberal state.

VII

Once the argument for the party system had been formulated by prominent politicians, it was not again lost sight of, and a growing acceptance of party can be seen in the pre-Civil War years among both theoretical writers and working politicians. But this does not mean that it had won a total victory. Many politicians who were living by the new code still paid lip service to the older anti-party ideal—how significant a por-

---

[38] *Autobiography*, 50.

tion will be known only when we have a full history of the doctrine of party. But of one thing we can be sure: the anti-party doctrine did not at once collapse before the arguments of the Van Buren school. John C. Calhoun, the most arresting thinker among American politicians between Madison and the Progressives a hundred years later, once again adapted anti-party thought to a new and special purpose.

Calhoun was dominated by two great urges: he wanted to be president, and with increasing urgency as time went on, he wanted to defend the interests of the slave-holding South. In part his views were a private reaction against men like Van Buren, Crawford, and Andrew Jackson, who blocked his ambitions, and in part they voiced his most enduring public anxiety: how could the South's institutions survive under a strong federal government animated by the democratic forces now at work, and simultaneously strengthened and corrupted by party rivalry and the spoils system?

As a South Carolinian, Calhoun came from a political culture in which, despite the presence of factions and sectional tensions, no clear two-party struggle existed, and in which the leading planters preferred the older arts of political management.[39] There the dominant political ideal still envisaged firm leadership by high-minded patricians, based in large measure upon their prestige and enlightenment. When Calhoun became a leader in national politics soon after the War of 1812, this prejudice in favor of patrician leaders strengthened his revulsion against the political spoilsmen who were now barring his way to the presidency: first, William H. Crawford, the coarse and aggressive Georgian, an ally of some of Calhoun's enemies in South Carolina and his chief rival among the Southern aspirants; then Van Buren, who helped forge the alliance that put Jackson into the White House and who completed the work

[39] William W. Freehling, *Prelude to Civil War* (1966), 105–106 and chap. 9.

that Crawford had begun of alienating Jackson from Calhoun. Both belonged to a breed detested by Calhoun, but were more fit than he for the rough game of practical politics. As the Democratic party endorsed with increasing candor the idea of rotation in office and the use of the spoils, Calhoun's prejudices were confirmed. After 1827 his convictions about parties and spoils were animated by his fear that they were weapons sure to be used against the South's interest.

In the course of his defense of slavery Calhoun developed the famous doctrine of the concurrent majority which found full expression near the end of his life in his *A Disquisition on Government* and *A Discourse on the Constitution and Government of the United States*. As William Freehling has pointed out, Calhoun's fear of the majority was intimately associated with his fear of party politics and of the use of patronage by the spoilsmen to build a strong federal executive. This he predicted would create a powerful national state under which the simple numerical majority could mount a fatal attack upon the South.[40]

Calhoun's conception of the concurrent majority, which in effect required a formal minority veto or consent, has been so much discussed that it needs no rehearsal here. What is important for our purpose is that party was a central fact in the system of the simple numerical majority which Calhoun was concerned to prevent. He was convinced that under the numerical majority the party system would become the instrument of demagogic spoilsmen, and he was also fearful that the power of partisan conflict would pull society apart. Rome had declined, he thought, under the impact of partisan conflict, until at last it came under "the despotic rule of the chieftain

---

[40] Freehling, "Spoilsmen and Interests in the Thought and Career of John C. Calhoun," *Journal of American History*, 52 (1965), 25–42. Quotations in the following paragraphs are documented in this article, to which I am much indebted.

of the successful party;—the sad, but only alternative which remained to prevent universal violence, confusion and anarchy." He was convinced that an equipoise between a major and minor party could be only temporary. Sooner or later, "the conflict between the two parties must be transferred . . . from an appeal to the ballot box to an appeal to force." The feature which distinguished a government of the numerical majority from that of the concurrent majority, he asserted, was that under the numerical majority, "each faction, in the struggle to obtain the control of the government, elevates to power the designing, the artful, and unscrupulous, who, in their devotion to the party,—instead of aiming at the good of the whole,—aim exclusively at securing the ascendency of party." By contrast, under the restraining influence of the concurrent majority principle, a state of social harmony (not much dissimilar to the unanimity that Washington and Monroe had striven for) could be achieved. Enlightened men would be chosen for office, and "instead of faction, strife, and struggle for party ascendency, there would be patriotism, nationality, harmony, and a struggle only for supremacy in promoting the common good of the whole."

None of this would be possible if partisanship and patronage were allowed to control the fate of the nation. An unrestrained use of the spoils would put a premium on the skills of unscrupulous party politicians rather than wise statesmen, and make government an affair of party organization and jobs rather than policies or principles. It would induce corruption and selfishness in the whole body politic, and by strengthening the executive would put him in a position to choose his own successor, thus circumventing the true procedures of republican government. No doubt Calhoun here had the formidable example of Jackson foremost in mind.

In portraying the corrupting effect of partisan spoils upon the quality and honor of political leadership and upon the tone of politics, Calhoun not only made pertinent observations on the state of politics in his time but also laid down a critique of the party system that anticipated Mugwump reformers of a later generation. The cogency of his argument, and its stature as a categorical defense of minority rights, have often been overestimated. Some recent writers have taken Calhoun as a spokesman of American pluralism in the Madisonian tradition who was merely expressing a special concern for the protection of minority rights. To me it seems that he was in fact breaking sharply with Madisonian pluralism to set up a rigid dualistic system. Where Madison had seen the majority as a changing and fluctuating coalition, now gaining and now losing interests from among the body politic, Calhoun defined the majority and the minority as more or less fixed quantities, behind which we have little difficulty in discerning simply the North and the South. His defense of minority rights, moreover, shades off all too rapidly into a demand for a minority veto which could easily become minority control. Moreover, his position on abolitionist agitation led him, as it did other Southern spokesmen, into repressive counter-measures which defy the fundamental minority right of criticism and dissent. Calhoun here marks not a primary contribution to the mainstream of American political thought but a suggestive and interesting byway.

Calhoun spoke for a retrogressive outlook in more senses than one, and in his lifetime a significant new note was struck in the discussion of political parties by political commentators and historians who showed a better grasp than he of the function of party. One cannot pretend to measure their influence in the country as a whole, but their work is a token of the drift of thought.

Truly significant nineteenth-century comment on the American polity probably began with Alexis de Tocqueville, whose *Democracy in America* was widely read in the United States after its translation in 1835. But Tocqueville, who so seldom disappoints, is not rewarding on the subject of party. Here Tocqueville is significant chiefly for what he did not say, since he eschewed the characteristic anti-party cant of earlier political theorists. He rather matter-of-factly accepted parties as a reality of the political order he was describing. But he showed a clear preference for the older political parties of the age of Hamilton and Jefferson, which he called "great parties"— that is, parties dedicated to principles and ideas and not to men —over current American parties which he regarded as minor parties. "Society," he admitted, "is convulsed by great parties, it is only agitated by minor parties. . . . America has had great parties, but has them no longer; and if her happiness is thereby considerably increased, her morality has suffered." But he showed no disposition to sound the implications of what he had said. He scorned the materialistic orientation of the current parties and the petty character of their quarrels, but he failed to confront the startling problem posed by his own idea that if major parties had fostered "morality," minor parties, after all, had succeeded in increasing the happiness of the country.[41]

A sharp new note in the discussion of parties was struck in 1838 and 1839 by the immigrant political scientist Francis Lieber of South Carolina College, one of the nation's leading

---

[41] *Democracy in America*, I, chap. 10; but see the interesting remarks on political associations, *ibid.*, chap. 12, and II, chap. 7. In the latter Tocqueville suggested that "freedom of association in political matters is not so dangerous to public tranquillity as is supposed, and that possibly, after having agitated society for some time, it may strengthen the state in the end. In democratic countries political associations are, so to speak, the only powerful persons who aspire to rule the state. . . . It may perhaps be easy to demonstrate that freedom of association in political matters is favorable to the prosperity and even to the tranquillity of the community." *Ibid.*, Phillips Bradley ed. (1945), II, 126–127.

academic men. Drawing upon his European education and experience as well as his observations of America, Lieber espoused the legitimacy of political parties with a vigor seldom seen before in political discussions and incarnated his reflections in his two-volume *Manual of Political Ethics* (1838–39), the first systematic treatment of political science written in the United States, and, despite its limited original sale, long a standard book on the subject. Lieber began with a positive definition of party which, if somewhat more elaborate, is reminiscent of Burke's: "By a party we understand a number of citizens, who, for some period and not momentarily, act in unison respecting some principles, interest or measure, by lawful means, keeping therefore within the bounds of the fundamental law and for the real or sincerely supposed common good of the whole commonwealth." What followed was a very appreciative discussion, clear if somewhat abstract, of the function of political parties in a free polity. Barring brief emergency periods that could unite a nation, Lieber found no instance of a free state without parties. Indeed, he concluded, "it is impossible for civil liberties to exist without parties." "Nor is it ... desirable that no parties should exist. Without parties there could be no loyal, steady, lasting and effective opposition, one of the surest safeguards of public peace. . . . Without parties many of the wisest measures could never be carried, and many of the best intended measures would remain harsh, unmodified, absolute. . . ."[42]

Lieber did not fail to acknowledge the presence of certain dangers in parties, not least the possibility of a drift toward violence; but he remarked that any sound principle is subject

---

[42] *Manual*, II, 413, 414, 415. If one is to judge by a brief statement on party in 1835 (*Miscellaneous Writings* [1880] I, 189–190), Lieber's views in his *Manual* represented a change of views. But he continued to hold to the pro-party position he had arrived at by 1839. *Writings*, I, 325–326.

to occasional exaggeration and misuse. A sound party, he explained, was one which was animated by an enlarged and noble principle worthy of moving masses of men, which drew large numbers to its support so that it had the capacity to become national; one which was consistent and well organized, whose members were moved by a spirit of civic dedication, and which did not assume the prerogative of persecuting occasional deviation among its members. He was much concerned also that the spirit of party should not infect private life and destroy the comity of the community. Exemplary restraint had been shown in this respect, he thought, during the battle over nullification in South Carolina, when "several of the most active leaders of the opposite parties remained on terms of amity, and showed themselves to be so in public." Lieber argued that the good citizen should indeed feel obliged to join a political party, particularly during periods of public danger, so long as he could find a party whose principles did no violence to his conscience. The idea of independence from party, once so highly valued as a civic virtue, he considered only a mask for "political vacillation, weakness, inconsistency of temperament, or self interest." Lieber's discussion of party was followed by a long account of the function of opposition. He concluded: "Without well-understood, lawful and loyal opposition, that support of all substantial civil liberty, namely, that the minority be protected, and have every fair chance of converting the majority secured, would be either a mockery, or lead to continued violences. . . . Without well-understood opposition liberty cannot co-exist with peace and order."[43]

The historian George Bancroft was another prominent writer of the period who began to grope his way toward a

---

[43] *Ibid.*, 418 ff., 423, 430, 433–434; Austin Ranney, "The Reception of Political Parties into American Political Science," *Southwestern Social Science Quarterly*, 32 (1951), 188, minimizes Lieber's appreciation of party.

conception of the function of partisan conflict. In an oration of 1854 he spoke of competing parties as embodying the necessary forces of liberty and order, but parties here seem to be little more than transcendental entities, and it was not until some years afterward, in looking back on the United States in the period after the Revolution, that the historian praised the historic parties as agencies that met distinct social needs, provided an apparatus for controlling conflict, and, by their competition, animated the civic interests and enlarged the political education of the people.[44] It was not Bancroft, however, but a relatively obscure writer, Jabez D. Hammond, who wrote the first major historical celebration of party; and it was neither Tocqueville nor Lieber but an even more obscure Ohio jurist, Frederick Grimke, who made the most articulate statement on the subject in political theory.

Jabez Hammond, born in Vermont in 1778, had turned to history after a brief career as a lawyer and politician in up-state New York. Formerly a follower of DeWitt Clinton, but as his occasional sallies show, a sharply critical and disillusioned one, he published in 1843 the first two substantial volumes of his *History of Political Parties in the State of New York*, which carried his story from the adoption of the Constitution to 1840, and followed it six years later with a third volume which combined a biography of Silas Wright with a narrative carrying events almost to the moment of its composition. Aside from its patient affection for detail, its absorbed interest in the year-by-year happenings in the political game, and its impressive spirit of fairness and detachment, the remarkable thing about this book is that it is not simply a conventional history of political events—as the first supposed histories of parties tended to be—but actually the history of *parties* that its title promises, and, what is more, a narrative that

---

[44] Bancroft, *Literary and Historical Miscellanies* (1857), 486–487, and Russell Nye, *George Bancroft* (1964), 90–91.

simply assumes parties to be a central phenomenon of the natural political world instead of taking them as unwelcome intrusions upon it. A work still widely used and respected by historians, Hammond's volumes provide a striking monument to the complex New York political culture of the period he records. He understood too well how much of the important political life of the nation went on at the state level to think of his heroic efforts as expended on too parochial a story, and he had the imagination to seize even upon such a workaday politician as Silas Wright as a significant American type.

In his preface, Hammond dedicated his book to the comity of the political system, addressing it to the "young politician" with the hope that its tendency would be to "assuage the bitterness of party zeal" and "to promote kind and good feelings between individuals belonging to adverse parties, and to cause the great laws by which all parties ought to be governed in their conduct towards their own members, and towards their opponents, to be better understood."[45] Hammond plainly hoped to enable politicians to serve the general interest not by forsaking party warfare but by conducting it in the proper spirit and under the proper limitations. His work was one of the first in America to meet Hume's demand that the historian aim to develop a spirit of moderation in the public's political consciousness.

The philosophy of party that occasionally breaks the surface of Hammond's dense narrative is essentially that of the Albany Regency, but it is set forward in a disinterested manner. Parties, Hammond says, will always exist—and should exist—in a free state. But their only legitimacy lies in their differences of opinion over measures, or on occasion over men. It is noteworthy here that in referring to measures and men, and not to *principles*, Hammond recedes somewhat from the commitment to

---

[45] *The History of Political Parties in the State of New York*, I (1842), v.

ideology that had marked the first parties, and which can be found in leading Regency spokesmen.[46]

Parties perform the function of clarifying public issues. They underwrite liberty by providing scope for opposition; they check corruption by providing a structure committed to examining the conduct of public business; and they aid social peace by providing an institutional, non-violent means for expressing conflict and changing administrations. For the legitimate purposes of party conflict, Hammond considered the two-party system the only natural one. Condemning Clinton's idea of party amalgamation, he wrote: "The idea of an amalgamation of parties in a free state is chimerical, and the notion that three great parties can, for any considerable time exist, is ridiculous." On another occasion he referred to a tri-partite party battle as being "as unnatural as a battle between three ships at sea, each fighting against the other two." Not only should there be precisely two parties, but the public interest and the internal discipline of parties would be best served if neither party had an overwhelming preponderance, but if they were closely matched. "That statesman is safest who stands at the head of a well organized party, which is opposed by another party nearly equal to it in numerical strength."[47]

Hammond accepted as a necessity of life the use of patronage to give parties discipline and coherence. He thought that men like Marcy who stressed this fact were merely being candid, and that party politicians who denounced him for it were hypocritical in repudiating as a principle what all of them found necessary in practice. Indeed he could see the cogency of the argument, he said, that to use spoils to further the cause of a party in which one conscientiously believes is not merely justified but even obligatory.[48]

[46] On the necessity of parties, see *ibid.*, II, 312; III, 670: on the legitimacy of parties, I, 226; II, 79–80; III, 670.

[47] *Ibid.*, II, 308–309; I, 476, 535–536, 445.

[48] *Ibid.*, I, 565–566; II, 312, 429; I, 95–96.

Hammond's acceptance of the imperatives of party organization led him to adopt the code of the Regency and to hail as virtues those qualities of discipline and dedication that the party demanded of its members. With cordial approval he quoted Horatio Seymour's characterization of Silas Wright: "Mr. Wright was a great man, an honest man: if he committed errors, they were induced by devotion to his party. He was not selfish: to him his party was every thing—himself nothing." The catalogue of civic virtue had been markedly changed and enlarged since the days when an Edmund Pendleton could be praised for his complete freedom from party prejudices or party connections.[49]

Frederick Grimke, who wrote the most imposing statement on parties made before the 1870's, was the brother of Sarah and Angelina Grimké (they kept, while he dropped, the acute accent), the better-known abolitionist and feminist reformers of South Carolina. After taking a B.A. at Yale in 1810 and practicing law briefly in Charleston, Grimke moved to Ohio where his career in the judiciary finally led to election to the Supreme Court of the State in 1836. In 1842 he resigned from the bench to study and write, and in 1848 he published his lengthy political commentary, *The Nature and Tendency of Free Institutions*. Although he did not share the abolitionism of his sisters, Grimke, in contrast to Calhoun, exiled himself to the freer culture of the North and preferred the vigorous popular democracy analyzed in his book to the older patrician world in which he had been reared.

Grimke, who led a secluded life, read widely—he particularly admired Comte and Tocqueville. His book shows him to be not so much a traditional political theorist as a forerunner of modern descriptive political sociology. Focal concerns of modern political thought and investigation—not merely the relations of property and power, but the phenomena of class and

---

[49] *Ibid.*, III, 53; for Pendleton see p. 13 above.

public opinion, of social structure and social status, even generational differences and antagonisms—were integral to his thought; and he realized far better than most of his contemporaries that nineteenth-century government was being reshaped by the advance of public opinion and mass suffrage. His great indebtedness to Tocqueville, to whom he referred as having "powers of generalization absolutely unrivaled in the department of political philosophy,"[50] is evident not only in his style of thought but in his literary manner. Like Tocqueville, he was more concerned with political culture than with politics: he was interested in the reciprocal effects that civil institutions and the mental habits of masses of men could have upon each other. Although his work is an immensely sympathetic account of the libertarian and democratic aspects of the American system and of the role of the masses in politics, it achieves its end not through a rhetorical celebration of democracy but through a fine-textured, if at points somewhat idealized, analysis of the workings of the democratic system. His book, though all but forgotten when he died in 1863, deserves a place among the more important works of nineteenth-century political speculation. Today one can read it with a pleasure quite akin to that which one derives from Tocqueville—and on at least one count, his discussion of parties, Grimke far outdid his master in subtlety and penetration.

As a critic of political society who grasped the functional role of conflict, Grimke was quite at home with the idea of a party system. "The democratic principle," he said in one of his arresting maxims, "has come into the world not to bring peace, but a sword; or rather to bring peace by a sword." It was not

---

[50] *The Nature and Tendency of Free Institution* (1848), ed. by John William Ward (1968), 669; this edition uses the text of the revised edition of 1856. Quotations and relevant passages from this work are from 172–175; 178–180, 186, 187, 188, 527; italics have been added in two cases.

enough simply to say that parties are necessary or even that they are useful. Indeed: "It is most certain that the *distinguishing excellence of free institutions consists in their giving birth to popular parties* and that the annoyance and inconvenience which these occasion to individuals, both in public and private life, are productive of incalculable advantage. . . . Popular parties are not only the natural result of elective government but, what is of much more consequence, they are absolutely necessary to uphold and preserve it." In the United States, he boasted, "in consequence of the conflict of parties the public will has been more steadily directed to the advancement of the public weal than in any other country. The disputes and contentions of parties have been favorable to that unity of purpose which is demanded in all human affairs."

Emphasizing the role of opinion in government, Grimke looked upon party conflict as a conflict of opinions which was at once instructive, stimulating, and chastening. Probably the first American writer to think deeply about the shaping effect of political life on public habits, he saw clearly the role of party conflict in mobilizing intelligent and interested mass action: "Party spirit at bottom is but the conflict of different opinions, to each of which some portion of truth almost invariably adheres; and what has ever been the effect of this mutual attraction of mind upon mind, but to sharpen men's wits, to extend the circle of their knowledge, and to raise the general mind above its former level. Therefore it is that an era of party spirit, whether religious, philosophical, or political, has always been one of intellectual advancement." Since it arouses and yet at the same time instructs the masses, party should be regarded as "a special and extraordinary provision for furthering the interests and advancing the intelligence of the most numerous class of society." Party conflict, he thought, exercises the mind, and even stimulates industry. "The regular deportment and habits of reflection which these produce, counteract the vicious tendencies of the system and operate as a safeguard against the extreme excesses and the violent revolutions which occur in other countries."

In discussing the place of checks and balances in government, Grimke, as a theorist of party, went a long step beyond Madison. Since in a republic a very large part of political authority is intentionally vested in the whole population, he argued, it is necessary to have something more than "a scheme of checks and balances within the government. As the forces which are set in motion are so much more extensive, we must contrive some machinery equally extensive for the purpose of controlling them. And thus popular parties very naturally, not to say necessarily, take the place of that curious system of checks and balances which are well enough adapted to a close aristocracy or pure monarchy, but which play only a subordinate part in representative government." So, in a republic, "parties take the place of the old system of balances and checks. *The latter balance the government only, the former balance society itself.*"

There was, it will be apparent, a hard core of conservatism under Grimke's democratic ardor. He put great stock in the disciplining effect of party conflict, arguing that when opinions have to pass through a great number of minds before they are embodied in a policy, society does not experience a violent shock, as it would upon a sudden and unpublicized adoption of the same policy. "The wider the arena on which parties move, the more numerous the persons who compose them, the less dangerous are they to the state; which is the reverse of the conclusion to which the great majority of men are inclined to lean." Deftly Grimke disposes of the old idea of unanimity: "In the imperfect condition of man unanimity would not be desirable. As in the individual, one faculty is set over against another in order to elicit the greatest amount of judgment, wisdom, and experience; so the mutual encounter of rival opinions in different sections of society constitutes a discipline of the same character on a much larger scale. Unanimity, which has the appearance of being the only rightful rule would, if it were conceivable, render society absolutely stationary. . . . Constituted as human nature is, there would be no virtue without some conflict of interests and no wisdom without some conflict of opinions." Grimke was even convinced that the party system, while consonant with majority rule, also gave the minority a decisive influence upon the course of public affairs through its access to public opinion. He was eloquent about the chastening and instructive effects upon a party's leaders of first holding and then losing power, which he thought induced "prudence and moderation" in everyone; and he put great stock in the alternately chastening and disciplinary effect on both parties of a system in which power is rotated between them, and each has to experience in its turn the responsibilities of decision and the education of defeat.[51]

Political theorists like Grimke and Lieber registered, if they did not in any significant way strengthen, an acceptance of party that was also growing among working politicians. It is possible that the idea of party was embraced with less enthusiasm by some older Whig leaders than by the Democrats, since the generation of Clay and Webster had been raised on the old republican distrust of party spirit. Their argument against Andrew Jackson and the spoilsmen may have confirmed the conviction that an anti-party posture was appropriate for them.[52] But the men who grew up in the era of Thurlow

---

[51] Grimke regarded the participation of the masses in government as a kind of discipline—one of his favorite words—and it may help to understand the direction of his thought to think of him as having developed a theory of politics as a discipline somewhat comparable to Veblen's conception of the "industrial discipline."

[52] See, for example, Henry Clay, *Works*, ed. by Calvin Colton (1904), IV, 226–227; but see also *ibid.*, VII, 372, 380–381; VIII, 207. Clay's utterances suggest a growing acceptance of the idea of party during

Weed and Martin Van Buren were used to parties. They showed an increasing consciousness of belonging to a nation which had had by now a long history of two-party division.[53] Party managers on both sides showed their respect for and proficiency in the principles of party organization, made skillful use of the spoils, and, at least after the demagogic Whig campaign of 1840, used much the same tactics to reach the common man.

In the 1850's, as the old parties cracked under the impact of the slavery question and the modern Republican party arose, Republican spokesmen were not hesitant to found their new party upon a firm consciousness of the value of a principled party organization. The Republican remedy for the decayed and obsolescent state of the old parties was not to condemn the party system as such but to form and justify a new party which was portrayed from the outset as ready to take its place among the great parties of the American political tradition. The major imperative for Republican spokesmen was not to justify their new organization for being a party—that was assumed—but to deny that it was a sectional party, and to affirm the national character of its leading principles. They stressed the current "degeneracy" of the Democratic party and set up the Republican party as the legitimate inheritor of the best principles of *both* the old parties—a rationale appropriate to

---

the 1830's. For Webster, see his *Writings and Speeches* (1903), II, 5–7; IV, 95–96, 181. In "The Strange Stillbirth of the Whig Party," *American Historical Review*, 72 (1967), 445–468, Lynn L. Marshall argues, perhaps overargues, the case that Whig leaders were very far behind the Jacksonians in accepting party and practicing its techniques.

[53] See, for example, R. McKinley Ormsby, *A History of the Whig Party* (1859), 45–46, 47, 355, and passim. On the growing and quite self-conscious acceptance of the idea of party in the 1830's and afterward, and the increasing regard for the personal qualities most consistent with party discipline, see Perry M. Goldman's forthcoming Columbia University doctoral dissertation, "The Republic of Virtue."

a new party that was recruiting both ex-Democrats and ex-Whigs.

Thoughtful Republican leaders embraced with enthusiasm the oppositional character of their party. Charles Sumner spoke in 1860 of the "political necessity for a great party of Opposition to act as a check upon the Administration." "Parties," he explained, "are unknown in despotic countries. They belong to the machinery of free governments. Through parties, public opinion is concentrated and directed. Through parties, principles are maintained above men. And through parties, men in power are held to a just responsibility." William H. Seward, one of the most interesting minds among the politicians of his day, while paying tribute to the past glories of the two major parties and lamenting their current condition, made it clear how thoroughly he accepted the principle of party itself: "Solid, enduring and consistent parties, inspired by love of country, reverence for virtue and devotion to human liberty, bold in their conceptions of measures, moderate in success, and resolute throughout reverses, are essential to effective and benevolent administration in every free State. Unanimity, even in a wise, just and necessary policy, can never be expected in any country all at once, and without thorough debate and earnest conflicts of opinion. All public movements are therefore undertaken, and prosecuted through the agencies, not of individuals, but of parties, regulated, excited and moderated, as occasion may require, by their representatives. He who proposes means so impracticable that he can win no party to his support may be a philanthropist but he cannot be a statesman."[54]

Abraham Lincoln never wrote a systematic statement about

---

[54] Sumner, "The Republican Party: Its Origin, Necessity, and Permanence: A Speech before the Young Men's Republican Union of New York City, June 11, 1860," (1860), 2–3; Seward, "Political Issues of the Day," *Tribune Tracts No. 8* (1860), 2; cf. 3 ff.

the place of parties in political life, but he was from his early days a good party man, and throughout his entire career showed an extraordinary deference to the imperatives of party. In 1861 he was among those who refused to compromise fundamental party principles in order to avoid the threat of civil war. As President, fully aware of the need to weld the heterogeneous new party into an effective instrument of government, Lincoln used the patronage with the virtuoso skill of an inveterate spoilsman, and became instrumental in "the most sweeping removal of federal office holders up to that time in American history."[55]

By the end of the Civil War no politician in either party had any excuse for being unfamiliar with standard intellectual defenses of the party and its functions. When an anti-party argument was resumed by the Mugwumps and other reformers of the Gilded Age, orthodox party men had ready answers.[56] The argument over party, in one form or another, has never stopped; but the characteristic criticisms of parties have undergone a cyclical change. It is, in fact, the very drastic nature of this change that makes it necessary for us to recreate with care the early development of the argument for parties. In the eighteenth century, parties had been charged with creating gratuitous strife and with destroying the unity and harmony of civil society. By the middle of the nineteenth century and af-

---

[55] H. J. Carman and R. H. Luthin, *Lincoln and the Patronage* (1943), 331. For Lincoln in 1861, see Kenneth M. Stampp, *And the War Came* (1950), 184–187.

[56] On the party argument in the Gilded Age, see David J. Rothman, *Politics and Power: The United States Senate, 1869–1901* (1966), chap. 8; for later nineteenth-century advocates (e.g., Woodrow Wilson, A. Lawrence Lowell) and critics (e.g., M. I. Ostrogorski and Herbert Croly) of parties, see Austin Ranney, *The Doctrine of Responsible Party Government* (1954). For a forthright reformer's view of party in the post-Civil War era, see Albert Stickney, *A True Republic* (1879), especially chaps. 4 and 5.

terward, the party system was charged with creating a corrupt (and perhaps overcentralized) government and with barring the ablest men from politics. In the twentieth century the characteristic criticism of the eighteenth has been all but reversed, since the party system is now most typically criticized not for divisiveness but for offering a superficial and false conflict to the voters, for failing to pose the "real" issues with clarity and responsibility, and for blocking out dissent—in effect, for protecting the unity and harmony of civil society all too completely, for blunting and minimizing conflict at too high a cost.

Index

Index

Harper, Robert Goodloe, 36–37, 106–107, 116 n, 148, 153
High Federalists. See Federalists on war
Hillhouse, James, 139 n
History of Political Parties in the State of New York (Hammond), 260–263
House of Representatives, 87, 128, 141, 147, 157 n, 175, 177, 179, 228
Human nature: and political parties, 14, 21; Hume on, 24–27; Jefferson on, 27, 115–116, 153 n, 168; Founding Fathers on, 49; Madison on, 64, 65; Washington on, 101; Van Buren on, 225; Grimke on, 266–267
Hume, David, 24–27, 56, 66 n

Idea of a Patriot King, The. See Bolingbroke, Henry St. John
Independent Reflector (Livingstone), 57–58

Jackson, Andrew, 182, 195, 237, 238, 254, 255
Jay, John, 53, 136, 146–147
Jay Treaty, 87, 90 n, 124, 180
Jefferson, Thomas, 1, 18, 44, 54, 56–57, 70, 80, 91, 94, 150, 201; on political parties, 2, 22, 27, 114–116, 122–128, 153 n, 167, 168, 182, 204–206; on Federalists as monarchists, 123–128, 165, 168, 182, see also conciliation and absorption; on Hamilton's banking system, 88, 158–161; letters quoted, 88 n, 89, 115–120, 122–128, 158, 163, 168, 181, 182–183, 204, 206; as moderate, 117–120, 150–158; for conciliation and absorption, 127–128, 151, 154, 166–168, 183, 193; election,

128–151; and patronage, 133–136, 146, 151, 156–158, 193; in office, 151–169, 172–180; inaugural address of, 151–153; assault on judiciary, 161–165; and war, 175; embargo, 151, 172, 175–180
Johnson, Samuel, 11
Judiciary, 107–108; Jefferson's assault on, 161–165

Kelsen, Hans, 7
Kentucky Resolutions, 109, 112, 117–118
Kenyon, Cecelia, 53–54
King, Rufus, 145–146
Koch, Adrienne, 112

Levy, Leonard, 127–128 n
Liberty: gives rise to parties, 24, 26–29, 35; protected by parties, 36; and power, 49–50; religious, 55–63, 75; protected by checks and balances, 70; political, 75. *See also* Opposition, social idea of
Lieber, Francis, 257–259
Lincoln, Abraham, 269–270
Livingston, William, 57–59
Lloyd, James, 107
Louisiana Purchase, 150–151, 161
Loyalty: to political parties, negative view of, 13, 25; Monroe on, 190–194; Van Buren and, 217, 225; and Albany Regency, 241–249; and party discipline, 244–245
Lyman, Samuel, 104

McDonald, Forrest, 71–72
McHenry, James, 140, 147
Machiavelli, Niccolò, 51–52 n

276

Index